Russian
for
Everybody

Workbook

Р. Бейкер

Русский язык для всех

Рабочая тетрадь

Москва
«Русский язык»
1984

R. Baker

Russian
for
Everybody

Workbook

Moscow
Russky Yazyk
1984

ББК 81 2Р—96
Р 89

Robert L. Baker

Middlebury College

Р 4602010000-097   (66-67)-84
015(01)-84

TABLE OF CONTENTS

INTRODUCTION TO THE RUSSIAN SOUND SYSTEM

УРОК
LESSON I

WORKSHEET

A. *Remember that Russian vowels are fuller and richer than English vowels. Make a check mark by the appropriate number if you feel that the vowel quality was acceptable in the non-native pronunciation.*

1. _____ ма́ма
2. _____ до́ма
3. _____ тут

4. _____ па́па
5. _____ дом

B. *Remember that Russian vowels are pronounced without diphthongization. Make a check mark by the appropriate number if the non-native pronounced the word without diphthongization.*

6. _____ до́ма.
7. _____ тут
8. _____ Анто́н

9. _____ ма́ма
10. _____ дом

C. *Remember that the Russian vowels [o] and [u] are pronounced with great lip-rounding. Mark the appropriate number if the non-native pronounced the vowel with adequate lip rounding.*

11. _____ тут
12 _____ дом
13. _____ до́ма

14. _____ тут
15. _____ он

D. *Remember that Russian stop consonants are pronounced without aspiration. Mark the appropriate number if the non-native pronounced the word without aspiration.*

16. _____ па́па
17. _____ па́па
18. _____ па́па

19. _____ па́па
20. _____ па́па

E. *Remember that final stop consonants in Russian must be released. Mark the appropriate number if the non-native pronounced the syllable with released final consonant.*

21. _____ уп
22. _____ оп
23. _____ ап

24. _____ оп
25. _____ тут

F. *You will now hear ten syllables pronounced by a native speaker of Russian. Mark which syllable you hear in each case.*

	Voiceless		Voiced		Voiceless		Voiced
26. ____	пу	____	бу	31. ____	по	____	бо
27. ____	пу	____	бу	32. ____	по	____	бо
28. ____	пу	____	бу	33. ____	па	____	ба
29. ____	по	____	бо	34. ____	па	____	ба
30. ____	по	____	бо	35. ____	па	____	ба

G. *Remember that Russian dental consonants must be pronounced on the teeth. Mark the appropriate number if the non-native pronounced the consonant correctly.*

36. _____ та   39. _____ та

37. _____ та   40. _____ та

38. _____ та

H. *You will now hear ten syllables pronounced by a native speaker. Mark which syllable you hear in each case.*

	Voiceless		Voiced		Voiceless		Voiced
41. ____	там	____	дам	46. ____	том	____	дом
42. ____	там	____	дам	47. ____	ту	____	ду
43. ____	там	____	дам	48. ____	ту	____	ду
44. ____	том	____	дом	49. ____	ту	____	ду
45. ____	том	____	дом	50. ____	там	____	дам

I. *You will now hear five sentences. Mark the appropriate number if the non-native pronounced the sentences correctly without raising the pitch of the voice before the fall.*

51. _____ Это дом.   54. _____ Это ма́ма.

52. _____ Это дом.   55. _____ Это ма́ма.

53. _____ Это ма́ма.

J. *You will now hear five sentences. Mark which sentence you hear in each case.*

56. _____ Это дом.   59. _____ Ма́ма до́ма.

      _____ Это он.   _____ Ма́ма там.

57. _____ Это ма́ма.   60. _____ Анто́н тут.

      _____ Это па́па.   _____ Анто́н там.

58. _____ Это она́.

      _____ Это Анна.

УРОК
LESSON II

WORKSHEET

A. *You will now hear ten syllables pronounced by a native speaker. Mark which syllable you hear in each case.*

Voiceless	Voiced	Voiceless	Voiced
1. _____ фу	_____ ву	6. _____ фо	_____ во
2. _____ фу	_____ ву	7. _____ фо	_____ во
3. _____ фу	_____ ву	8. _____ фа	_____ ва
4. _____ фо	_____ во	9. _____ фа	_____ ва
5. _____ фо	_____ во	10. _____ фа	_____ ва

B. *You will now hear ten syllables pronounced by a native speaker. Mark which syllable you hear in each case.*

Voiceless	Voiced	Voiceless	Voiced
11. _____ са	_____ за	16. _____ со	_____ зо
12. _____ са	_____ за	17. _____ со	_____ зо
13. _____ са	_____ за	18. _____ са	_____ за
14. _____ со	_____ зо	19. _____ са	_____ за
15. _____ со	_____ зо	20. _____ са	_____ за

C. *Remember that the Russian vowel [i] must be pronounced very high in the mouth and must not be diphthongized. Mark the appropriate number if the vowel is pronounced correctly by the non-native.*

21. _____ им
22. _____ им
23. _____ из
24. _____ иду́
25. _____ Ива́н

D. *You will now hear ten syllables pronounced by a native speaker of Russian. Mark which syllable you hear in each case.*

Voiceless	Voiced		Voiceless	Voiced
26. _____ ку	_____ гу		31. _____ ко	_____ го
27. _____ ку	_____ гу		32. _____ ко	_____ го
28. _____ ку	_____ гу		33. _____ ка	_____ га
29. _____ ко	_____ го		34. _____ ка	_____ га
30. _____ ко	_____ го		35. _____ ка	_____ га

E. *Remember that the Russian word «кто» must be pronounced as one syllable. Mark the appropriate number if the word is pronounced properly by the non-native.*

36. _____ кто

37. _____ кто

38. _____ кто

39. _____ кто

40. _____ кто

F. *Remember that the Russian sound* [n] *must always be pronounced on the teeth. Mark the appropriate number if the word is pronounced properly by the non-native.*

41. _____ банк

42. _____ банк

43. _____ банк

44. _____ банк

45. _____ банк

G. *You will now hear five syllables pronounced first by a native speaker, then by a non-native. Mark the appropriate number if the vowel is pronounced correctly by the non-native.*

46. _____ ты

47. _____ мы

48. _____ сын

49. _____ умы́

50. _____ быт

H. *You will now hear five syllables pronounced by a native speaker. Mark which word you hear in each case.*

Fricative	Stop		Fricative	Stop
51. _____ ух	_____ ук		54. _____ хо	_____ ко
52. _____ ух	_____ ук		55. _____ ха	_____ ка
53. _____ ох	_____ ок			

I. *Remember that the Russian consonant* [x] *must be pronounced without a stop sound at the beginning. Mark the appropriate number if the word is pronounced properly by the non-native.*

56. _____ ход

57. _____ ход

58. _____ сух

59. _____ у́хо

60. _____ их

J. *You will now hear five sentences. Mark which sentence you hear in each case.*

61. _____ Вот вы́ход.
     _____ Вот вход.

62. _____ Ма́ма и па́па иду́т домо́й.
     _____ Ма́ма и па́па е́дут домо́й.
     _____ Како́й э́то звук?

     _____ Кака́я э́то бу́ква?
64. _____ Это мой па́па.
     _____ Это мо́й папа.

65. _____ Вот твоя́ ма́ма.
     _____ Вот твоя́ ма́ма.

WRITTEN ASSIGNMENT

A. *Write a full line of each capital and lower-case letters.*

А *А* а *а*

О *О* о *о*

Э *Э* э *э*

У *У* у *у*

М *М* м *м*

П *П* п *п*

Б *Б* б *б*

- -

Н *Н* н *н*

- -

Т *Т* т *т*

- -

Д *Д* д *д*

- -

B. *Write each sentence three times.*

Это папа.   *Это папа.*

- -

Он тут.   *Он тут.*

- -

Это мама.   *Это мама.*

- -

Она там. *Она там.*

- -

Это Анна.   *Это Анна.*

- -

Она дома.   *Она дома.*

_ _

А Антон тут.   *А Антон тут.*

_ _

Мама дома.   *Мама дома.*

_ _

Папа там.   *Папа там.*

_ _

Это дом.   *Это дом.*

_ _

Дом там.   *Дом там.*

_ _

Анна там.   *Анна там.*

_ _

WORKSHEET

A. *You will now hear ten sentences pronounced by a native speaker of Russian. Mark which sentence you hear in each case.*

1. _____ Это дом? _____ Это дом!   6. _____ Она́ поёт? _____ Она́ поёт!

2. _____ Это дом? _____ Это дом!   7. _____ Она́ поёт? _____ Она́ поёт!

3. _____ Это дом? _____ Это дом!   8. _____ Это он? _____ Это он!

4. _____ Анна там? _____ Анна там!   9. _____ Это он? _____ Это он!

5. _____ Анна там? _____ Анна там!   10. _____ Это он? _____ Это он!

B. *Remember that the Russian intonation contour No. 3 must be pronounced with a very sharp rise in pitch. Mark a check mark if the intonation of the non-native is satisfactory for Russian questions.*

11. _____ Это дом?   14. _____ Анна там?

12. _____ Это он?   15. _____ Она́ поёт?

13. _____ Это она́?

C. *Remember that the sharp rise of intonation contour No. 3 is followed by a fall in tone if there are syllables after the sharp rise. Mark the appropriate number if the intonation of the non-native is correct for neutral questions.*

16. _____ Это ма́ма?   19. _____ Па́па до́ма?

17. _____ Это па́па?   20. _____ Па́па до́ма?

18. _____ Ма́ма до́ма?

D. *You will now hear five sentences pronounced by a native speaker of Russian. Mark which sentence you hear in each case.*

21. _____ Это ма́ма? _____ Это ма́ма.   24. _____ Па́па до́ма? _____ Па́па до́ма.

22. _____ Это па́па? _____ Это па́па.   25. _____ Па́па до́ма? _____ Па́па до́ма.

23. _____ Ма́ма до́ма? _____ Ма́ма до́ма.

E. *You will now hear five questions. Mark the answer which is appropriate in each case.*

26. _____ Да, до́ма. _____ Да, ма́ма.

27. _____ Да, там. _____ Да, Анна.

14

28. _____ Да, поёт. _____ Да, она́.
29. _____ Да, поёт. _____ Да, она́.
30. _____ Да, до́ма. _____ Да, ма́ма.

F. *You will now hear ten syllables pronounced by a native speaker of Russian. Mark which syllable you hear in each case.*

31. _____ ня _____ на
32. _____ ню _____ ну
33. _____ тя _____ та
34. _____ ти _____ ты
35. _____ дё _____ до

36. _____ ди _____ ды
37. _____ сё _____ со
38. _____ си _____ сы
39. _____ зя _____ за
40. _____ зи _____ зы

G. *You will now hear ten syllables. Mark the appropriate number if the non-native pronounces the syllables correctly, without superfluous [y] between the consonant and the vowel.*

41. _____ ня
42. _____ нё
43. _____ тю
44. _____ тя
45. _____ дё

46. _____ дю
47. _____ ся
48. _____ сё
49. _____ зя
50. _____ зю

H. *You will now hear five syllables. Mark the appropriate number if the non-native pronounces the consonant sufficiently softened before the vowel [i].*

51. _____ ни
52. _____ ти
53. _____ ди

54. _____ си
55. _____ зи

I. *You will now hear ten syllables pronounced by a native speaker of Russian. Mark which syllable you near in each case.*

56. _____ нья _____ ня
57. _____ нья _____ ня
58. _____ нью _____ ню
59. _____ нью _____ ню
60. _____ ньё _____ нё

61. _____ ньё _____ нё
62. _____ ньи _____ ни
63. _____ ньи _____ ни
64. _____ нье _____ не
65. _____ нье _____ не

J. *You will now hear ten syllables pronounced by a native speaker of Russian. Mark which syllable you hear in each case.*

66. _____ тя _____ тья _____ та
67. _____ тю _____ тью _____ ту
68. _____ тё _____ тьё _____ то

69. _____ те _____ тье
70. _____ ти _____ тьи _____ ты
71. _____ дя _____ дья _____ да

15

| 72. _____ дю | _____ дью | _____ ду | 74. _____ де | _____ дье |
| 73. _____ дё | _____ дьё | _____ до | 75. _____ ди | _____ дьи | _____ ды |

K. *You will now hear five words pronounced by a native speaker of Russian. Mark which word you hear in each case.*

76. _____ сядь	_____ сад	79. _____ звони́ть	_____ звони́т
77. _____ есть	_____ ест	80. _____ звони́ть	_____ звони́т
78. _____ есть	_____ ест		

WRITTEN ASSIGNMENT

A. *Write a full line of each capital and lower-case letters.*

И *И* и *и*

_ _

Я *Я* я *я*

_ _

Ё *Ё* ё *ё*

_ _

Е *Е* е *е*

_ _

Ю *Ю* ю *ю*

_ _

Ы *ы*   й *й*

_ _ _ _ _ _ _ _ _ _ _ _   _ _ _ _ _ _ _ _ _ _

Ф *Ф* ф *ф*

— — — — — — — — — — — — — — — — — — —

В *В* в *в*

— — — — — — — — — — — — — — — — — — —

С *С* с *с*

— — — — — — — — — — — — — — — — — — —

З *З* з *з*

— — — — — — — — — — — — — — — — — — —

К *К* к *к*

— — — — — — — — — — — — — — — — — — —

Г *Г* г *г*

— — — — — — — — — — — — — — — — — — —

Х *Х* х *х*

— — — — — — — — — — — — — — — — — — —

B. *Write each sentence three times.*

— Кто это?   — *Кто это?*

— — — — — — — — — — — — — — — — — — —

— Это мой папа.   — *Это мой папа.*

А это твоя мама.   *А это твоя мама.*

Вот твоя бумага.   *Вот твоя бумага.*

— Кто поёт?   — *Кто поёт?*

— Иван и Анна поют.   — *Иван и Анна поют.*

И я пою.   *И я пою.*

— Кто ест суп?   — *Кто ест суп?*

— Я ем суп.   — *Я ем суп.*

Вот выход. *Вот выход.*

Как вас зовут? *Как вас зовут?*

Мама и папа едут в Москву. *Мама и папа едут в Москву.*

УРОК
LESSON IV

WORKSHEET

A. *You will now hear five words pronounced by a native speaker of Russian. Mark which word you hear in each case.*

1. _____ ви́дит   _____ ви́дят   4. _____ сто́ит   _____ стоя́т
2. _____ ви́дит   _____ ви́дят   5. _____ сто́ит   _____ стоя́т
3. _____ ку́пит   _____ ку́пят

B. *You will now hear ten words. Mark the appropriate number if the non-native pronounces the consonant* [r] *correctly, as a tap sound.*

6. _____ пра́вда   11. _____ ста́рый
7. _____ Ве́ра   12. _____ ры́ба
8. _____ ра́но   13. _____ спорт
9. _____ уро́к   14. _____ парк
10. _____ друг   15. _____ до́брый

WRITTEN ASSIGNMENT

A. *Write a full line of lower-case letter.*

ь ь
— — — — — — — — — — — — — — — — —

B. *Write each sentence three times.*

— Кто это?   — *Кто это?*

— —

20

— Это Антон. — *Это Антон.*

— Кто он? — *Кто он?*

— Он новый студент? — Да. — *Он новый студент? — Да.*

Вот идёт Зина. *Вот идёт Зина.*

— Она новая студентка? — Нет. — *Она новая студентка? — Нет.*

— Это твоя статья? — *Это твоя статья?*

— Да, моя. — *Да, моя.*

— Где моя книга? — *Где моя книга?*

— На окне. — *На окне.*

Нина идёт домой. *Нина идёт домой.*

— Это факт? — *Это факт?*

— Да, это факт. — *Да, это факт.*

— Зина и Нина поют.   — *Зина и Нина поют.*

— И Максим поёт.   — *И Максим поёт.*

WORKSHEET

A. *You will now hear ten words. Mark the appropriate number if the non-native pronounces the consonant* [l] *correctly.*

1. _____ столы́
2. _____ до́лго
3. _____ ла́мпа
4. _____ ла́дно
5. _____ дал

6. _____ по́лка
7. _____ холо́дный
8. _____ знал
9. _____ ел
10. _____ в углу́

B. *You will now hear ten words. Mark the appropriate number if the non-native pronounces the consonant soft* [l] *correctly.*

11. _____ и́ли
12. _____ купи́ли
13. _____ гуля́ть
14. _____ лю́ди
15. _____ фильм

16. _____ апре́ль
17. _____ е́ли
18. _____ ель
19. _____ люблю́
20. _____ то́лько

C. *You will now hear ten words. Mark the appropriate number if the non-native pronounces the fricative consonants hard.*

21. _____ хожу́
22. _____ жа́рко
23. _____ жаль
24. _____ жить
25. _____ пишу́

26. _____ Са́ша
27. _____ шесть
28. _____ маши́на
29. _____ ви́жу
30. _____ ша́пка

D. *You will now hear five words. Mark the appropriate number if the non-native pronounces the affricate* [ts] *hard.*

31. _____ офице́р
32. _____ центр
33. _____ сце́на

34. _____ цирк
35. _____ ци́фра

WRITTEN ASSIGNMENT

A. *Write a full line of each capital and lower-case letter.*

Р *Р* р *р*

B. *Write each sentence three times.*

Здравствуйте!   *Здравствуйте!*

Доброе утро!   *Доброе утро!*

Добрый день!   *Добрый день!*

Простите!   *Простите!*   Извините!   *Извините!*

Мои сигареты на окне.   *Мои сигареты на окне.* ·

— Куда идёт Максим?   *— Куда идёт Максим?*

— В кино. — *В кино.*

— —

— Вы курите? — *Вы курите?*

— —

— Хотите сигарету? — *Хотите сигарету?*

— —

— —

— Нет, спасибо. — *Нет, спасибо.*

— —

— —

— Я не курю. — *Я не курю.*

— —

— Это моя новая знакомая. — *Это моя новая знакомая.*

— —

— —

— —

— Как её зовут? — Вера. — *Как её зовут? — Вера.*

— —

— —

— Кто она?— Физик.   — *Кто она? — Физик.*

_ _ _ _ _ _ _ _ _ _ _ _ _ _ _ _ _ _ _

_ _ _ _ _ _ _ _ _ _ _ _ _ _ _ _ _ _ _

— Это мой дядя.   — *Это мой дядя.*

_ _ _ _ _ _ _ _ _ _ _ _ _ _ _ _ _ _ _

_ _ _ _ _ _ _ _ _ _ _ _ _ _ _ _ _ _ _

— Как его зовут?   — *Как его зовут?*

_ _ _ _ _ _ _ _ _ _ _ _ _ _ _ _ _ _ _

_ _ _ _ _ _ _ _ _ _ _ _ _ _ _ _ _ _ _

— Максим.   — *Максим.*

_ _ _ _ _ _ _ _ _ _ _ _ _ _ _ _ _ _ _

— Кто он?   — *Кто он?*

_ _ _ _ _ _ _ _ _ _ _ _ _ _ _ _ _ _ _

— Химик.   — *Химик.*

_ _ _ _ _ _ _ _ _ _ _ _ _ _ _ _ _ _ _

УРОК 1

WORKSHEET

A. *You will now hear three statements. Mark which picture corresponds to the statement you hear.*

1. A._____   B. _____   C. _____

2. A._____   B. _____   C. _____

3. A. _____   B. _____   C. _____

B. *You will now hear three questions. Mark which picture could represent an answer to each question.*

4. A. _____   B. _____

5. A. _____   B. _____

6. A._____   B. _____

C. *You will now hear two questions. Mark the correct answer for each question, based on the picture clue given.*

7.   8.

A. _____ Он здесь.   A. _____ Они́ здесь.
B. _____ Она́ здесь.   B. _____ Она́ там.
C. _____ Она́ там.   C. _____ Она́ здесь.

D. *You will now hear seven questions. Mark the appropriate answer in each case.*

9. A._____ Он здесь.   12. A._____ Это письмо́.
   B._____ Оно́ здесь.   B. _____ Это Макси́м.
   C._____ Они́ здесь   13. A._____ Это газе́та.
10. A._____ Он там.   B. _____ Это Ива́н Ива́нович.
    B._____ Она́ там.   14. A._____ Это Анна Петро́вна.
    C._____ Оно́ там.   B. _____ Это кни́га и газе́та.
11. A._____ Он здесь.   15. A._____ Это журна́л.
    B._____ Она́ там.   B. _____ Это Макси́м и Ни́на.
    C._____ Они́ здесь.

ПИСЬМЕННОЕ ЗАДАНИЕ (WRITTEN ASSIGNMENT)

A. *Write a full line of each capital and lower-case letter.*

Л *Л* л *л*

Ж *Ж* ж *ж*

Ш *Ш* ш *ш*

Ц *Ц* ц *ц*

Ч *Ч* ч *ч*

Щ *Щ* щ *щ*

B. *Write each sentence three times.*

Познакомьтесь, это мой брат Валерий.
Познакомьтесь, это мой брат Валерий.

Мою сестру зовут Наташа.   *Мою сестру зовут Наташа.*

Скажите, пожалуйста, чьи это вещи?
Скажите, пожалуйста, чьи это вещи?

Нина ученица.   *Нина ученица.*

А Наташа студентка.   *А Наташа студентка.*

— Ваше имя и отчество?   — *Ваше имя и отчество?*

— Иван Иванович.   — *Иван Иванович.*

— Национальность?   — *Национальность?*

— Русский.   — *Русский.*

Я немного говорю по-русски.   *Я немного говорю по-русски.*

Я изучаю русский язык.   *Я изучаю русский язык.*

Всего хорошего!   *Всего хорошего!*

WORKSHEET

You will now hear a number of incomplete Russian sentences. Complete each sentence by marking the appropriate space here.

1. _____ сын.
   _____ дочь.
   _____ жена́.

2. _____ мать (ма́ма).
   _____ оте́ц (па́па).
   _____ сестра́.

3. _____ брат.
   _____ оте́ц (мать).
   _____ жена́.

4. _____ брат.
   _____ сестра́.
   _____ муж.

5. _____ жена́.
   _____ мать (ма́ма).
   _____ сестра́.

6. _____ роди́тели.
   _____ де́ти.
   _____ брат и сестра́.

7. _____ муж.
   _____ брат.
   _____ сын.

8. _____ роди́тели.
   _____ де́ти.
   _____ брат и сестра́.

9. _____ его́ брат.
   _____ её брат.
   _____ их брат.

10. _____ его́ кни́га.
    _____ её кни́га.
    _____ их кни́га.

11. _____ его́ роди́тели.
    _____ её роди́тели.
    _____ их роди́тели.

12. _____ его́ сын.
    _____ её сын.
    _____ их сын.

13. _____ его́ ма́ма.
    _____ её ма́ма.
    _____ их ма́ма.

14. _____ его́ де́ти.
    _____ её де́ти.
    _____ их де́ти.

15. _____ чита́ет кни́гу.
    _____ чита́ют кни́гу.

16. _____ слу́шает стихи́.
    _____ слу́шают стихи́.

17. _____ слу́шает ра́дио.
    _____ слу́шают ра́дио.

18. _____ чита́ет газе́ту.

    _____ чита́ют газе́ту.

19. _____ гуля́ет.

    _____ гуля́ют.

20. _____ гуля́ет.

    _____ гуля́ют.

21. _____ газе́та.

    _____ газе́ту.

22. _____ кни́га.

    _____ кни́гу.

23. _____ кни́га.

    _____ кни́гу.

24. _____ му́зыка.

    _____ му́зыку.

25. _____ газе́та.

    _____ газе́ту.

ПИСЬМЕННОЕ ЗАДАНИЕ

Образе́ц: (де́ти) Вот Ива́н Ива́нович и Анна Петро́вна.— *Их де́ти то́же здесь.*

1. (муж) Вот Анна Петро́вна._____

2. (роди́тели) Вот Макси́м и Ни́на._____

3. (брат) Вот Ни́на._____

4. (сын) Вот Ива́н Ива́нович. _____

5. (сестра́) Вот Макси́м._____

Образе́ц: (де́ти) Вот Ива́н Ива́нович и Анна Петро́вна.— *А где же их де́ти?*

6. (сын) Вот Анна Петро́вна и Ива́н Ива́нович._____

7. (дочь) Вот Васи́лий Никола́евич._____

8. (роди́тели) Вот Ни́на и Макси́м._____

9. (жена́) Вот Ива́н Ива́нович._____

10. (па́па) Вот Ни́на._____

Запо́лните про́пуски. (Fill in the blanks with proper form of the verbs given in parentheses.)

11. (слу́шает/слу́шают) Ма́ма и Макси́м_____му́зыку.

12. (де́лает/де́лают) Что сейча́с _____ их роди́тели?

13. (чита́ет/чита́ют) Ива́н Ива́нович _____ кни́гу.

14. (слу́шает/слу́шают) Васи́лий Никола́евич _____ ра́дио.

15. (гуля́ет/гуля́ют) Анна Петро́вна и Ива́н Ива́нович _____.

16. (чита́ет/чита́ют) Ни́на _____ журна́л.

17. (чита́ет/чита́ют) Анна Петро́вна и её муж _____ письмо́.

18. (де́лает/де́лают) А что _____ их де́ти?

19. (гуля́ет/гуля́ют) Макси́м сейча́с_____.

20. (слу́шает/слу́шают) Ни́на и её ма́ма _____му́зыку.

3*

Образе́ц: Это кни́га. Ма́ма чита́ет *кни́гу.*

21. Это письмо́. Ни́на чита́ет _____.

22. Это стихи́. Макси́м чита́ет _____.

23. Это газе́та. Васи́лий Никола́евич чита́ет _____.

24. Это ра́дио. Па́па слу́шает _____.

25. Это журна́л. Ма́ма чита́ет _____.

26. Это упражне́ние № 2. Де́ти чита́ют _____.

27. Это кни́га. Па́па чита́ет _____.

28. Это газе́та. Ни́на чита́ет _____.

Образе́ц: Это Ни́на.— *Что де́лает Ни́на?*

Это она́. — *Что она́ де́лает?*

29. Это её роди́тели. _____

30. Это Макси́м. _____

31. Это он. _____

32. Это Васи́лий Никола́евич и его́ дочь. _____

_____

33. Это Анна Петро́вна. _____

34. Это Ива́н Ива́нович. _____

35. Это он. _____

36. Это его́ де́ти. _____

37. Это ма́ма и па́па. _____

38. Это они́. _____

Запо́лните про́пуски. (Use и *or* а.)

39. — Это па́па и ма́ма.— _____ э́то?

40. Ни́на слу́шает ра́дио, _____ Макси́м гуля́ет.

41. Это газе́та _____ журна́л.

42. Па́па _____ ма́ма гуля́ют.

43. Макси́м гуля́ет, _____ Ни́на гуля́ет.

44. Ива́н Ива́нович чита́ет журна́л, _____ Васи́лий Никола́евич чита́ет газе́ту.

45. Ма́ма слу́шает му́зыку, _____ Ни́на чита́ет стихи́.

46. — Это Ни́на и Макси́м.— _____ где же их роди́тели?

47. Это Макси́м _____ Ни́на.

48. Ма́ма слу́шает ра́дио, _____ Макси́м слу́шает ра́дио.

WORKSHEET

Complete each sentence you hear by marking the appropriate space.

1. _____ гуля́ю.
   _____ гуля́ешь.
   _____ гуля́ем.

2. _____ слу́шаем ра́дио.
   _____ слу́шаете ра́дио.
   _____ слу́шают ра́дио.

3. _____ гуля́ешь.
   _____ гуля́ем.
   _____ гуля́ют.

4. _____ де́лаю?
   _____ де́лаешь?
   _____ де́лаете?

5. _____ чита́ет журна́л.
   _____ чита́етс журна́л.
   _____ чита́ют журна́л.

6. _____ не рабо́таю.
   _____ не рабо́таем.
   _____ не рабо́таете.

7. _____ чита́ет газе́ту.
   _____ чита́ем газе́ту.
   _____ чита́ют газе́ту.

8. _____ живу́ в Москве́.
   _____ живёшь в Москве́.
   _____ живёте в Москве́.

9. _____ слу́шаю му́зыку.
   _____ слу́шаешь му́зыку.
   _____ слу́шаете му́зыку.

10. _____ живу́ в Новосиби́рске.
    _____ живём в Новосиби́рске.
    _____ живу́т в Новосиби́рске.

11. _____ Москва́.
    _____ Москве́.

12. _____ Москва́.
    _____ Москве́.

13. _____ институ́т.
    _____ институ́те.

14. _____ кни́га.
    _____ кни́гу.
    _____ кни́ге.

15. _____ газе́та.
    _____ газе́ту.
    _____ газе́те.

16. _____ газе́та.
    _____ газе́ту.
    _____ газе́те.

17. _____ журна́л.
    _____ журна́ле.

18. _____ журна́л.
    _____ журна́ле.

19. ____ библиоте́ка.

    ____ библиоте́ке.

20. ____ библиоте́ка.

    ____ библиоте́ке.

Complete the dialogs you hear by marking the appropriate response.

21. ____ — Да, входи́те, пожа́луйста.

    ____ — Нет, он уже́ на пе́нсии.

    ____ — Спаси́бо.

22. ____ — Пожа́луйста.

    ____ — Спаси́бо.

    ____ — Входи́те, пожа́луйста.

23. ____ — Да, она́ до́ма.

    ____ — Нет, э́то Ни́на.

    ____ — Входи́те, пожа́луйста.

24. ____ — Пожа́луйста.

    ____ — Нет, в Москве́.

    ____ — Ива́н Ива́нович.

25. ____ — Анна Петро́вна на рабо́те.

    ____ — Это Анна Петро́вна.

    ____ — Это кни́га.

26. ____ — Спаси́бо.

    ____ — Пожа́луйста.

    ____ — Да, в Новосиби́рске.

27. ____ — Пожа́луйста.

    ____ — Да, э́то дом № 2.

    ____ — В институ́те.

28. ____ — Пожа́луйста.

    ____ — Познако́мьтесь.

    ____ — Она́ уже́ до́ма.

29. ____ — Спаси́бо.

    ____ — Ни́на гуля́ет в па́рке.

    ____ — Нет, до́ма.

30. ____ — Он фи́зик.

    ____ — Она́ фи́зик.

    ____ — Она́ рабо́тает в Москве́.

ПИСЬМЕННОЕ ЗАДАНИЕ

Запо́лните про́пуски. (Use the words in parentheses in the required form.)

1. (жить, рабо́тать) Ива́н Ива́нович и его́ жена́ _____ и _____ в Москве́.

   (жить, жить, рабо́тать) Васи́лий Никола́евич то́же _____ там, а его́ сын Оле́г _____ и _____ в Новосиби́рске.

2. (жить; жить) — Где ты _____, Макси́м? — Я _____ в кварти́ре № 2.

3. (жить; жить) — Где вы _____, де́ти? — Мы _____ в до́ме № 1.

4. (де́лать; чита́ть) — Что вы _____, де́ти? — Мы _____ письмо́.

   (гуля́ть) — Где ва́ши роди́тели?— Они́ _____ в па́рке.

5. (де́лать; слу́шать) — Что ты _____, Зи́на? — Я _____ му́зыку.

   (чита́ть) — А твоя́ ма́ма?— Она́ _____ журна́л.

Образец: (кварти́ра № 2) — Где живёт Макси́м?— *Он живёт в кварти́ре № 2.*

6. (дом № 3) — Где строи́тель?_____

7. (институ́т) — Где сейча́с Зи́на?_____

_____

8. (парк) — Где гуля́ют Ни́на и Макси́м?_____

_____

9. (шко́ла) — Где рабо́тает Анна Петро́вна?_____

_____

10. (Москва́) — Где живёт Ива́н Ива́нович?_____

11. (библиоте́ка) — Где рабо́тает их ма́ма?_____

12. (Новосиби́рск) — Где рабо́тает Оле́г?_____

_____

13. (кварти́ра № 3) — Где живёт Зи́на?_____

_____

14. (Москва́) — Где она́ рабо́тает?_____

_____

15. (дом № 1) — Где живёт её семья́?_____

_____

Переведи́те на ру́сский язы́к. (*Give English equivalents.*)

When doing this type of exercise, remember that exact translation is almost never possible. Don't translate *words* — use the words and structures you already know to express the *ideas*.

16. "Who's that?" "It's their neighbor, Ivan Ivanovich." "And what is he?" "He's a driver."

_____

_____

_____

17. Oleg is now living not in Moscow but in Novosibirsk. He's a construction worker. But his father lives in Moscow. He's no longer working, he's retired.

_____

_____

_____

_____

18. Anna Petrovna works in a school. She's a teacher. And her neighbor Zina is a physicist and works at an institute.

_____

_____

_____

19. "Is Ivan Ivanovich home yet?" "No, he's still at work."

_____

_____

20. Is Oleg reading the second or the third lesson?

21. "Is Anna Petrovna still at work?" "No, she's at home already. Come in, please." "Thank you."

_____

_____

_____

22. Boris is not a teacher but a construction worker. His sister Larisa is also a construction worker. Their father and mother are already retired.

_____

_____

_____

_____

23. Ivan Ivanovich lives in building No. 1, in apartment No. 2. And his neighbor Vasily Nikolaevich lives in apartment No. 3.

_____

_____

_____

_____

WORKSHEET

Complete the sentences you hear by marking the appropriate space in each case.

1. _____ мой?
   _____ моя́?
   _____ моё?
   _____ мой?

2. _____ твой?
   _____ твоя́?
   _____ твоё?
   _____ твой?

3. _____ наш?
   _____ на́ша?
   _____ на́ше?
   _____ на́ши?

4. _____ ваш?
   _____ ва́ша?
   _____ ва́ше?
   _____ ва́ши?

5. _____ твой?
   _____ твоя́?
   _____ твоё?
   _____ твой?

6. _____ мой?
   _____ моя́?
   _____ моё?
   _____ мой?

7. _____ ваш?

   _____ ва́ша?
   _____ ва́ше?
   _____ ва́ши?

8. _____ наш?
   _____ на́ша?
   _____ на́ше?
   _____ на́ши?

9. _____ твой?
   _____ твоя́?
   _____ твоё?
   _____ твой?

10. _____ ваш?
    _____ ва́ша?
    _____ ва́ше?
    _____ ва́ши?

11. _____ отдыха́ю.
    _____ отдыха́ем.
    _____ отдыха́ете.
    _____ отдыха́ют.

12. _____ за́втракаю.
    _____ за́втракает.
    _____ за́втракаем.
    _____ за́втракают.

13. _____ рабо́тает.
    _____ рабо́таем.

_____ рабо́таете.

_____ рабо́тают.

14. _____ зна́ю.

_____ зна́ешь.

_____ зна́ем.

_____ зна́ете.

15. _____ у́жинаю.

_____ у́жинаешь.

_____ у́жинает.

_____ у́жинаете.

16. _____ обе́даешь.

_____ обе́дает.

_____ обе́даем.

_____ обе́даете.

17. _____ слу́шаю ра́дио.

_____ слу́шаешь ра́дио.

_____ слу́шаем ра́дио.

_____ слу́шаете ра́дио.

18. _____ обе́даю.

_____ обе́даете.

_____ обе́даем.

_____ обе́дают.

19. _____ у́жинаю.

_____ у́жинаешь.

_____ у́жинает.

_____ у́жинают.

20. _____ отдыха́ю.

_____ отдыха́ем.

_____ отдыха́ете.

_____ отдыха́ют.

ПИСЬМЕННОЕ ЗАДАНИЕ

Образе́ц: — _Чей э́то га́лстук? (ты)_ — _Э́то твой га́лстук._

1. — _____ э́то руба́шка? (я) _____

2. — _____ э́то де́ти? (мы) _____

3. — _____ э́то пальто́? (вы) _____

4. — _____ э́то кварти́ра? (я) _____

5. — _____ э́то газе́та? (ты) _____

6. — _____ э́то письмо́? (я) _____

7. — _____ э́то га́лстук? (вы) _____

8. — _____ э́то портфе́ль? (ты) _____

9. — _____ э́то стихи́? (он) _____

10. — _____ э́то журна́л? (я) _____

11. — _____ э́то кни́га? (я) _____

12. — _____ э́то сигаре́ты? (он) _____

13. — _____ э́то упражне́ние? (ты) _____

14. — _____ э́то кварти́ра? (мы) _____

15. — _____ э́то пальто́? (ты) _____

Use the words provided to make up Russian sentences. Do not change the order in which the words are given. Provide any necessary prepositions.

Образе́ц: мы/за́втракай + /у́тром — *Мы за́втракаем у́тром.*

16. я/сейча́с/опа́здывай + _____

17. мы/отдыха́й + /дом о́тдыха _____

18. мой/сигаре́ты/портфе́ль _____

19. вы/обе́дай + /институ́т _____

20. ве́чером/они́/у́жинай + _____

21. ты/за́втракай + /до́ма _____

22. вы/не/знай + /где/наш/де́ти? _____

23. ваш/де́ти/опа́здывай + _____

24. где/ты/отдыха́й + ? _____

25. наш/роди́тели/жить/Москва́ _____

26. а/мы/жить/Новосиби́рск _____

27. его́/жена́/не/рабо́тай + /она́/пе́нсия _____

28. ты/не/знай + /где/мой/пальто́? _____

29. их/ма́ма/отдыха́й + /дом о́тдыха _____

30. я/обе́дай + /шко́ла _____

Переведи́те на ру́сский язы́к.

31. "Why doesn't Nina know where her briefcase is?" "Because her mama is now vacationing at a resort."

_____

_____

32. "Please meet my daughter." "Very pleased to meet you."

_____

33. "You don't happen to know what Zina's doing now?" "She's having supper."

_____

_____

34. Their father still works in Novosibirsk. He's a construction worker. But their mother is no longer working, she's retired.

_____

_____

_____

35. When Mama's at home we eat breakfast calmly. When she's at the vacation center we don't eat breakfast because we're late.

_____

_____

_____

36. "When do you eat dinner?" "We eat dinner in the afternoon."

_____

_____

37. "What do you do in the evening?" "In the evening we rest, read, listen to music."

_____

_____

_____

38. "Is Anna Petrovna still at school?" "No, she's already home."

_____

39. "What's in the briefcase?" "My newspaper and your book are in the briefcase."

_____

_____

40. "Who's that?" "That's my son Vladimir." "What is he?" "He's a teacher."

_____

_____

WORKSHEET

Complete the sentences you hear by marking the appropriate space in each case.

1. _____ говорю́.
   _____ говори́шь.
   _____ говори́м.
   _____ говоря́т.

2. _____ говори́т.
   _____ говори́м.
   _____ говори́те.
   _____ говоря́т.

3. _____ говори́шь?
   _____ говори́т?
   _____ говори́те?
   _____ говоря́т де́ти?

4. _____ говорю́!
   _____ говори́шь!
   _____ говори́м!
   _____ говори́те!

5. _____ говорю́.
   _____ говори́шь.
   _____ говори́те.
   _____ говоря́т.

6. _____ говори́шь.

   _____ говори́т.
   _____ говори́м.
   _____ говоря́т.

7. _____ ру́сский язы́к.
   _____ по-ру́сски.

8. _____ ру́сский язы́к.
   _____ по-ру́сски.

9. _____ англи́йский язы́к.
   _____ по-англи́йски.

10. _____ ру́сский язы́к.
    _____ по-ру́сски.

11. _____ францу́зский язы́к.
    _____ по-францу́зски.

12. _____ ру́сский язы́к.
    _____ по-ру́сски.

13. _____ англи́йский язы́к.
    _____ по-англи́йски.

14. _____ францу́зский язы́к.
    _____ по-францу́зски.

15. _____ францу́зский язы́к.
    _____ по-францу́зски.

ПИСЬМЕННОЕ ЗАДАНИЕ

Образец: Здесь мой журнал. — *Ваши журналы там.*

1. Здесь моя книга._____

2. Здесь моё пальто._____

3. Здесь мой галстук._____

4. Здесь моё письмо._____

5. Здесь мой портфель._____

6. Здесь моё окно._____

7. Здесь моя газета._____

8. Здесь моё упражнение. _____

9. Здесь моя квартира._____

10. Здесь моя рубашка._____

11. Здесь мой дом._____

Use plural forms of the words given in parentheses.

12. Максим и Антон уже здесь. (мать) А где же их _____ ?

13. Нина и Зина уже здесь. (отец) А где же их _____ ?

14. Лариса уже здесь. (сестра) А где же её _____ ?

15. Антон Иванович уже здесь. (дочь) А где же его _____ ?

16. Зинаида Петровна уже здесь. (сын) А где же её _____ ?

17. Дети уже здесь. (учительница) А где же _____ ?

18. Антон уже здесь. (брат) А где же его _____ ?

19. Дети уже здесь. (учитель) А где же _____ ?

20. Профессор уже здесь. (студент) А где же _____ ?

21. Максим и Антон уже здесь. (мама) А где же их _____ ?

Переведите на русский язык.

22. "About whom are the stewardesses talking?" "About John. He's an American and he speaks only English."

_____

_____

_____

23. "Tell me, please, what's the teacher talking about?" "About Lesson No. 5." "Thanks." "Don't mention it."

_____

_____

_____

24. "What do you think, is Anna Petrovna already at work?" "I don't think so."

_____

25. The American still knows Russian poorly, but he already understands Russian.

_____

26. "I don't know whether Vera speaks French." "I don't know either."

_____

27. The teacher asks in Russian, but the children answer in English. They're studying Russian, but still speak Russian poorly.

_____

_____

_____

28. I'm studying German, but my brother is studying Spanish.

_____

_____

29. "You don't happen to know where Larisa works?" "She's a stewardess and works at Aeroflot."

_____

_____

_____

30. Zina asks, "Are these your cigarettes?" I answer, "Yes, mine." "Here you are," Zina says. Then she asks if I know where her cigarettes are.

_____

_____

_____

_____

УРОК-ОБОБЩЕНИЕ (1-5) I

Переведите на русский язык.

1. Whose cigarettes are these, yours or his?

2. Nina's studying English in school. She already understands a little English, but still speaks poorly.

3. "Who's that?" "That's our neighbor." "What is she?" "She's a construction worker."

4. "Papa's already home." "I know he's at home."

5. "Please meet my daughters, Anna and Vera." "Very pleased to meet you, Victor."

6. "You don't happen to know what Nina's doing?" "She's out playing."

7. Their teacher is not a Russian but an American.

8. He says he's retired and is no longer working.

9. About what are the children talking, about the magazine or the book?

10. John lives in Moscow, but he doesn't understand Russian.

11. I'm an American and don't understand what you're saying.

_____

12. "This isn't your shirt, but mine." "And where in the world is my shirt?" "Here it is."

_____

_____

13. Anna Petrovna works not at the library, but at a school.

_____

_____

14. Maxim's reading a book about Paris.

_____

15. "Is Ivan Ivanovich still at work?" "No, he's already at home." "Thank you."
"You're welcome."

_____

_____

_____

16. "About whom is he asking?" "About the stewardess."

_____

17. "Come in, please." "Thank you."

_____

18. Tell me, please, where is Oleg working now?

_____

_____

19. "What do you think, is Anna Petrovna still at home?" "I think so."

_____

_____

20. Do you have dinner in the afternoon or in the evening?

_____

_____

21. "What's this?" "It's a book." "Whose book is it?"

_____

_____

WORKSHEET

Complete each sentence you hear by marking the appropriate space here.

1. _____ пешко́м.
   _____ на маши́не.

2. _____ пешко́м.
   _____ на трамва́е.

3. _____ пешко́м.
   _____ на метро́.

4. _____ пешко́м.
   _____ на тролле́йбусе.

5. _____ пешко́м.
   _____ на авто́бусе.

You will now hear a number of questions. Mark the appropriate answer in each case.

6. _____ Он до́ма.
   _____ Он идёт домо́й.
   _____ Он е́дет домо́й.

7. _____ Они́ до́ма.
   _____ Они́ иду́т домо́й.
   _____ Они́ е́дут домо́й.

8. _____ Она́ до́ма.
   _____ Она́ идёт домо́й.
   _____ Она́ е́дет домо́й.

9. _____ Они́ до́ма.
   _____ Они́ иду́т домо́й.
   _____ Они́ е́дут домо́й.

10. _____ Я до́ма.
    _____ Я иду́ домо́й.
    _____ Я е́ду домо́й.

You will now hear a number of statements. Mark the appropriate question in each case.

11. _____ Где они́?
    _____ Куда́ они́ иду́т?
    _____ Куда́ они́ е́дут?

12. _____ Где они́?
    _____ Куда́ они́ иду́т?
    _____ Куда́ они́ е́дут?

13. _____ Где она́?
    _____ Куда́ она́ идёт?
    _____ Куда́ она́ е́дет?

14. _____ Где она́?
    _____ Куда́ она́ идёт?
    _____ Куда́ она́ е́дет?

15. _____ Где он?
    _____ Куда́ он идёт?
    _____ Куда́ он е́дет?

Complete the dialogs you hear by marking the appropriate space here.

16. _____ Это говори́т Зи́на.

_____ Вот она́.

_____ Спаси́бо.

17. _____ Подожди́те мину́точку.

_____ Входи́те, пожа́луйста.

_____ Это говори́т Анто́н.

18. _____ Входи́те, пожа́луйста.

_____ Вот хорошо́!

_____ До́ма. Подожди́те мину́точку.

19. _____ Это говори́т Макси́м.

_____ Вот хорошо́! Спаси́бо.

_____ Пожа́луйста.

20. _____ Спаси́бо.

_____ Вот они́.

_____ Подожди́те мину́точку.

ПИСЬМЕННОЕ ЗАДАНИЕ

Запо́лните про́пуски. (Use the words in parentheses in the required form.)

1. (е́хать, до́ма/домо́й) На́ша ма́ма _____ _____ на тролле́йбусе.

2. (где/куда́, идти́) — _____ _____ Макси́м и Ни́на? (идти́, до́ма/домо́й) — Они́ уже́ _____ _____ .

3. (е́хать, до́ма/домо́й, идти́) Мы _____ _____ на трам-ва́е, а на́ша ма́ма _____ пешко́м.

4. (где/куда́) — _____ твой па́па?— Он сейча́с в до́ме о́тдыха.

5. (е́хать, до́ма/домо́й) Мари́я Влади́мировна сейча́с _____ _____ на метро́, а её муж Васи́лий Никола́евич уже́ _____ .

6. (идти́, до́ма/домо́й) Ма́ма и па́па _____ _____ пешко́м. (до́ма/домо́й, смотре́ть; идти́) А Ма́ша и ба́бушка уже́ _____ и _____ в окно́. Ма́ша говори́т: «Ба́бушка, вот _____ ма́ма и па́па вме́сте».

7. (где/куда́, до́ма/домо́й) — _____ сейча́с Макси́м и Ни́на?— Макси́м _____ , а Ни́на в шко́ле.

8. (смотре́ть; идти́, е́хать) Я _____ в окно́. Вот на́ша у́лица. _____ маши́ны, авто́бусы, тролле́йбусы.

9. Де́ти хорошо́ игра́ют вме́сте. (смотре́ть) Ма́ша, почему́ ты _____ в окно́?

10. (е́хать, до́ма/домо́й) Как вы _____ _____ , на такси́ и́ли на метро́?

Answer the following questions, using the words given in parentheses.

11. (портфе́ль) — Где ва́ши кни́ги? _____

12. (у́жинать) — Что вы де́лаете ве́чером? _____

13. (у́тром) — Когда́ вы за́втракаете? _____

14. (чита́ть газе́ты) — Что вы де́лаете в библиоте́ке? _____

_____

15. (Ива́н Ива́нович) — Кто живёт в кварти́ре № 2? _____

_____

Supply questions which would elicit the following answers.

16. Днём мы обе́даем. _____

17. Анна Петро́вна рабо́тает в шко́ле. _____

_____

18. В библиоте́ке рабо́тает Мари́я Бори́совна. _____

_____

19. В портфе́ле пи́сьма и газе́ты. _____

_____

20. Де́ти уже́ до́ма. _____

Переведи́те на ру́сский язы́к.

21. "How are you going home, by metro or by bus?" "Maxim's going home alone on the metro, and we're going home by taxi."

_____

_____

_____

22. "Is your mother still at work?" "No, she's already coming home. Here she comes now. Wait a minute." "Thank you."

_____

_____

23. "Oleg and Zina are walking home together". "Who else is walking home?" "Masha is walking home."

_____

_____

_____

24. "Why don't the passengers answer?" "They don't answer because they're Americans and don't understand Russian."

_____

_____

_____

25. "About whom are you asking?" "About Maxim and Nina. You wouldn't happen to know whose children they are?"

_____

_____

_____

26. "Hello, Ivan Ivanovich. Is this your car?" "Yes. I'm going home now. Are you going home too? Please [offering a ride]." "What a break! Thank you."

_____

_____

_____

_____

27. Telephone conversation: "Hello. Nina? This is Vasily Nikolaevich. Is your father at home yet?" "Yes, he's at home. Just a minute, please."

_____

_____

_____

_____

28. "Tell me, please, where's the bus stop?" "Here it is." "Thank you." "You're welcome."

_____

_____

29. Grandma asks why the children are looking out the window.

_____

WORKSHEET

You will now hear a number of questions. Mark here the appropriate answer in each case.

1. _____ — В шко́лу.
   _____ — В шко́ле.
2. _____ — В институ́т.
   _____ — В институ́те.
3. _____ — В дом о́тдыха.
   _____ — В до́ме о́тдыха.
4. _____ — На рабо́ту.
   _____ — На рабо́те.
5. _____ — На заво́д.
   _____ — На заво́де.

6. _____ — На заня́тия.
   _____ — На заня́тиях.
7. _____ — На ле́кцию.
   _____ — На ле́кции.
8. _____ — На уро́к.
   _____ — На уро́ке.
9. _____ — В гара́ж.
   _____ — В гараже́.
10. _____ — В парк.
    _____ — В па́рке.

You will now hear a number of sentences to which you are to react here by marking the appropriate spaces.

11. _____ — Како́й хоро́ший!
    _____ — Кака́я хоро́шая!
    _____ — Како́е хоро́шее!
    _____ — Каки́е хоро́шие!
12. _____ — Како́й краси́вый!
    _____ — Кака́я краси́вая!
    _____ — Како́е краси́вое!
    _____ — Каки́е краси́вые!
13. _____ — Како́й симпати́чный!
    _____ — Кака́я симпати́чная!
    _____ — Како́е симпати́чное!
    _____ — Каки́е симпати́чные!
14. _____ — Како́й ста́рый!
    _____ — Кака́я ста́рая!

    _____ — Како́е ста́рое!
    _____ — Каки́е ста́рые!
15. _____ — Како́й краси́вый!
    _____ — Кака́я краси́вая!
    _____ — Како́е краси́вое!
    _____ — Каки́е краси́вые!
16. _____ — Како́й хоро́ший!
    _____ — Кака́я хоро́шая!
    _____ — Како́е хоро́шее!
    _____ — Каки́е хоро́шие!
17. _____ — Како́й плохо́й!
    _____ — Кака́я плоха́я!
    _____ — Како́е плохо́е!
    _____ — Каки́е плохи́е!

18. _____ — Како́й краси́вый!   _____ — Како́е серьёзное!

_____ — Кака́я краси́вая!   _____ — Каки́е серьёзные!

_____ — Како́е краси́вое!   20. _____ — Како́й краси́вый!

_____ — Каки́е краси́вые!   _____ — Кака́я краси́вая!

19. _____ — Како́й серьёзный!   _____ — Како́е краси́вое!

_____ — Кака́я серьёзная!   _____ — Каки́е краси́вые!

Complete the sentences you hear by marking the appropriate space here.

21. _____ час.   24. _____ час.

_____ часа́.   _____ часа́.

_____ часо́в.   _____ часо́в.

22. _____ час.   25. _____ час.

_____ часа́.   _____ часа́.

_____ часо́в.   _____ часо́в.

23. _____ час.   26. _____ час.

_____ часа́.   _____ часа́.

_____ часо́в.   _____ часо́в.

You will now hear a number of questions. Mark the appropriate answer in each case.

27. _____ — Да, я.   _____ — Да, е́дет.

_____ — Нет, не о́чень хорошо́.   _____ — Нет, в Новосиби́рск.

_____ — Да, ру́сский.   32. _____ — Да, я.

28. _____ — Да, я.   _____ — Да, иду́.

_____ — Нет, не иду́.   _____ — Нет, в библиоте́ку.

_____ — Да, на рабо́ту.   33. _____ — Да, э́то.

29. _____ — Да, Зи́на.   _____ — Да, моё.

_____ — Да, идёт.   _____ — Нет, э́то моя́ руба́шка.

_____ — Нет, на рабо́ту.   34. _____ — Да, э́та.

30. _____ — Да, Лари́са.   _____ — Да, на́ша.

_____ — Да, рабо́тает.   ___ — Да, кварти́ра.

_____ — Да, в Аэрофло́те.   35. _____ — Да, я.

31. _____ — Да, па́па.   _____ — Да, говорю́.

_____ — Да, по-англи́йски.

ПИСЬМЕННОЕ ЗАДАНИЕ

Образе́ц: (де́тский сад) — Куда́ иду́т де́ти? — *Де́ти иду́т в де́тский сад.*

1. (магази́н) — Куда́ спеши́т Аня? _____

2. (завóд) — Где рабóтает ваш сын? _____

3. (Новосибúрск) — Где живёт Олéг? _____

4. (урóк) — Кудá идёт Нúна? _____

5. (Москвá) — Кудá éдет Ларúса? _____

6. (рабóта) — Кудá спешúт вáша сестрá? _____

_____

7. (квартúра № 7) — Где живýт Соколóвы? _____

8. (гарáж) — Где сейчáс Вáня? _____

9. (Амéрика) — Кудá éдет Вадúм? _____

10. (библиотéка) — Кудá идёт Мáша? _____

Образéц: (серьёзный) — Вот идёт Нúна.— *Какáя онá серьёзная!*

11. (симпатúчный) — Вот идýт мои брáтья. _____

12. (красúвый) — Вот идёт Ларúса. _____

13. (серьёзный) — Вот идёт Максúм. _____

14. (красúвый) — Вот идýт нáши дóчери. _____

15. (симпатúчный) — Вот идёт Вадúм. _____

Образéц: (стáрый) Это óчень _____ пальтó.— *Это óчень стáрое пальтó.*

16. (хорóший) Это óчень _____ кнúги.

17. (дéтский) Это _____ кнúга.

18. (симпатúчный, рýсский) Это óчень _____ _____ дéвушка.

19. (хорóший) Это _____ пальтó.

20. (плохóй) Это _____ сигарéты.

21. (нóвый) Это нáши _____ студéнты.

22. (нóвый, рýсский) Это _____ _____ кнúги и журнáлы.

23. (хорóший, дéтский) Это _____ _____ письмó.

24. (симпатúчный, серьёзный) Это _____ и óчень _____ лю́ди.

25. (стáрый, плохóй) Это _____ _____ рубáшки.

Образéц: (5) — Скóлько сейчáс врéмени?— *Сейчáс пять часóв.*

26. (2) — Котóрый час? _____

27. (4) — Скóлько врéмени? _____

28. (1) — Скóлько сейчáс врéмени? _____

29. (5) — Скóлько врéмени? _____

30. (3) — Котóрый сейчáс час? _____

31. (6) — Кото́рый час? _____

32. (7) — Ско́лько вре́мени? _____

Переведи́те на ру́сский язы́к. (Always write numbers out fully as words.)

33. Vadim Petrovich is late today and is going to work at the library by taxi.

_____

_____

34. Masha is telling (narrating) what she does in the morning.

_____

35. Our mother now is vacationing at a resort.

_____

_____

36. "Where are Maxim and Nina Petrov?" "They're out playing in the park."

_____

_____

37. Tell me, please, does trolleybus No. 6 go downtown?

_____

_____

38. I'm in a big hurry. After all it's already 7 o'clock.

_____

_____

39. "Is nobody working today?" "No, everybody is resting."

_____

_____

40. Larisa's very nice and is always smiling.

_____

41. I know Russian very poorly. You don't happen to know what this means in Russian?

_____

_____

42. "About whom are you talking?" "About the American in the plane."

_____

_____

43. Victor is late to classes at the university and is going by taxi.

_____

_____

УРОК **8**

WORKSHEET

Answer each question you hear by marking the appropriate space here.

1. _____ Сейча́с 7 часо́в.
   _____ В 7 часо́в.

2. _____ Час.
   _____ В час.

3. _____ Три часа́.
   _____ В 3 часа́.

4. _____ Сейча́с 8 часо́в.
   _____ В 8 часо́в.

5. _____ Два часа́.
   _____ В 2 часа́.

6. _____ Среда́.
   _____ В сре́ду.

7. _____ Суббо́та.
   _____ В суббо́ту.

8. _____ Сего́дня пя́тница.
   _____ В пя́тницу.

9. _____ Сего́дня вто́рник.
   _____ Во вто́рник.

10. _____ Воскресе́нье.
    _____ В воскресе́нье.

11. _____ Он не прав.
    _____ Она́ не права́.
    _____ Они́ не пра́вы.

12. _____ Он прав.
    _____ Она́ права́.
    _____ Они́ пра́вы.

13. _____ Он не прав.
    _____ Она́ не права́.
    _____ Они́ не пра́вы.

14. _____ Он прав.
    _____ Она́ права́.
    _____ Они́ пра́вы.

15. _____ Он не прав.
    _____ Она́ не права́.
    _____ Они́ не пра́вы.

ПИСЬМЕННОЕ ЗАДАНИЕ

Образе́ц:— Когда́ они́ иду́т на рабо́ту? (3)— *Они́ иду́т на рабо́ту в три часа́.*

1. — Когда́ Макси́м идёт в де́тский сад? (8) _____

   _____

2. — Когда́ вы обы́чно обе́даете? (3) _____

   _____

58

3. — Когда́ начина́ется уро́к? (1) _____

4. — Когда́ конча́ется де́тская переда́ча? (4) _____

_____

5. — В кото́ром часу́ за́втракают Ивано́вы? (7) _____

_____

6. — Когда́ ты у́жинаешь? (6) _____

7. — Когда́ ди́ктор начина́ет переда́чу? (2) _____

_____

8. — Когда́ вы конча́ете рабо́тать? (5) _____

_____

Запо́лните про́пуски. (Use the appropriate pronouns based on context.)

9. Я ру́сский. Вы понима́ете _____, когда́ я говорю́?

10. Вы но́вый студе́нт? Как _____ зову́т?

11. Ты зна́ешь, я _____ не понима́ю, когда́ ты говори́шь по-англи́йски.

12. Вот идёт но́вая студе́нтка. Ты не зна́ешь, как _____ зову́т?

Add the particle -ся in those blanks where it is needed.

13. В 8 часо́в начина́ет _____ переда́ча «Москва́ и москвичи́».

14. Де́тские переда́чи обы́чно конча́ют _____ в 5 часо́в.

15. Ди́ктор всегда́ начина́ет _____ переда́чу в час.

16. Заня́тия обы́чно начина́ют _____ в 2 часа́.

17. Её уро́к конча́ет _____ в 3 часа́.

18. Снача́ла на́ши де́ти у́жинают, пото́м начина́ют _____ игра́ть.

19. Сейча́с начина́ет _____ друга́я интере́сная переда́ча.

Переведи́те на ру́сский язы́к.

20. "Are you leaving already? Let's watch TV. After all there's an interesting show starting now." "OK, let's. I consider that this's a very good program."

_____

_____

_____

21. Anna Petrovna's been vacationing for a long time at a resort and Ivan Ivanovich doesn't want to watch TV alone. Therefore he comes to apartment No. 3 and he and his neighbors watch TV together. After all there are very interesting programs in the evening. At 8 o'clock, for example, the program "Moscow and the Muscovites" begins.

_____

_____

_____

_____

_____

_____

22. You're wrong, Anya. That's an interesting book.

_____

23. Pardon me, I'm in a big hurry. I'm late to work at the plant.

_____

_____

24. You're right, Ivan Ivanovich. Anton Nikolaevich plays chess very well.

_____

_____

25. "The program's coming to an end. Let's play a game of chess!" "Let's!"

_____

_____

26. "Papa and Anton Nikolaevich are watching TV." "So they're not playing chess? But after all Anton Nikolaevich comes to play chess."

_____

_____

_____

_____

27. Our sons and daughters usually come Friday evening and we eat supper together.

_____

_____

_____

28. On Tuesday I always start working at 8 o'clock and finish working at 5. At 2 o'clock I have dinner at the institute. I arrive home at 6 o'clock.

_____

_____

_____

29. Here are our neighbors, Vasily Nikolaevich and Maria Vladimirovna Sokolov. They've been living in apartment No. 3 a long time.

_____

_____

_____

WORKSHEET

Answer each question you hear by marking the appropriate space here.

1. _____ Да, есть.
_____ Да, ру́сские.

2. _____ У меня́ есть.
_____ Он у меня́.

3. _____ Да, есть.
_____ Да, но́вая.

4. _____ Да, есть.
_____ Нет, не у меня́.

5. _____ Да, есть.
_____ Да, у меня́.

6. _____ У меня́ есть.
_____ У меня́.

7. _____ Да, есть.
_____ Да, больша́я.

8. _____ Да, есть.
_____ Да, горя́чая.

9. _____ Да, есть.
_____ Нет, не у меня́.

10. _____ Да, есть.
_____ Да, де́ти.

Complete each sentence you hear by marking the appropriate space here.

11. _____ входи́!
_____ входи́те!

12. _____ дава́й поговори́м!
_____ дава́йте поговори́м!

13. _____ здра́вствуй!
_____ здра́вствуйте!

14. _____ подожди́!
_____ подожди́те!

15. _____ прости́!
_____ прости́те!

16. _____ скажи́, пожа́луйста, где Зи́на?
_____ скажи́те, пожа́луйста, где Зи́на?

17. _____ смотри́!
_____ смотри́те!

18. _____ дава́й посмо́трим переда́чу!
_____ дава́йте посмо́трим переда́чу!

19. _____ спроси́, до́ма ли Анна Петро́вна?
_____ спроси́те, до́ма ли Анна Петро́вна?

20. _____ узна́й, что де́лает ба́бушка.
_____ узна́йте, что де́лает ба́бушка.

Complete each conversation you hear by marking the appropriate space here.

21. _____ Всё равно́ в го́роде лу́чше.

  _____ С удово́льствием.

  _____ Как живёте?

22. _____ Спаси́бо, хорошо́.

  _____ Коне́чно, есть.

  _____ С удово́льствием.

23. _____ Хорошо́.

  _____ Как его́ зову́т?

  _____ Мо́жет быть, до́ма.

24. _____ Спаси́бо, хорошо́.

  _____ Всё равно́ в дере́вне лу́чше.

  _____ Здра́вствуй. Как живёшь?

25. _____ Дава́й!

  _____ Ну и как?

  _____ Идём вме́сте!

26. _____ С удово́льствием!

  _____ Идём вме́сте!

  _____ Мо́жет быть.

27. _____ С удово́льствием!

  _____ Как живёшь?

  _____ Как её зову́т?

28. _____ Мой. Спаси́бо.

  _____ С удово́льствием!

  _____ Всё равно́ здесь лу́чше.

ПИСЬМЕННОЕ ЗАДАНИЕ

Образе́ц: Вот моя́ маши́на.— *У меня́ есть маши́на.*

1. Вот твои́ сигаре́ты. _____

2. Вот их де́ти. _____

3. Вот её роди́тели. _____

4. Вот мой портфе́ль. _____

5. Вот наш де́душка. _____

6. Вот ва́ши ша́хматы. _____

7. Вот их маши́на. _____

8. Вот твои́ бра́тья. _____

9. Вот его́ ба́бушка. _____

10. Вот ва́ши сёстры. _____

Запо́лните про́пуски.

11. (хоро́ший, но́вый) У неё о́чень _____ _____ пальто́.

12. (большо́й) У нас в кварти́ре о́чень _____ о́кна.

13. (ма́ленький, большо́й) У него́ в ко́мнате _____ окно́, а у меня́ _____ .

14. (горя́чий, холо́дный) У них в кварти́ре есть и _____ , и _____ вода́.

15. (большо́й, хоро́ший) У нас _____

ку́хня.

Отвеча́йте! (Give short-form answers in the positive.)

Образе́ц: — У вас есть маши́на? — *Да, есть.*

16. — У вас но́вая кварти́ра? _____

17. — У неё есть ба́бушка? _____

18. — У них есть де́ти? _____

19. — У них ма́ленькие де́ти? _____

20. — У них есть горя́чая вода́? _____

21. — У вас но́вый телеви́зор? _____

22. — У вас есть бра́тья? _____

23. — Мой журна́л у тебя́? _____

24. — У вас есть ру́сские газе́ты? _____

Переведи́те на ру́сский язы́к.

25. "Do you have a car?" "Yes, I do." "What kind of car do you have?" "It's small, but very good."

_____

_____

_____

26. "Do you have my chess set?" "No, they have it."

_____

27. "Who has my chess set?" "I have it." "Where is it?" "It's on the table."

_____

_____

28. My grandfather and grandmother are now retired and live in the country. They have a big apartment. In their apartment they have both hot and cold water, gas and a television set. But all the same, I think that it's better in the city.

_____

_____

_____

_____

29. "Do you have Russian newspapers?" "Yes, we do."

_____

_____

30. "Do you have the Russian newspaper?" "No, it's on the table." "Not here." "Maybe it's in the drawer." "Not here either."

_____

_____

31. "What's here?" "It's our kitchen, bathroom and toilet."

_____

32. "Do you have (any) big shirts?" "Yes, here they are. These are very good shirts."

_____

33. "Are you leaving? What time is it?" "It's already 8 o'clock."

_____

34. While they're listening to music, I read a book.

_____

35. "Who has a car?" "I do."

_____

36. "Who has the program?" "I don't. Here comes Vanya. Maybe he has it?"

_____

37. "Is this your magazine?" "No, it's not my magazine. Here comes Zina. Maybe it's her magazine."

_____

_____

38. "What's on TV today? Where's the program?" "Our neighbor Vadim is appearing at 9 o'clock." "Good! I always watch his program with pleasure."

_____

_____

_____

_____

WORKSHEET

Complete each sentence you hear by marking the appropriate space here.

1. _____ отдыха́ет.
   _____ отдыха́ла.
   _____ отдыха́ли.

2. _____ на столе́.
   _____ бы́ло на столе́.
   _____ бы́ли на столе́.

3. _____ гуля́ют.
   _____ гуля́ла.
   _____ гуля́ли.

4. _____ рабо́таем.
   _____ рабо́тал.
   _____ рабо́тали.

5. _____ живёт в Москве́.
   _____ жил в Москве́.
   _____ жила́ в Москве́.

6. _____ до́ма.
   _____ был до́ма.
   _____ была́ до́ма.

7. _____ рабо́тает на заво́де.
   _____ рабо́тал на заво́де.
   _____ рабо́тала на заво́де.

8. _____ смо́трят телеви́зор.
   _____ смотре́л телеви́зор.
   _____ смотре́ли телеви́зор.

9. _____ не рабо́тает.
   _____ не рабо́тал.
   _____ не рабо́тали.

10. _____ гуля́ют в па́рке.
    _____ гуля́ла в па́рке.
    _____ гуля́ли в па́рке.

11. _____ Вади́м.
    _____ Вади́ма.
    _____ о Вади́ме.

12. _____ Пе́тя.
    _____ Пе́тю.
    _____ о Пе́те.

13. _____ Ви́ктор?
    _____ Ви́ктора?
    _____ Ма́ша?

14. _____ де́душка.
    _____ де́душку.
    _____ о де́душке.

15. _____ преподава́тель.
    _____ преподава́теля.
    _____ о преподава́теле.

16. _____ Васи́лий Никола́евич.
    _____ Васи́лия Никола́евича.
    _____ о Васи́лии Никола́евиче.

17. ____	Вади́м.	19. ____	Ва́ня.
____	Вади́ма.	____	Ва́ню.
____	о Вади́ме.	____	Ви́тя.
18. ____	па́па.	20. ____	брат?
____	па́пу.	____	бра́та?
____	о па́пе.	____	о бра́те?

Continue each conversation you hear by marking the appropriate space here.

21. ____ — Как её зову́т?
    ____ — Как она́ называ́ется?
22. ____ — Как его́ зову́т?
    ____ — Как он называ́ется?
23. ____ — Как их зову́т?
    ____ — Как они́ называ́ются?
24. ____ — Как её зову́т?
    ____ — Как она́ называ́ется?
25. ____ — Как их зову́т?
    ____ — Как они́ называ́ются?

26. ____ — Почему́ вы прихо́дите сюда́?
    ____ — Заче́м вы прихо́дите сюда́?
27. ____ — Почему́ прихо́дит Ви́ктор?
    ____ — Заче́м прихо́дит Ви́ктор?
28. ____ — Почему́...?
    ____ — Заче́м...?
29. ____ — Почему́...?
    ____ — Заче́м...?

ПИСЬМЕННОЕ ЗАДАНИЕ

Образе́ц:— Макси́м сейча́с гуля́ет?— *Нет, но вчера́ он гуля́л.*

1. — Ма́ша сейча́с игра́ет? _____

2. — Вади́м сего́дня выступа́ет по телеви́зору? _____
   _____

3. — Ива́н Ива́нович сейча́с отдыха́ет? _____
   _____

4. — Та́ня сего́дня рабо́тает в кио́ске? _____
   _____

5. — Гали́на Васи́льевна сего́дня рабо́тает? _____
   _____

Образе́ц: Де́ти изуча́ют ру́сский язы́к.— *Ра́ньше они́ то́же изуча́ли ру́сский язы́к.*

6. Де́душка и ба́бушка живу́т в дере́вне. _____
   _____

7. Обéд начинáется в два часá. _____
_____

8. Вѝктор провóдит свобóдное врéмя в пáрке. _____
_____

9. Мой дéдушка рабóтает в институ́те. _____
_____

10. Олéг в Новосибѝрске. _____
_____

Образéц: Вот идёт Максѝм.— *Ты, навéрно, ужé знáешь Максѝма.*

11. Вот идёт егó дéдушка. _____

12. Вот идёт Васѝлий Николáевич. _____
_____

13. Вот идёт Галѝна Васѝльевна. _____
_____

14. Вот идёт её мать. _____

15. Вот идёт Ивáн Ивáнович. _____
_____

16. Вот идёт егó пáпа. _____

17. Вот идёт Ларѝса. _____

18. Вот идёт Мáша. _____

Переведѝте на рýсский язы́к.

19. Formerly Tanya spent (her) free time at the library. There she would read *Pravda* and the magazines *Soviet Woman* and *Family & School*. But now she buys *Soviet Sport* and *Chess in the USSR* at the newsstand.
_____
_____
_____
_____
_____

20. The girl who was working at the kiosk last night is called Tanya.
_____
_____

21. "Who's working at the kiosk this evening, a man or a woman?" "There's an elderly man working there."

_____

_____

22. Do you know the physicist and construction worker who appeared on TV last night?

_____

_____

23. "What magazines do you subscribe to?" "I subscribe to *Moscow* and to the newspaper *Evening Moscow*."

_____

_____

_____

24. "*Pravda*, please." "Here you are. What else?" "Nothing else today, thank you."

_____

_____

25. Have you already seen our new chairs?

_____

26. "I have some tickets to the movies." "Tonight I'm working." "That's a pity. It's a very good film." "What's it called?" "*Uncle Vanya*."

_____

_____

_____

27. Today Victor is in a big hurry. Therefore he walks past and doesn't buy anything at the newsstand.

_____

_____

28. I hear Maxim and Masha, but I don't see them.

_____

29. "Why do you always come here in the morning?" "I come here to buy *Pravda*."

_____

_____

30. "Why does Victor come here?" "He comes here because Tanya's been working at the kiosk for a long time."

_____

_____

УРОК-ОБОБЩЕНИЕ (6-10) II

Упражнение № 10. *Переведите на русский язык.*

1. "Anton Nikolaevich says that in the evening he usually plays chess. Therefore he doesn't buy a TV. But on Saturday evening at 8 he usually comes here." "Why does he come?" "He comes to watch the show 'Moscow and the Muscovites.'"

   _____

   _____

   _____

2. Formerly classes began at 9. Now they begin at 8.

   _____

3. While the men are playing chess, Anna Petrovna is showing the apartment. They have a new apartment and she shows it with pleasure. In the kitchen they have gas and both hot and cold water. Of course they have both a bathroom and a toilet.

   _____

   _____

   _____

4. I usually go to work at the factory by metro, but when I'm in a big hurry I go by taxi.

   _____

   _____

5. Maxim and Nina Petrov live close and usually go to school on foot.

   _____

6. "Who's that?" "It's my grandfather and grandmother. They live in the country, but now they're in Moscow."

_____

_____

7. When Tanya's working at the kiosk Victor spends (his) free time there. He even reads *Family & School.*

_____

_____

8. I don't know if Larisa was at home last night.

_____

9. Hello, Galina Vasilyevna. Tell me, please, what magazines do you have today?

_____

10. Hello, Tanya. You wouldn't happen to know where Mashenka is?

_____

_____

11. Formerly Larisa never smiled, but now she is always smiling.

_____

12. "Whose cigarettes are these?" "I don't know, they're not my cigarettes. Maybe they're your cigarettes."

_____

13. "Where is the magazine which I was reading?" "It's there on the table." "No, it's not here." "Maybe it's in the drawer." "Not here either."

_____

_____

14. It's good that I now finish working at 4 on Friday. I come home at 5, have supper and rest.

_____

15. "Why doesn't Vasya play chess?" "He says he plays chess poorly and therefore he doesn't want to play."

_____

16. "I don't have your new book. It's on the chair." "This isn't my book."

_____

_____

17. "Are you leaving? Where are you going?" "To a lecture at the library."

_____

18. "How are you?" "Fine. And you?"

_____

19. On Friday evening there are good programs on TV and they all watch TV together.

_____

_____

20. "Maybe you're right, Anna Petrovna." "Of course, I'm always right."

_____

_____

21. "Let's watch the new movie tonight." "I'm working tonight." "That's a pity. It's a very good movie."

_____

_____

_____

22. "Where does Vasily Nikolaevich work?" "He doesn't work anyplace now, he's been retired for a long time."

_____

_____

_____

УРОК **11**

WORKSHEET

React to each sentence you hear by marking the appropriate space here.

1. _____ — Вот э́тот?
   _____ — Вот э́та?
   _____ — Вот э́то?
   _____ — Вот э́ти?

2. _____ — Вот э́тот?
   _____ — Вот э́та?
   _____ — Вот э́то?
   _____ — Вот э́ти?

3. _____ — Вот э́тот?
   _____ — Вот э́та?
   _____ — Вот э́ту?
   _____ — Вот э́ти?

4. _____ — Вот э́тот?
   _____ — Вот э́та?
   _____ — Вот э́ту?
   _____ — Вот э́то?

5. _____ — Вот э́тот?
   _____ — Вот э́та?
   _____ — Вот э́то?
   _____ — Вот э́ти?

6. _____ — Вот э́тот?
   _____ — Вот э́та?
   _____ — Вот э́ту?
   _____ — Вот э́то?

7. _____ — Вот э́тот?
   _____ — Вот э́та?
   _____ — Вот э́ту?
   _____ — Вот э́то?

8. _____ — Вот э́тот?
   _____ — Вот э́та?
   _____ — Вот э́ту?
   _____ — Вот э́то?

9. _____ — Вот э́тот?
   _____ — Вот э́та?
   _____ — Вот э́ту?
   _____ — Вот э́то?

10. _____ — Вот э́тот?
    _____ — Вот э́та?
    _____ — Вот э́то?
    _____ — Вот э́ти?

Complete each sentence you hear by marking the appropriate space here.

11. _____ час.
    _____ часа́.
    _____ часо́в.

12. _____ мину́ту.
    _____ мину́ты.
    _____ мину́т.

13. _____ час.
_____ часа́.
_____ часо́в.

14. _____ год.
_____ го́да.
_____ лет.

15. _____ год.
_____ го́да.
_____ лет.

16. _____ мину́ту.
_____ мину́ты.
_____ мину́т.

17. _____ час.
_____ часа́.
_____ часо́в.

18. _____ год.
_____ го́да.
_____ лет.

19. _____ год.
_____ го́да.
_____ лет.

20. _____ час.
_____ часа́.
_____ часо́в.

React to each sentence you hear by marking the appropriate space here.

21. _____ — Так до́лго?
_____ — Так давно́?

22. _____ — Так до́лго?
_____ — Так давно́?

23. _____ — Так до́лго?
_____ — Так давно́?

24. _____ — Так до́лго?
_____ — Так давно́?

25. _____ — Так до́лго?
_____ — Так давно́?

Complete each sentence you hear by marking the appropriate space here.

26. _____ стро́или.
_____ постро́или.

27. _____ стро́или.
_____ постро́или.

28. _____ чита́л.
_____ прочита́л.

29. _____ чита́л.
_____ прочита́л.

30. _____ расска́зывал.
_____ рассказа́л.

31. _____ расска́зывала о рабо́те.
_____ рассказа́ла о рабо́те.

32. _____ пока́зывать фотогра́фии.
_____ показа́ть фотогра́фии.

33. _____ пока́зывать кварти́ру.
_____ показа́ть кварти́ру.

34. _____ пока́зывала фотогра́фии.
_____ показа́ла фотогра́фии.

35. _____ пока́зывала фотогра́фии.
_____ показа́ла фотогра́фии.

ПИСЬМЕННОЕ ЗАДАНИЕ

Запо́лните про́пуски. (Supply the correct form of the modifiers given in parentheses.)

1. (оди́н) Мы здесь зна́ем то́лько _____ челове́ка.

2. (весь, э́тот) Я уже́ прочита́л _____ _____ кни́гу.

3. (весь) В воскресе́нье мы _____ день гуля́ли в лесу́.

4. (ваш, ваш) Мы нигде́ не ви́дели _____ бра́та и _____ сестру́.

5. (твой, наш) В кинотеа́тре мы ви́дели _____ ма́му и _____ учи́тельницу.

6. (весь) Он _____ суббо́ту рабо́тал в саду́.

7. (оди́н) Подожди́те нас _____ мину́ту!

8. (э́тот) Мы все уже́ зна́ем _____ гео́лога.

9. (мой) Са́ша, ты не ви́дел _____ кни́ги?

10. (э́тот) Когда́ конча́ется _____ переда́ча?

Запо́лните про́пуски.

11. (all day and all evening) Они́ _____ рабо́тали в саду́.

12. (10 minutes) В кафе́ идти́ _____ .

13. (6 hours) Мы _____ е́хали в Москву́.

14. (2 years; 8 years) В Новосиби́рске мы живём _____ , а в Москве́ мы жи́ли _____ .

15. (2 minutes) Подожди́те _____ !

16. (the whole day on Friday) Вади́м _____ рабо́тал в библиоте́ке.

17. (4 hours) В Москву́ е́хать _____ .

18. (for five years) Наш го́род стро́или _____ .

19. (a year) Оле́г уже́ _____ рабо́тает в Академгородке́.

20. (3 hours) Оле́г _____ расска́зывал об Академгородке́.

Запо́лните про́пуски. (Use verbs in parentheses in the correct form.)

21. (стро́ить/постро́ить) Го́род _____ до́лго, но сейча́с уже́ _____ дома́, шко́лы, теа́тр, институ́т.

22. (чита́ть/прочита́ть) Весь ве́чер брат _____ , а мы смотре́ли телеви́зор. Он _____ все газе́ты и на́чал чита́ть э́ту кни́гу.

23. (расска́зывать/рассказа́ть; пока́зывать/показа́ть) Сего́дня Лари́са весь ве́чер _____ , как она́ отдыха́ла на мо́ре. Она́ всё _____ и начала́ _____ фотогра́фии, кото́рые она́ сде́лала.

74

24. (пока́зывать/показа́ть) Зи́на о́чень до́лго _____ фотогра́фии, кото́рые она́ сде́лала в Пари́же. А сейча́с она́ уже́ _____ все фотогра́фии.

25. (начина́ться/нача́ться) Ра́ньше переда́ча _____ в 8 часо́в, а сего́дня она́ _____ в 9 часо́в.

26. (чита́ть/прочита́ть) Ната́ша 3 часа́ _____ журна́л, а сейча́с она́ его́ уже́ _____ .

27. (пока́зывать/показа́ть) Ма́ша до́лго _____ кварти́ру. Сейча́с она́ _____ сад.

28. (чита́ть/прочита́ть) Ве́ра уже́ давно́ _____ э́ту кни́гу, а я её _____ ещё вчера́ ве́чером.

29. (стро́ить/постро́ить) — Этот го́род _____ четы́ре го́да. — Когда́ его́ на́чали _____ ?

30. (чита́ть/прочита́ть) Вы уже́ ко́нчили _____ э́ту кни́гу? Я хочу́ её _____ .

31. (стро́ить/постро́ить) — Это на́ше кафе́.— Како́е краси́вое! Его́ давно́ _____ ?

32. (стро́ить/постро́ить) Ра́ньше Оле́г 10 лет _____ дома́ в Москве́, а тепе́рь он уже́ 2 го́да _____ дома́ в Новосиби́рске.

33. (расска́зывать/рассказа́ть) Ма́ма ча́сто _____ о до́ме о́т-дыха.

Переведи́те на ру́сский язы́к.

34. "What did you do last night?" "We read magazines and played chess."

_____

_____

35. "What did you accomplish today?" "I read this book."

_____

36. I don't know whether Vitya has finished that book yet.

_____

37. Don't you know if there are any Russian magazines at the stand?

_____

38. Do you happen to know how long it took them to build this modern theater?

_____

_____

39. "How are your sons and daughters?" "OK, they're all studying at the institute now. It's a very good institute where future physicists and geologists study."

_____

_____

_____

40. "How long does it take to go downtown by trolleybus?" "Ten minutes."

_____

_____

41. In the photograph we see the ancient Russian city Suzdal.

_____

_____

42. Oleg has been living and working for a long time in Novosibirsk. He has been building houses there. Therefore he seldom visits Moscow.

_____

_____

_____

WORKSHEET

Complete each sentence you hear by marking appropriate space here.

1. _____ ему́.
   _____ ей.
   _____ им.

2. _____ ему́.
   _____ ей.
   _____ им.

3. _____ ему́.
   _____ ей.
   _____ её.

4. _____ ему́.
   _____ ей.
   _____ им.

5. _____ мне.
   _____ меня́.
   _____ тебя́.

6. _____ нам.
   _____ нас.
   _____ вас.

7. _____ его́.
   _____ ему́.
   _____ ей.

8. _____ их.
   _____ им.

9. _____ ей.
   _____ меня́.
   _____ тебя́.

10. _____ тебя́.
    _____ вас.
    _____ вам.

11. _____ до́лжен пойти́ в шко́лу.
    _____ должна́ пойти́ в шко́лу.
    _____ должны́ пойти́ в шко́лу.

12. _____ до́лжен прийти́ за́втра.
    _____ должна́ прийти́ за́втра.
    _____ должны́ прийти́ за́втра.

13. _____ до́лжен пригото́вить уро́ки.
    _____ должна́ пригото́вить уро́ки.
    _____ должны́ пригото́вить уро́ки.

14. _____ до́лжен купи́ть хлеб.
    _____ должна́ купи́ть хлеб.
    _____ должны́ купи́ть хлеб.

15. _____ до́лжен почи́стить ры́бу.
    _____ должна́ почи́стить ры́бу.
    _____ должны́ почи́стить ры́бу.

You will now hear a number of complex sentences. Indicate whether the two actions are simultaneous or consecutive.

16. _____ simultaneous
    _____ consecutive
17. _____ simultaneous
    _____ consecutive
18. _____ simultaneous
    _____ consecutive

19. _____ simultaneous
    _____ consecutive
20. _____ simultaneous
    _____ consecutive.

Complete each sentence you hear by marking the appropriate space here.

21. _____ приду́.
    _____ пойду́.
    _____ пойдёшь.
22. _____ приду́.
    _____ приду́т.
    _____ пойду́т.
23. _____ спрошу́.
    _____ спро́сишь.
    _____ спро́сим.
24. _____ почи́щу.
    _____ почи́стит.
    _____ почи́стим.
25. _____ куплю́?
    _____ ку́пишь?
    _____ ку́пите?

26. _____ пригото́влю обе́д.
    _____ пригото́вишь обе́д.
    _____ пригото́вите обе́д.
27. _____ начну́.
    _____ начнём.
    _____ начну́т.
28. _____ пригото́влю за́втрак.
    _____ пригото́вишь за́втрак.
    _____ пригото́вят за́втрак.
29. _____ куплю́.
    _____ ку́пишь.
    _____ ку́пим.
30. _____ пригото́влю.
    _____ пригото́вишь.
    _____ пригото́вят.

ПИСЬМЕННОЕ ЗАДАНИЕ

Запо́лните про́пуски. (Use the pronouns in parentheses in the required form.)

1. (мы) Оле́г _____ рассказа́л, как стро́или Академгородо́к.
2. (ты) В пя́тницу я _____ пригото́влю вку́сный обе́д.
3. (я) Зи́на всегда́ улыба́ется _____ и говори́т: «Здра́вствуйте».
4. (она́) Когда́ ба́бушка гото́вит у́жин, Ма́ша всегда́ помога́ет _____ .
5. (они́) Когда́ вы пока́жете _____ но́вые фотогра́фии, кото́рые вы сде́лали в Нью-Йо́рке?
6. (вы) Я уже́ сказа́л _____ , что он придёт за́втра у́тром.
7. (он) Вот идёт Вади́м. Расскажи́ _____ , что ты вчера́ де́лал.

8. (кто) _____ ты купи́л э́ти сигаре́ты?

9. (я) Ты _____ никогда́ не помога́ешь.

Запо́лните про́пуски. (Use forms of the future tense.)

10. (пойти́; прийти́, пригото́вить) За́втра у́тром мы вме́сте _____
на рабо́ту. Когда́ я _____ домо́й, я _____ тебе́
вку́сный обе́д.

11. (рассказа́ть) Когда́ вы нам _____, как стро́или э́ту шко́лу?

12. (нача́ть) За́втра ве́чером я _____ чита́ть э́ту кни́гу.

13. (ко́нчиться) Когда́ _____ вече́рние переда́чи?

14. (купи́ть, купи́ть) Я _____ мя́со и ры́бу, а ты _____
о́вощи и фру́кты.

15. (почи́стить, положи́ть) Когда́ я все о́вощи _____, ты их
_____ в кастрю́лю.

16. (спроси́ть) Я не зна́ю ничего́ об э́том, я сейча́с _____ па́пу.

17. (постро́ить) Вы не зна́ете, когда́ _____ э́ту библиоте́ку?

18. (пообе́дать, посмотре́ть) Когда́ мы _____, мы _____
переда́чу «Москва́ и москвичи́».

19. (показа́ть) Когда́ ты мне _____ э́тот журна́л?

20. (ко́нчиться, сыгра́ть) Когда́ _____ э́та переда́ча, мы
_____ в ша́хматы.

21. (пойти́, купи́ть) Де́ти сейча́с _____ в магази́н и _____
хлеб и фру́кты.

22. (нача́ть) Когда́ ты _____ гото́вить уро́ки?

23. (прийти́) Ива́н Ива́нович сказа́л, что он _____ домо́й то́лько
в 7 часо́в.

24. (спроси́ть) Я зна́ю, что Вади́м меня́ _____, где я был вчера́
ве́чером.

Переведи́те на ру́сский язы́к.

25. "This evening I have to finish reading this book." "So you won't go to the movies?
That's too bad. It's a very interesting film."

_____

_____

_____

26. While the wife prepared dinner her husband watched soccer on TV. When the

wife had prepared everything they started to dine. When they had finished dinner the husband said it had been very delicious.

_____

_____

_____

_____

_____

27. Why did he put vegetables in the pan? I haven't finished cleaning them yet.

_____

28. I wonder what's for supper. Again fish and vegetables! Then I'll go to a restaurant.

_____

29. "Have they been building this city for long?" "No, they began building it recently."

_____

30. When Vera had cleaned the vegetables, Anton came to the kitchen and put them in the pan. Then he went back to watch TV. He considers he's a modern husband and understands that he must help her, but he wants to watch soccer on TV.

_____

_____

_____

_____

_____

31. "Would you like tea or coffee?" "Tea for me, please. What delicious tea!" "The coffee's also delicious."

_____

_____

32. When I finish reading this book I'll go to the library.

_____

33. "For us, please, soup, meat, vegetables and fruit. And of course bread." "Right away."

_____

_____

WORKSHEET

Complete each sentence you hear by marking the appropriate space here.

1. _____ , что ну́жно.
   _____ , кото́рые у него́ бы́ли.

2. _____ , что ну́жно.
   _____ , кото́рые бы́ли на столе́.

3. _____ , что ну́жно.
   _____ , кото́рые она́ прочита́ла.

4. _____ , что ну́жно.
   _____ , кото́рые у неё есть.

5. _____ , что ей ну́жно.
   _____ , кото́рые ей ну́жно купи́ть.

6. _____ , что ну́жно.
   _____ , кото́рые он сде́лал в Су́здале.

7. _____ , что он зна́ет об Академгородке́.
   _____ , кото́рые рабо́тают в Академ-
   городке́.

8. _____ , что ну́жно.
   _____ , кото́рые бы́ли на окне́.

9. _____ , что ну́жно.
   _____ , кото́рые бы́ли на сту́ле.

10. _____ , что у него́ бы́ло в портфе́ле.
    _____ , кото́рые бы́ли у него́ в порт-
    фе́ле.

11. _____ свой портфе́ль.
    _____ его́ портфе́ль.

12. _____ свой сын.
    _____ её сын.

13. _____ свой чемода́н.
    _____ его́ чемода́н.

14. _____ свой ту́фли.
    _____ её ту́фли.

15. _____ свой чемода́н.
    _____ его́ чемода́н.

16. _____ свой но́вый журна́л.
    _____ его́ но́вый журна́л.

17. _____ свои́ но́вые брю́ки.
    _____ его́ но́вые брю́ки.

18. _____ свою́ бри́тву.
    _____ его́ бри́тву.

19. _____ свой де́ти.
    _____ её де́ти.

20. _____ своего́ сы́на.
    _____ его́ сы́на.

Respond to each sentence you hear by marking the appropriate space here.

21. _____ — Сейча́с дам.
    _____ — Сейча́с дади́м.

    _____ — Сейча́с даду́т.

22. _____ — Сейча́с дади́м.

_____ — Сейча́с дади́те.　　　　　_____ — Сейча́с даст.

_____ — Сейча́с даду́т.　　　　　_____ — Сейча́с даду́т.

23. _____ — Сейча́с дам.　　　　25. _____ — Сейча́с дашь.

_____ — Сейча́с дашь.　　　　　_____ — Сейча́с даст.

_____ — Сейча́с даду́т.　　　　　_____ — Сейча́с дади́м.

24. _____ — Сейча́с дашь.

Complete each sentence you hear by marking the appropriate space here.

26. _____ купи́ть сигаре́ты.　　　　_____ пойти́!

_____ покупа́ть сигаре́ты.　　30. _____ Он хо́чет игра́ть.

27. _____ купи́ть.　　　　　　　　_____ Он опя́ть придёт за́втра.

_____ покупа́ть.　　　　　　31. _____ Он хо́чет смотре́ть телеви́зор.

28. _____ пойти́ в магази́н.　　　　_____ Он опя́ть придёт ве́чером.

_____ идти́ в магази́н.　　　32. _____ взять.

29. _____ идти́!　　　　　　　　　_____ брать.

ПИСЬМЕННОЕ ЗАДАНИЕ

Запо́лните про́пуски. (_Use proper forms of present/future tense or imperative._)

1. (дать; дать) — Мы вам _____ э́ти журна́лы за́втра. — Нет, _____ их нам, пожа́луйста, сейча́с!

2. (купи́ть, взять) Я не _____ э́ту кни́гу, я её _____ в библиоте́ке.

3. (отве́тить; отве́тить) — Когда́ ты _____ на э́то письмо́? — За́втра _____ .

4. (взять) Макси́м за́втра придёт и _____ э́ти ве́щи.

5. (взять; прийти́) Эти кни́ги _____ мой сын. Он _____ за́втра у́тром.

6. (дать; дать) — Когда́ ты мне _____ э́ти ру́сские журна́лы? — За́втра _____ .

7. (забы́ть) Оле́г никогда́ не _____ шко́лу, где он учи́лся.

Образе́ц: — У него́ есть бри́тва?— _Нет, ему́ ну́жно купи́ть бри́тву._

8. — У тебя́ есть чемода́н? _____

9. — У нас есть хлеб? _____

10. — У вас есть зубны́е щётки? _____

11. — У неё есть спи́чки? _____

12. — У нас есть сигаре́ты? _____

Образе́ц: — Анто́н хо́чет пригото́вить у́жин.— *Пусть пригото́вит.*

13. — Макси́м хо́чет купи́ть но́вые ту́фли. _____

14. — Ве́ра хо́чет учи́ть англи́йский язы́к. _____

15. — Васи́лий Никола́евич хо́чет отдохну́ть. _____

16. — Анто́н Никола́евич хо́чет игра́ть в футбо́л. _____

17. — Вади́м хо́чет дать ей свою́ кни́гу. _____

Запо́лните про́пуски.

18. (his) Макси́м не зна́ет, где _____ роди́тели.

19. (her, her) Ма́шенька пошла́ в _____ ко́мнату и взяла́ _____ кни́ги.

20. (his) Анто́н всегда́ забыва́ет _____ ве́щи, когда́ он е́дет на юг.

21. (her, his; her, his) Ве́ра дала́ ему́ _____ ту́фли и _____ брю́ки. Он положи́л в чемода́н _____ ту́фли и _____ брю́ки.

22. (their) Де́ти должны́ взять _____ кни́ги.

23. (her; her) Ни́на забы́ла, где _____ портфе́ль. Она́ забы́ла _____ портфе́ль в шко́ле.

24. (your) Не забу́дь взять _____ бри́тву.

25. (their) Де́ти, наве́рно, не по́мнят, где _____ зубны́е щётки.

26. (his) Макси́м не забы́л, куда́ он положи́л _____ журна́л.

27. (his) Са́ша забы́л взять в дом о́тдыха _____ но́вый костю́м.

Переведи́те на ру́сский язы́к.

28. "He needs to get a good rest." "Then have him go to the south. He'll get a good rest there."

_____

_____

_____

29. You don't need to buy that newspaper. I already have it. Take my newspaper.

_____

_____

_____

_____

30. Vera put in the suitcase everything they need. They're now in the south and Vera doesn't know yet that her husband forgot the suitcase in Moscow.

_____

_____

_____

31. You're doing that the wrong way. You need to do it this way.

_____

_____

32. "Why doesn't the passenger answer my questions?" "Probably because she's an American and doesn't understand Russian."

_____

_____

_____

33. I forgot to buy matches at the kiosk.

34. When we were at the resort in the north we walked all day and all evening. The resort stands in a forest.

_____

_____

_____

35. Excuse me, it's already 11 o'clock. I need to go, I must be home at 12 o'clock.

_____

_____

36. We've already received the pictures you made in America. Thanks very much.

_____

37. "While you were at work Vadim came. He forgot his magazine on the windowsill." "That's OK, he'll come this evening anyway."

_____

_____

_____

WORKSHEET

Answer each question you hear by marking the appropriate spaces here.

1. _____ Не хочу́.
   _____ Не хоти́те.
   _____ Не хотя́т.

2. _____ Не хочу́.
   _____ Не хо́чешь.
   _____ Не хо́чет.

3. _____ Не хочу́.
   _____ Не хо́чешь.

   _____ Не хоти́м.

4. _____ Не хоти́м.
   _____ Не хоти́те.
   _____ Не хотя́т.

5. _____ Не хо́чет.
   _____ Не хоти́м.
   _____ Не хоти́те.

You will now hear a number of sentences including quoted speech. Indicate the correct sentences including indirect speech.

6. _____ Вади́м сказа́л, что он пое́хал отдыха́ть на юг.
   _____ Вади́м сказа́л, что он е́дет отдыха́ть на юг.
   _____ Вади́м сказа́л, что он пое́дет отдыха́ть на юг.

7. _____ Лари́са сказа́ла, что она́ была́ в Нью-Йо́рке.
   _____ Лари́са сказа́ла, что она́ в Нью-Йо́рке.
   _____ Лари́са сказа́ла, что она́ бу́дет в Нью-Йо́рке.

8. _____ Наш сосе́д сказа́л, что они́ пое́хали в Су́здаль.
   _____ Наш сосе́д сказа́л, что они́ е́дут в Су́здаль.
   _____ Наш сосе́д сказа́л, что они́ пое́дут в Су́здаль.

9. _____ Ива́н Ива́нович сказа́л, что он в суббо́ту купи́л но́вый телеви́зор.
   _____ Ива́н Ива́нович сказа́л, что он покупа́ет но́вый телеви́зор.
   _____ Ива́н Ива́нович сказа́л, что он в суббо́ту ку́пит но́вый телеви́зор.

10. _____ Макси́м сказа́л, что его́ ма́ма была́ до́ма.
    _____ Макси́м сказа́л, что его́ ма́ма до́ма.
    _____ Макси́м сказа́л, что его́ ма́ма бу́дет до́ма.

Complete each sentence you hear by marking the appropriate space here.

11. _____ день.

_____ дня.

_____ дней.

12. _____ час.

_____ часá.

_____ часóв.

13. _____ год.

_____ гóда.

_____ лет.

14. _____ год.

_____ гóда.

_____ лет.

15. _____ минýту.

_____ минýты.

_____ минýт.

16. _____ день.

_____ дня.

_____ дней.

17. _____ час.

_____ часá.

_____ часóв.

18. _____ год.

_____ гóда.

_____ лет.

19. _____ час.

_____ часá.

_____ часóв.

20. _____ год.

_____ гóда.

_____ лет.

21. _____ покупáть нóвое пальтó.

_____ купúть нóвое пальтó.

22. _____ покупáть.

_____ купúть.

23. _____ он придёт вéчером.

_____ он хóчет игрáть в шáхматы.

24. _____ он вернётся вéчером.

_____ он хóчет посмотрéть фотогрáфии.

25. _____ бýдем отдыхáть.

_____ отдохнём.

26. _____ отдыхáли на сéвере.

_____ отдохнýли на сéвере.

27. _____ идтú.

_____ пойтú.

28. _____ игрáли в шáхматы.

_____ сыгрáли в шáхматы.

29. _____ встал.

_____ встáну.

30. _____ вставáл в 9 часóв.

_____ встал в 9 часóв.

ПИСЬМЕННОЕ ЗАДАНИЕ

Запóлните прóпуски. (Use proper forms of the future tense. Note that verbs of both aspects are given in some cases. Choose the correct verb for the context.)

1. (отдыхáть, купáться, загорáть) Когдá Олéг _____ на юге, он

весь день _____ и _____ . (отды-

хáть/отдохнýть, вернýться, поднимáться) Когдá он хорошó _____ ,

86

он _____ в Москву́ и _____ на шесто́й эта́ж без ли́фта.

2. (конча́ть/ко́нчить, верну́ться, смотре́ть/посмотре́ть) Когда́ мы _____ _____ рабо́ту и _____ домо́й, мы весь ве́чер _____ _____ телеви́зор.

3. (отдыха́ть/отдохну́ть, встава́ть/встать) Когда́ мы _____ на се́вере, мы ка́ждый день _____ в пять часо́в.

4. (смотре́ть/посмотре́ть, идти́/пойти́) Когда́ мы _____ э́ту переда́чу, мы _____ в кафе́. (танцева́ть/потанцева́ть; верну́ться) Там мы немно́го _____. Мы _____ _____ домо́й в де́вять часо́в.

5. (встава́ть/встать) Они́ за́втра _____ в четы́ре часа́. (устава́ть/уста́ть) Я ду́маю, что они́ о́чень _____.

6. (дать) Когда́ я прочита́ю э́ту кни́гу, я _____ её тебе́.

7. (пригласи́ть) За́втра я _____ Зи́ну на у́жин.

8. (хоте́ть/захоте́ть) Ле́том она́, наве́рно, опя́ть _____ по-
е́хать отдыха́ть на юг.

9. (быть) Как вы ду́маете, она́ там _____ за́втра днём?

10. (верну́ться, у́жинать/поу́жинать, чита́ть/прочита́ть) Когда́ мы _____ _____ домо́й, мы _____ и пото́м _____ _____.

11. (верну́ться, начина́ть/нача́ть, гото́вить/пригото́вить) Когда́ они́ _____ _____, они́ _____ _____ обе́д.

Запо́лните про́пуски. (Use the expressions in parentheses in the required form.)

12. («Вече́рняя Москва́», «Моско́вская пра́вда») Я сейча́с куплю́ _____ _____ и _____.

13. (больша́я хоро́шая кварти́ра) Мы неда́вно получи́ли _____ _____.

14. (наш но́вый преподава́тель) Вы ещё не зна́ете _____ _____?

15. (хоро́шие де́тские переда́чи) Днём мы смо́трим _____ _____.

Переведите на русский язык.

16. In an hour, when we return home, we'll have dinner and then watch TV all evening.

17. Borya will come every week and we'll play chess or soccer.

18. "Anton said he would arrive at 2 o'clock, but I've been standing here for a long time already." "Wait a little, I think he'll come in five minutes."

19. "I wonder if this is a good movie." "I've heard it's not only very interesting, but also very beautiful." "Let's see it tomorrow."

20. When we're in the country, let's always get up at six o'clock.

21. "May I invite you to have dinner in the restaurant?" "Thanks, I've already eaten dinner."

22. The elevator isn't working right now. We must go up to the third floor on foot.

23. "You don't happen to know if Victor usually studies at the library?" "It seems he usually studies at home."

24. "Where are you hurrying?" "It's already 9 o'clock. I have to go to classes at the university."

WORKSHEET

Complete each sentence you hear by marking the appropriate space here.

1. _____ Василий Николаевич.
   _____ Василия Николаевича.
   _____ Василию Николаевичу.

2. _____ мать.
   _____ матери.
   _____ о матери.

3. _____ Вадим.
   _____ Вадима.
   _____ Вадиму.

4. _____ Максим.
   _____ Максима.
   _____ Максиму.

5. _____ Иван Иванович.
   _____ Ивана Ивановича.
   _____ Ивану Ивановичу.

6. _____ Вадим.
   _____ Вадима.
   _____ Вадиму.

7. _____ сын и дочь.
   _____ сына и дочь.
   _____ сыну и дочери.

8. _____ Лариса?
   _____ Ларису?
   _____ Ларисе?

9. _____ соседка.
   _____ соседку.
   _____ соседке.

10. _____ Галина Васильевна?
    _____ Галину Васильевну?
    _____ Галине Васильевне?

11. _____ , которого мы видели вчера.
    _____ , которую мы видели вчера.
    _____ , которые мы видели вчера.

12. _____ , которого ты ещё не знаешь.
    _____ , которую ты ещё не знаешь.
    _____ , которое ты ещё не знаешь.

13. _____ , который я купил утром.
    _____ , которое я купил утром.
    _____ , которые я купил утром.

14. _____ , который живёт в Академгородке.
    _____ , которую мы видели во дворе.
    _____ , которой улыбнулась Лариса.

15. _____ , которого мы видели в театре.
    _____ , которую мы видели в театре.
    _____ , которые были в библиотеке.

16. _____ покупать эту книгу.
    _____ купить эту книгу.

17. _____ ехать на юг отдыхать.

_____ поéхать на юг отдыхáть.   _____ прочитáть эту кни́гу.

18. _____ писáть емý письмó.   20. _____ вставáть в 5 часóв.

_____ написáть емý письмó.   встать в 5 часóв.

19. _____ читáть эту кни́гу.

Continue each dialog you hear by marking the appropriate space here.

21. _____ — Большóе спаси́бо.   _____ — С удовóльствием придём.

_____ — Хорошó. Обязáтельно куплю́. 24. _____ — Он, кáжется, пошёл в парк.

_____ — Рáзве ужé 12 часóв?   _____ — Рáзве он ещё не ýчится?

22. _____ — Дóброе ýтро. Как живёте?   _____ — Да, действи́тельно жáрко.

_____ — Дóбрый вéчер. Как живёшь? 25. ___ — Хорошó, обязáтельно придý.

_____ — Обязáтельно придý.   _____ — Рáзве Вáня там был?

23. _____ — Обязáтельно напишý.   _____ — Как, хóлодно? Тóлько —10°.

_____ — Да, действи́тельно, óчень хорóший день.

ПИСЬМЕННОЕ ЗАДАНИЕ

Запóлните прóпуски. (Use the words in parentheses in the required form.)

1. (Васи́лий Николáевич, женá, Мари́я Влади́мировна) Вéрочка, покажи́ свои́
   фотогрáфии. Я дýмаю, что не тóлько _____ ,
   но и егó _____ _____
   бýдет интерéсно их посмотрéть.

2. (Макси́м, Мáша, холóдный/хóлодно) Если _____ и _____
   бýдет _____ в пáрке, они́ придýт домóй.

3. (кто, писáть/написáть; бáбушка, дéдушка) — _____ ты сейчáс
   _____ ?— _____ и _____ .

4. (писáть/написáть, Аня, онá, éсли/ли) Тáня, когдá ты _____ ,
   спроси́ _____ , есть _____ у неё эта кни́га.

5. (пáпа, мáма) Мáма готóвит _____ обéд, а Мáша помогáет _____
   в кýхне.

6. (писáть/написáть, америкáнец, Джон; перепи́сываться) Ни́на сейчáс _____
   письмó _____ _____ . Они́ ужé давнó
   _____ .

7. (прия́тный/прия́тно; я, жáркий/жáрко) — В пáрке сейчáс так _____ .
   Пойдём в парк. _____ здесь _____ . (éсли,

писа́ть/на-) — Дава́й, но то́лько _____ ты уже́ ко́нчил _____
все пи́сьма, кото́рые ну́жно.

8. (де́лать/сде́лать) — Вади́м, что ты _____ в суббо́ту и воскресе́нье?
(е́хать/пое́хать, е́сли/ли, тёплый/тепло́) — Я ещё не зна́ю, мо́жет быть,
_____ на́ реку купа́ться, _____ бу́дет _____ .

9. (сове́товать/посове́товать, Зи́на) Я за́втра _____ _____
пое́хать на мо́ре отдыха́ть.

10. (хоро́ший/хорошо́, холо́дный/хо́лодно, неприя́тный/неприя́тно) — Сейча́с
до́ма так _____ , а на у́лице _____ и _____ .
(сове́товать/по-, идти́/пойти́) Я тебе́ не _____ _____
в кино́. Лу́чше пойдём в друго́й день.

11. (тёплый/тепло́) — По ра́дио сказа́ли, что в Ленингра́де сего́дня не о́чень
_____ и идёт дождь. (тако́й/так, хоро́ший/хорошо́) — Да, там не
_____ _____ кли́мат, как у нас.

12. (кото́рый) Де́вушка, _____ идёт ми́мо, живёт о́чень далеко́, но она́
всегда́ хо́дит в институ́т пешко́м.

13. (писа́ть/на-, я; писа́ть/на-) — _____ _____ , пожа́-
луйста, когда́ ты бу́дешь в Ки́еве. — Обяза́тельно_____ .

14. (писа́ть/на-, Оле́г; интере́сно) Та́ня сейча́с _____ письмо́
_____ . Она́ _____ расска́зывает, как она́ проводи́ла ле́то
в дере́вне.

15. (сын, дочь, кото́рый) Ива́н Ива́нович пока́зывает _____ и _____
фотогра́фии, _____ он сде́лал на се́вере.

Переведи́те на ру́сский язы́к.

16. "Good morning, Larisa. Please get acquainted. This is John, who lives in the U.S.A."
"Larisa. Very pleased to meet you." "Me too." "We're going to the movies. Allow
me to invite you. It seems it's a good film." "Thank you very much. I'm very sorry.
I'm in a big hurry, I'm late to classes at the university. Good-bye."

_____
_____
_____
_____
_____
_____
_____
_____

17. "It's not as cold today as it was last night. It's now only 25 degrees below." "All the same, in my opinion that's quite cold."

_____

_____

18. Even when it's raining Maxim wants to go out playing in the park. He says he's not at all cold.

_____

_____

19. In the south it's not as cold as it is in the north. There it almost never snows. But in my opinion it's interesting to live in the north.

_____

_____

20. "Tell me, please, what's the temperature outside?" "It's 32° Celsius." "Is it really that hot?" "Yes, it's really a hot day today. I don't remember when it was so hot."

_____

_____

21. In the autumn we often have warm days. Then the adults and children often spend their free time in the park unless it's raining.

_____

_____

22. "You haven't answered that letter yet? You received it a long time ago." "What do you mean 'a long time ago'? I just received this letter."

_____

_____

23. Did Petya leave already? I wanted to show him my new photos.

_____

_____

УРОК-ОБОБЩЕНИЕ (11-15) III

Упражнéние № 8. *Переведúте на рýсский язы́к.*

1. "Let Sasha and Misha get a good rest today. They studied all week and are very tired." "Then I'll ask them if they want to go to the beach to swim and sunbathe."

_____

_____

_____

2. He has to go to Moscow tomorrow and he'll get up at 6 o'clock. He'll return to Leningrad only in a week.

_____

_____

3. "It's not interesting to watch TV all evening. Let's go to the movies. They say, for example, that 'Anna Karenina' is a good movie." "It's so unpleasant outside. Let's play a game of chess instead!"

_____

_____

_____

_____

4. When Anton comes home I'll tell him I don't want to go anywhere tonight.

_____

_____

5. When Vera had bought everything she needed, she started to get supper ready. She prepared such a tasty supper. She always cooks so well!

_____

_____

_____

6. Please meet our new neighbor Vasily Petrovich.

_____

_____

7. Ask Galina Vasilyevna if she knows why Victor walks past and doesn't buy anything.

_____

_____

8. "Where did you buy this new book?" "I checked it out of the library." "When you've read it, give it to me, please."

_____

_____

_____

9. I usually spend all of my free time at home. I read a great deal.

_____

_____

10. "You must answer the letter you received today. When you've answered it I'll give you a new book." "I don't remember where I put the letter."

_____

_____

_____

11. "Is it so cold today?" "Yes, it's really cold weather. In Moscow it's sometimes quite cold in the fall."

_____

_____

_____

_____

12. Formerly we subscribed to this newspaper, but now we buy it at the stand.

_____

_____

_____

13. Larisa and John have been corresponding for two years. For a long time he's wanted very much to go to Moscow because she writes it's very interesting there.

_____

_____

_____

_____

14. Many want to rest in the woods or at the sea today.

    _____

    _____

15. "How long does it take to walk to the library?" "15 minutes." "It can't be!"

    _____

    _____

16. Pardon me, I'm in a hurry. There's a good show starting on TV in an hour.

    _____

    _____

17. Can it be that he doesn't have to study this evening?

    _____

WORKSHEET

Answer each question you hear by marking the appropriate space here.

1. _____ Неде́лю наза́д.

_____ Че́рез неде́лю.

2. _____ 3 дня наза́д.

_____ Че́рез 3 дня.

3. _____ Де́сять мину́т наза́д.

_____ Че́рез 10 мину́т.

4. _____ Ме́сяц наза́д.

_____ Че́рез ме́сяц.

5. _____ Три часа́ наза́д.

_____ Че́рез 3 часа́.

Respond to each utterance you hear by marking the appropriate space here.

6. _____ Я его́ уже́ ви́дел.

_____ Я ви́дел, что он чита́ет газе́ту.

7. _____ Я их ви́дел.

_____ Я ви́дел, что они́ игра́ют во дворе́.

8. _____ Я её уже́ ви́дел.

_____ Я ви́дел, что она́ чита́ет журна́л.

9. _____ Я её уже́ ви́дел.

_____ Я ви́дел, что она́ сего́дня рабо́тает.

Answer each question you hear by marking the appropriate space here.

10. _____ В кинотеа́тре.

_____ К сосе́ду.

11. _____ В дере́вне.

_____ К де́душке.

12. _____ На рабо́те.

_____ К сестре́.

13. _____ У меня́.

_____ Ко мне́.

14. _____ В библиоте́ке.

_____ К Ива́ну Ива́новичу.

15. _____ Он пошёл к Никола́ю Ива́новичу.

_____ Он ходи́л к Никола́ю Ива́новичу.

16. _____ Они́ пошли́ в де́тский сад.

_____ Они́ ходи́ли в де́тский сад.

17. _____ Я пошёл на ле́кцию.

_____ Я ходи́л на ле́кцию.

18. _____ Она́ пошла́ в магази́н.

_____ Она́ ходи́ла в магази́н.

19. _____ Она́ пошла́ в шко́лу.

_____ Она́ ходи́ла в шко́лу.

ПИСЬМЕННОЕ ЗАДАНИЕ

Заполните пропуски. (*Supply possessive modifiers, giving variants where possible.*)

1. Антóн не знáет, где _____ вéщи. Он ещё не знáет, что он забы́л _____ вéщи в Москвé.

2. Зимóй мы мнóго говори́м о _____ похóде.

3. Любóвь Ивáновна и её семья́ берýт _____ байдáрку, когдá идýт в похóд.

4. Ни́на, ты не забы́ла взять _____ кни́ги?

5. Почемý вы никогдá не знáете, где _____ вéщи?

Заполните пропуски. (*Use the words in parentheses in the required form.*)

6. (мы, наш) Сегóдня в газéте пи́шут о _____ и о _____ дóме.

7. (кто; оди́н) — О _____ вы говори́те? — Об _____ студéнтке.

8. (э́тот) Мы тóлько что говори́ли об _____ письмé, котóрое получи́ла Ни́на.

9. (э́тот) Вади́м нам дóлго расскáзывал об _____ фи́льме.

Заполните пропуски (пойти́ ~ ходи́ть).

10. — Где мáма? — Онá тóлько что _____ в магази́н. Онá сейчáс вернётся.

11. — Где ты был ýтром? — Я _____ в библиотéку и взял там э́ту кни́гу.

12. — Где вы бы́ли весь вéчер? — Мы _____ к Ни́не Николáевне.

13. — Ты не знáешь, где Макси́м? — Он _____ гуля́ть.

14. Ви́ктор ужé _____ в университéт на заня́тия. Он вернётся в четы́ре часá.

15. — Пáпа ещё дóма? — Нет, он _____ в гарáж на рабóту.

16. Когдá Вéра пришлá домóй, онá _____ в магази́н покупáть фрýкты и ры́бу.

17. Макси́м ýтром _____ в дéтский сад, а вéчером он был дóма.

18. — Где Вади́м? — Он _____ в киóск. Емý нýжно купи́ть сигарéты и спи́чки.

19. — Где вы бы́ли ýтром? — Я _____ в библиотéку.

Переведите на рýсский язык.

20. "I heard that you love to sing." "Yes, I sing a great deal. But my sisters say I sing too much and not very well."

_____

_____

21. "I advise you to take your skis tomorrow." "I always take my skis when I go on a hike in the winter."

_____

_____

22. "Lyubov Ivanovna and her family very much love sports and talk only of sports. They have both a big tent and a kayak.

_____

_____

23. Their acquaintances are always surprised when they see them taking even the children on their hikes. But they say that they really spend their time very well. Recently they spent an entire week on the Volga.

_____

_____

_____

_____

24. He never forgets to take his tent when he goes on a ski trip, but sometimes he forgets the little things.

_____

_____

25. Maxim is 7, and in the fall he'll go to school.

_____

26. Two years ago we spent a whole month in the south. We saw such beautiful places there!

_____

_____

27. Last Saturday Zina spent 4 hours at the beach and got a good suntan.

_____

_____

28. The students decided to sing Russian and French songs, but unfortunately I know only American songs. Therefore I didn't sing and only listened to them.

_____

_____

_____

_____

29. "You wouldn't happen to know where Victor is?" "It seems he went to the library to study."

_____

_____

30. Once we set out on a ski trip when it was ten below Celsius. But Maxim was cold and we returned home in an hour.

_____

_____

УРОК **17**

WORKSHEET

Respond to each utterance you hear by marking the appropriate space here.

1. _____ — Мы то́лько что спра́шива-
        ли о нём.
   _____ — Мы то́лько что спра́шива-
        ли о ней.
   _____ — Мы то́лько что спра́шива-
        ли о них.
2. _____ — Мы то́лько что спра́шива-
        ли о нём.
   _____ — Мы то́лько что спра́шива-
        ли о ней.
   _____ — Мы то́лько что спра́шива-
        ли о них.
3. _____ — Мы то́лько что спра́шива-
        ли о нём.
   _____ — Мы то́лько что спра́шива-
        ли о ней.
   _____ — Мы то́лько что спра́шива-
        ли о них.
4. _____ — Мы то́лько что спра́шива-
        ли о нём.
   _____ — Мы то́лько что спра́шива-
        ли о ней.

   _____ — Мы то́лько что спра́шива-
        ли о них.
5. _____ — Мы то́лько что спра́шива-
        ли о нём.
   _____ — Мы то́лько что спра́шива-
        ли о ней.
   _____ — Мы то́лько что спра́шива-
        ли о них.
6. _____ — Об э́том?
   _____ — Об э́той?
7. _____ — Об э́том?
   _____ — Об э́той?
8. _____ — Об э́том?
   _____ — Об э́той?
9. _____ — О моём?
   _____ — О мое́й?
10. _____ — О на́шем?
    _____ — О на́шей?

Answer each question you hear by marking the appropriate space here.

11. _____ — Мы е́здили в дере́вню.
    _____ — Мы пое́хали в дере́вню.
12. _____ — Они́ е́здили к ба́бушке.
    _____ — Они́ пое́хали к ба́бушке.
13. _____ — Мы е́здили в Су́здаль.

    _____ — Мы пое́хали в Су́здаль.
14. _____ — Он е́здил в Ки́ев.
    _____ — Он пое́хал в Ки́ев.
15. _____ — Он е́здил в Ленингра́д.
    _____ — Он пое́хал в Ленингра́д.

ПИСЬМЕННОЕ ЗАДАНИЕ

Заполните пропуски. (Use the words in parentheses in the required form.)

1. (какой, ста́рый, но́вый) О _____ кварти́ре вы говори́те, о
_____ и́ли о _____ ?

2. (свой, краси́вый) Он всё вре́мя говори́т о _____ _____
_____ до́чери.

3. (какой, букинисти́ческий) В_____ _____
_____ магази́не вы купи́ли э́ту кни́гу?

4. (э́тот, интере́сный) Мы говори́ли об _____ _____ письме́,
кото́рое нам написа́л Джон.

5. (э́тот, симпати́чный, кото́рый, газе́тный) Вади́м всё вре́мя ду́мает об _____
_____ де́вушке, _____ рабо́тает в _____
_____ кио́ске.

6. (свой, большо́й, хоро́ший) Анна Петро́вна о́чень лю́бит говори́ть о _____
_____ _____ са́де.

Заполните пропуски (е́зд-и-ть ~ пое́хать).

7. — Где вы бы́ли вчера́?— Мы _____ в Су́здаль.

8. — Где па́па?— Он уже́ _____ на рабо́ту.

9. — Вы не зна́ете, где Лари́са?— Она́ _____ в Ленингра́д к ма́тери.

10. — Где ва́ши де́ти бы́ли ле́том?— Они́ _____ в дере́вню к
ба́бушке.

11. — Где Бори́с?— Он уже́ _____ в институ́т.

12. — Вы не зна́ете, где Анто́н и Ве́ра?— Они́ _____ на юг отдыха́ть.

13. — Где вы бы́ли на про́шлой неде́ле?— Мы ___ _____ в Новосиби́рск
к сы́ну.

14. — Вот Ле́на и Га́ля.— Ра́зве они́ уже́ _____ в дере́вню?

15. — Когда́ Ве́ра пришла́ домо́й, она́ _____ в магази́н покупа́ть
ры́бу.

Заполните пропуски (с-пра́ш-ивай+/с-прос-и́-ть ~ прос-и́-ть/по-).

16. — О чём _____ Оле́г?— Он _____ , хоти́м ли
мы смотре́ть его́ но́вые фотогра́фии.

17. Мы _____ Лари́су рассказа́ть нам о Вашингто́не.

18. У меня́ ко́нчились сигаре́ты. Вот идёт Вади́м. Я _____ у него́
сигаре́ту.

19. Преподаватель всегда _____ нас по-русски, а мы иногда отвечаем ему по-английски.

20. Маша всё время _____ бабушку, когда приедет домой мама.

21. Маша _____ бабушку прочитать ей детскую книгу, которую ей вчера купил папа.

22. _____ , пожалуйста, Нину, будет ли она дома завтра вечером.

23. Мама _____ , что я буду делать вечером.

Заполните пропуски (тоже ~ и).

24. Максим сегодня в детском саду. Маша _____ сегодня там.

25. Сегодня Нина должна учить физику. Она должна учить _____ химию.

26. В чемодане мои туфли и твои брюки. Там _____ твой новый костюм.

27. Василий Николаевич собирает книги. Он собирает _____ пластинки.

28. Вадим всё время думает о Ларисе. Виктор _____ думает только о ней.

29. — Все дети играют в футбол.— Пусть Максим _____ играет.

30. Здесь работает Вадим. Его друг Валерий _____ работает здесь.

Переведите на русский язык.

31. Everybody has his hobbies. I collect rare art books in French and English. Once a week I drive downtown to the bookstore Friendship on Gorky Street. Then I go to a second-hand bookstore, which is located not far from here. Here they sell only old books.

_____

_____

_____

_____

_____

_____

32. "Good morning, Ira. What do you have on American music today?" "Unfortunately we have nothing new right now." "That's too bad. Good-bye."

_____

_____

33. "I don't understand what this Russian word means." "Look it up in the Russian-English dictionary."

_____

_____

34. Larisa already gave that book to Vasily Nikolaevich and I don't know what I ought to do. I've already asked both Vadim and Zina to advise me where to buy this book, but neither he nor she knows where it's for sale.

_____

_____

_____

_____

_____

35. "You don't happen to know if Petrov lives in this apartment?" "No, he lives in apartment No. 5." "Sorry to have bothered you." "Don't mention it."

_____

_____

_____

36. A girl friend of mine invited me to listen to records. Classical music is her hobby. But I like contemporary music better.

_____

_____

_____

УРОК **18**

WORKSHEET

Complete each sentence you hear by marking the appropriate space here.

1. _____ говори́те профе́ссору об э́том.
   _____ скажи́те профе́ссору об э́том.
2. _____ Входи́те! Ма́ма сейча́с придёт.
   _____ Войди́те! Ма́ма сейча́с придёт.
3. _____ пока́зывай мне э́то письмо́.
   _____ покажи́ мне э́то письмо́.
4. _____ приходи́те к нам.
   _____ приди́те к нам.
5. _____ Встава́й в 6 часо́в.
   _____ Встань в 6 часо́в.
6. _____ , чтобы ты верну́лся домо́й в 3 часа́.
   _____ , что ты верну́лся домо́й в 3 часа́.
7. _____ , чтобы я купи́л э́ту кни́гу.

_____ купи́ть э́ту кни́гу.
8. _____ , чтобы он верну́лся ве́чером.
   _____ , что он вернётся ве́чером.
9. _____ , чтобы я рабо́тал.
   _____ рабо́тать.
10. _____ , чтобы она́ учи́лась в МГУ.
    _____ , что она́ у́чится в МГУ.
11. _____ , чтобы ты отдыха́л на се́вере.
    _____ отдыха́ть на се́вере.
12. _____ , чтобы Макси́м пошёл в па́рк гуля́ть.
    _____ что Макси́м пошёл в па́рк гуля́ть.
13. _____ , чтобы ма́ма пошла́ на рабо́ту.
    _____ , что ма́ма пошла́ на рабо́ту.

ПИСЬМЕННОЕ ЗАДАНИЕ

Образе́ц: Тебе́ на́до купи́ть ко́фе.— *Купи́ ко́фе.*

1. Тебе́ на́до сдава́ть экза́мены. _____
2. Вам на́до бо́льше занима́ться. _____
3. Тебе́ не на́до волнова́ться. _____
4. Вам на́до сдава́ть экза́мены. _____
5. Тебе́ на́до э́то реши́ть сего́дня же. _____
6. Вам на́до отве́тить на э́тот вопро́с. _____

7. Тебе́ на́до пригото́вить уро́ки. _____

8. Вам на́до почи́стить о́вощи. _____

9. Вам на́до всегда́ встава́ть ра́но. _____

10. Тебе́ на́до пое́хать в Ленингра́д. _____

11. Тебе́ на́до пригласи́ть её в теа́тр. _____

12. Вам на́до ко́нчить э́ту рабо́ту сего́дня. _____

13. Тебе́ на́до написа́ть письмо́ ма́тери. _____

14. Вам на́до нача́ть занима́ться сейча́с же. _____

Образе́ц: Помога́й, пожа́луйста, ма́ме. — *Я хочу́, что́бы ты помога́л ма́ме.*

15. Спроси́те Оле́га об э́том. _____

16. Дай э́то письмо́ Мари́и Ива́новне. _____

17. Встань в 6 часо́в. _____

18. Пригласи́ их к нам за́втра. _____

19. Пригото́вь мне у́жин, пожа́луйста. _____

20. Забу́дь об э́том! _____

21. Прода́йте мне э́ти биле́ты. _____

22. Возьми́те свои́ ве́щи. _____

23. Не бери́ э́ти ве́щи. _____

24. Покажи́ мне своё письмо́. _____

Переведи́те на ру́сский язы́к.

25. "Hello, Anna Petrovna. How are things at home?" "Thank you. Very well. But we're all thinking about where Nina will go to study." "Isn't it early to worry about that? After all she'll graduate from school only in four years."

_____

_____

_____

_____

26. When Alyosha graduated from school he didn't feel like studying any more and he decided to go to work at a factory. But now he's entered the construction institute and is studying in the evening division.

_____

_____

_____

_____

27. Olya wants very much to enroll in the philological department at the university, but she doesn't feel like taking the exams this year.

_____

_____

_____

28. My whole family is worried about where I'll go to study when I graduate from school. But I'm thinking of going to work at a store.

_____

_____

_____

29. "I'll have a leave next week and it's difficult for me to decide where to go." "Go to the Black Sea. It's warm and pleasant there now."

_____

_____

_____

30. Most of all I'm afraid Yura won't return this week. Then I'll have to go to Leningrad alone.

_____

_____

_____

WORKSHEET

Complete each sentence you hear by marking the appropriate space here.

1. _____ нра́вится.
   _____ нра́вятся.

2. _____ понра́вился.
   _____ понра́вилась.
   _____ понра́вились.

3. _____ нра́вится?
   _____ нра́вятся?

4. _____ понра́вился?
   _____ понра́вилось?
   _____ понра́вились?

5. _____ не нра́вится.
   _____ не нра́вятся.

6. _____ ребёнок.
   _____ ребёнка.
   _____ дете́й.

7. _____ ребёнок.
   _____ ребёнка.
   _____ дете́й.

8. _____ ребёнок.
   _____ ребёнка.
   _____ дете́й.

9. _____ ребёнок.
   _____ ребёнка.
   _____ дете́й.

10. _____ ребёнок.
    _____ ребёнка.
    _____ дете́й.

11. _____ до́лжен пое́хать в Ки́ев.
    _____ до́лжен был пое́хать в Ки́ев.
    _____ до́лжен бу́дет пое́хать в Ки́ев.

12. _____ должны́ занима́ться.
    _____ должны́ бы́ли занима́ться.
    _____ должны́ бу́дем занима́ться.

13. _____ должна́ пригото́вить обе́д.
    _____ должна́ была́ пригото́вить обе́д.
    _____ должна́ бу́дет пригото́вить обе́д.

14. _____ должны́ написа́ть де́душке.
    _____ должны́ бы́ли написа́ть де́душке.
    _____ должны́ бу́дут написа́ть де́душке.

15. _____ должна выступа́ть по ра́дио.
    _____ должна́ была́ выступа́ть по ра́дио.
    _____ должна́ бу́дет выступа́ть по ра́дио.

ПИСЬМЕННОЕ ЗАДАНИЕ

Заполните пропуски. (Use the words in parentheses in the required form.)

1. (эта молодая девушка) Вадим улыбается _____
_____ .

2. (свой новый знакомый) Я пишу письмо _____
_____ .

3. (этот маленький мальчик) Дайте книгу _____
_____ .

4. (ваша маленькая дочь) Расскажите это _____
_____ .

5. (наш преподаватель) _____
очень понравилась моя работа.

Заполните пропуски (нрав-и-ть-ся/по-). (Use the words in parentheses in the required form.)

6. (американская девочка) Эта русская песня очень _____
_____ .

7. (моя сестра) Фильм, который мы вчера видели, очень _____
_____ .

8. (Юрий Васильевич) Какие имена особенно _____
_____ ?

9. (наш сын) Мы вчера ездили в Суздаль. Этот старинный город очень _____
_____ .

10. (моя мама) Моя новая знакомая очень _____
_____ .

11. (Мария Владимировна) _____
очень _____ настоящие русские имена.

12. (Алексей Павлович) _____
очень _____ новая пластинка, которую мы ему вчера
дали.

13. (вы) Посмотрите этот новый фильм. Я думаю, что он _____ _____
_____ .

14. (наш сын) _____ очень _____
_____ новый детский сад.

15. (Тамара Юрьевна) Ваша работа о русской музыке очень _____
_____ .

Заполните пропуски (ребёнок/дети).

16. — У вас есть _____ ? — Да, у нас один _____ .

17. Нина Николаевна — мать-героиня. У неё десять _____ .

18. Вы не знаете, как соседи назвали своего _____ ?

19. Дайте вашему _____ эту книгу.

20. О каком _____ вы говорите?

Заполните пропуски (самый).

21. Считают, что Оля и Юра _____ серьёзные студенты в институте.

22. Виктор пригласил танцевать _____ симпатичную девушку в нашем институте.

23. Любовь Ивановна часто рассказывает о своём _____ интересном походе.

24. Все студенты сейчас говорят о _____ трудном экзамене.

Переведите на русский язык.

25. "Good morning. How are things at your place?" "My sister Lyuba will soon be a heroine-mother." "Is it true that she wants to name the girl Clara?" "Yes, that's true and I don't like that at all. I like only real Russian names." "But she already has 9 children, and it's very difficult to decide what to name this child."

_____

_____

_____

_____

_____

_____

_____

_____

26. "What's the name of the street you live on now?" "University Prospect. It's completely new and we like it very much."

_____

_____

_____

_____

_____

27. "I'm afraid I'll have to go to the library this evening. But I don't feel like going. It's 20 below Celsius and it's snowing." "Is it really that cold?"

_____

_____

_____

_____

28. All our friends are congratulating us. We had a boy and a girl yesterday. We thought only one child would be born and we haven't decided yet what to name the boy.

_____

_____

_____

_____

29. Some (people) consider that Maxim doesn't look like his father at all.

_____

_____

30. Permit me to ask, what's your name and patronymic?

_____

31. "How much do we owe?" "A rouble 38." "That's too little!"

_____

32. You're right. She is really very nice.

_____

WORKSHEET

Complete each utterance you hear by marking the appropriate space here.

1. _____ рубль.
   _____ рубля́.
   _____ рубле́й.
2. _____ рубль.
   _____ рубля́.
   _____ рубле́й.
3. _____ рубль.
   _____ рубля́.
   _____ рубле́й.
4. _____ копе́йку.
   _____ копе́йки.
   _____ копе́ек.
5. _____ копе́йку.
   _____ копе́йки.
   _____ копе́ек.
6. _____ копе́йку.
   _____ копе́йки.
   _____ копе́ек.
7. _____ копе́йку.
   _____ копе́йки.
   _____ копе́ек.
8. _____ копе́йку.
   _____ копе́йки.
   _____ копе́ек.
9. _____ копе́йку.

_____ копе́йки.
_____ копе́ек.
10. _____ рубль.
   _____ рубля́.
   _____ рубле́й.
11. _____ консервато́рия.
   _____ консервато́рии.
12. _____ институ́т.
   _____ институ́та.
13. _____ Ива́н Ива́нович.
   _____ Ива́на Ива́новича.
14. _____ маши́на.
   _____ маши́ны.
15. _____ Мари́я Влади́мировна.
   _ Мари́и Влади́мировны.
16. _____ Ни́на.
   _____ Ни́ны.
17. _____ Васи́лий Никола́евич.
   _____ Васи́лия Никола́евича.
18. _____ Оле́г?
   _____ Оле́га?
19. _____ остано́вка тролле́йбуса.
   _____ остано́вки тролле́йбуса.
20. _____ ста́нция метро́.
   _____ ста́нции метро́.

ПИСЬМЕННОЕ ЗАДАНИЕ

Заполните пропуски. (Use the words in parentheses in the required form.)

1. (Антон, Вера; они) — _____ и _____ сейчас дома? — Нет, _____ сейчас нет.

2. (он) Ты не знаешь, где мой портфель? _____ на моём столе нет.

3. (музей, Пушкин) Вы не скажете, как доехать до _____ имени _____ ?

4. (сын, дочь) Без _____ и _____ мы в поход не пойдём.

5. (Юрий Васильевич, семья) Вот новая фотография _____ _____ и его _____ .

6. (ресторан, кафе) В нашем городе нет _____ , но есть _____ _____ .

7. (институт, техникум) Это не _____ , а _____ _____ .

8. (билет; билет) — У вас есть _____ на этот фильм? — Нет, у меня нет _____ .

9. (отец, эта девочка) Вы знаете _____ _____ ?

10. (Таня) _____ не дома, она на занятиях.

11. (мать-героиня, Ольга Юрьевна, дети) — У _____ _____ уже десять _____ .

12. (мелочь; деньги) — Ах, я забыл, у меня нет _____ . — У меня тоже нет сейчас _____ .

13. (Олег) Когда мы приехали в Новосибирск, нам сказали, что _____ в городе нет.

14. (Серёжа, Шура) Почему _____ и _____ нет сегодня на занятиях?

15. (девушка) Это вещи _____ , которая приходила вчера вечером.

Образец: — Сколько это стоит? (1 р.) — *Один рубль.*

16. — Сколько стоит билет в трамвае? (3 к.) _____

17. — Сколько стоит «Комсомольская правда»? (4 к.) _____

18. — Сколько стоит этот хлеб? (18 к.) _____

19. — Сколько стоят эти брюки? (13 р.) _____

20. — Сколько стоит эта книга? (4 р.) _____

21. — Сколько стоит этот журнал? (30 к.) _____

22. — Ско́лько сего́дня гра́дусов? (22°) _____
23. — Ско́лько гра́дусов бы́ло вчера́? (-21°) _____
24. — Вы давно́ стои́те здесь? (15 мин.) _____
25. — Ско́лько неде́ль вы там бу́дете? (4) _____
26. — Ско́лько ме́сяцев он здесь был? (2) _____
27. — Ско́лько лет вы там жи́ли? (21) _____
28. — Ско́лько дней вы бы́ли на Оке́? (3) _____
29. — Ско́лько вре́мени стро́или э́тот дом? (5 мес.) _____
30. — Ско́лько вре́мени е́хать в центр? (35 мин.) _____

Переведи́те на ру́сский язы́к.

31. "Why are you alone, (little) girl?" "My father's lost." "Don't be upset. We'll find him right away."

_____

_____

_____

32. "Call your mother to the phone." "Mama's not at home." "Who else is at home?" "Brother is." "Then call your brother." "But he's very small. He's just 3 months old."

_____

_____

_____

33. At Children's World suddenly they announced on the radio that a little girl named Masha was lost. Then, in 10 minutes, her mother had found her.

_____

_____

_____

34. "Excuse me, I'm a foreigner and am riding a Moscow bus for the first time. How much does a ticket cost?" "5 kopecks." "Will Red Square be soon?" "This bus doesn't go there. You need to transfer to bus No. 5."

_____

_____

_____

_____

35. "Will you get the tickets?" "Yes, I have change, ten kopecks."

_____

36. "Is the Bolshoi Theater still far from here?" "Yes, quite far." "Why is the bus going so slowly? I'm afraid I'll be late." "Unless you want to be late, I advise you to transfer to the metro."

_____

_____

_____

_____

37. "I'm getting off at the next stop. Pardon me for bothering you." "Don't mention it."

_____

_____

38. At Children's World there's a telephone on each floor and a nursery on the first floor of the store.

_____

_____

УРОК-ОБОБЩЕНИЕ (16-20) IV

Упражнéние № 5. *Переведúте на рýсский язык.*

1. I love sports very much. I go to my neighbor's to play chess once a week. Then we watch soccer on TV together.

2. "Are you getting off at the next stop?" "No, after 3 stops." "And I'm getting off at the next. Pardon me for bothering you." "Don't mention it."

3. "Unfortunately, I have no change at all." "I'll get the tickets. I have change, 8 kopecks."

4. "What happened?" "When I was shopping for pants for my little son I suddenly noticed he was missing. What should I do?" "Don't worry. Go to the nursery on the first floor. They'll announce about it on the radio. They'll probably find him very quickly."

5. "I just found out Olya's had a son!" "Yes, I heard they want to name him Yury." "That's good. I like real Russian names. Foreign names aren't fashionable now."

6. "Where's Ira studying?" "She isn't studying anyplace. She didn't pass the entrance exams to the university and now she is working at a factory. Nevertheless she wants to take the exams again next year."

_____

_____

_____

7. "If you have some free time, come to our place Wednesday evening." "We'll come with pleasure."

_____

8. "Why isn't Mama at home?" "She went to Children's World." "Why did she go there?" "She went to shop for a new coat for Nina."

_____

_____

_____

9. I collect not only fiction but also physics books in English. Tomorrow afternoon I'll go to the second-hand bookstore to buy some books.

_____

_____

_____

10. "Is it far from here to the Bolshoi Theater?" "This bus doesn't go there. You'll have to transfer to a trolleybus."

_____

_____

11. Have you really already read that book? Then ask Vasily Nikolaevich for another book.

_____

12. "Drive to the country to Grandma's." "I don't feel like driving to the country today. I went there last week."

_____

_____

13. Don't buy that book. I don't think you'll like it.

_____

_____

14. It's a pity you don't like to go on ski trips.

_____

15. "Congratulate me! We had a daughter a week ago. We haven't decided yet what to name her. It's so difficult to name a baby."

_____

_____

_____

16. I don't understand why some think Irochka looks like me.

_____

_____

17. I envy Nina. She passed the entrance exams and will enroll at the physics department at the university.

_____

_____

WORKSHEET

Complete each utterance you hear by marking the appropriate space here.

1. _____ с ним.
   _____ с ней.
   _____ с ни́ми.

2. _____ с ним.
   _____ с ней.
   _____ с ни́ми.

3. _____ с на́ми.
   _____ с ва́ми.
   _____ с ни́ми.

4. _____ с тобо́й.
   _____ с ним.
   _____ с ней.

5. _____ со мной.
   _____ с на́ми.
   _____ с ни́ми.

6. _____ со мной?
   _____ с тобо́й?
   _____ с ва́ми?

7. _____ с ним?
   _____ с на́ми?
   _____ с ни́ми?

8. _____ со мной.
   _____ с тобо́й.
   _____ с ва́ми.

9. _____ с на́ми.
   _____ с ва́ми.
   _____ с ни́ми.

10. _____ со мной?

_____ с ним?
_____ с ни́ми?

11. _____ ешь?
    _____ еди́те?
    _____ едя́т?

12. _____ ем?
    _____ ешь?
    _____ еди́те?

13. _____ ешь?
    _____ ест?
    _____ едя́т?

14. _____ ем.
    _____ еди́м?
    _____ едя́т?

15. _____ ешь?
    _____ еди́те?
    _____ едя́т?

16. _____ ве́чером.
    _____ ве́чера.

17. _____ ве́чером.
    _____ ве́чера.

18. _____ но́чью.
    _____ но́чи.

19. _____ у́тром.
    _____ утра́.

20. _____ днём.
    _____ дня.

ПИСЬМЕННОЕ ЗАДАНИЕ

Заполните пропуски.

1. Я иду́ в кино́. (я) Кто хо́чет пойти́ с _____ ?
2. Эти ма́льчики живу́т в до́ме, в кото́ром живёт Макси́м. (они́) Он игра́ет в хокке́й с _____ .
3. Вот идёт Га́ля. (она́) У́тром я це́лый час разгова́ривал с _____ по телефо́ну.
4. (кто) Ва́ня, с _____ ты разгова́ривал сейча́с на у́лице?
5. Вот идёт Анто́н Никола́евич. (он) Раз в неде́лю Ива́н Ива́нович игра́ет с _____ в ша́хматы.
6. (мы) Мы е́дем на юг. Кто е́дет с _____ ?
7. (ты) Та́ня, кто э́то сейча́с танцева́л с _____ ?
8. (вы) Бори́с Петро́вич, вы не зна́ете, кто э́то сиде́л ря́дом с _____ в теа́тре?

Заполните пропуски.

9. (откры́ться; откры́ться) — Когда́ _____ ваш но́вый кинотеа́тр? — Он _____ неде́лю наза́д.
10. (пить; вы́пить) — Де́ти ещё _____ чай? — Нет, они́ уже́ _____ _____ чай.
11. (пить, пить) Ра́ньше Лари́са никогда́ не _____ ко́фе, а тепе́рь она́ его́ ча́сто _____ .
12. (есть; есть) — Что э́то ты _____ , Макси́м? — Я _____ моро́женое.
13. (съесть) Когда́ Ма́ша _____ весь суп, ба́бушка дала́ ей моро́женое.
14. (есть, есть) Я о́чень ре́дко _____ ры́бу, но э́ту ры́бу я _____ с удово́льствием.
15. (есть, есть) Ни́на с удово́льствием _____ о́вощи, а мно́гие де́ти их совсе́м не _____ .
16. (мочь; мочь) — Ты _____ дать мне ме́лочь? — Коне́чно, _____ .
17. (мочь) Вади́м и Ви́ктор не _____ прийти́ к нам сего́дня ве́чером, они́ в Ленингра́де.
18. (мочь; мочь) Вчера́ вы не _____ прийти́ к нам. А сего́дня вы _____ _____ ?
19. (оста́ться) Все де́ти сейча́с пойду́т в библиоте́ку, а Ле́на _____ до́ма.
20. (остава́ться/оста́ться) Ве́ра о́чень лю́бит дете́й, и Макси́м ча́сто _____ _____ с ней, когда́ его́ роди́тели иду́т в кино́ и́ли в теа́тре.

Образец: — Ка́жется, здесь был (бу́дет) газе́тный кио́ск.— *Нет, здесь не́ было (не бу́дет) газе́тного кио́ска.*

21. — Ка́жется, здесь была́ де́тская библиоте́ка. _____

_____

22. — Ка́жется, здесь бы́ло ма́ленькое кафе́. _____

23. — Ка́жется, здесь была́ моя́ пала́тка. _____

24. — Ка́жется, здесь бу́дет но́вая шко́ла. _____

25. — Ка́жется, здесь бу́дет кни́жный магази́н. _____

26. — Ка́жется, здесь бы́ли Оля и Га́ля. _____

_____

Переведи́те на ру́сский язы́к.

27. "Why are you walking so slowly? I'm afraid we'll be late to the showing. There's only ten minutes left until the beginning." "Don't worry, we'll arrive on time."

_____

_____

_____

28. "There's a good movie showing at the new movie theater. I've just called the box office and ordered 3 tickets for the showing at 9 p. m. [Use 24-hour clock.]" "But I haven't eaten supper yet." "Never mind, there's an excellent snack bar in the lobby. We'll have a cup of coffee. One can also have ice cream or sandwiches there."

_____

_____

_____

_____

_____

29. "Where are you calling?" "The movie theater. I want to find out what's showing." "They've just announced on the radio that a new American film is playing."

_____

_____

120

30. When we arrived at the movie theater we saw that there were already a great many people in the lobby. A young singer was performing.

31. After the showing we all went to a new restaurant which is near our house and for a long time drank coffee and talked about the film. We all had a very good time and returned home very late, at 12 o'clock at night.

32. It turns out that everybody was there except for your sister Zina.

33. I almost forget to tell you that Vadim would like to go to the movies with us. He wants to see that film again.

WORKSHEET

Complete each utterance you hear by marking the appropriate space here.

1. _____ гаража́.
   _____ рабо́ты.
   _____ сосе́да.

2. _____ де́тского са́да.
   _____ пля́жа.
   _____ знако́мого.

3. _____ институ́та.
   _____ ле́кции.
   _____ Ива́на Ива́новича.

4. _____ магази́на.
   _____ ле́кции.
   _____ Мари́и Влади́мировны.

5. _____ поликли́ники.
   _____ заво́да.
   _____ врача́.

6. _____ неде́лю.
   _____ на неде́лю.

7. _____ ме́сяц.
   _____ на ме́сяц.

8. _____ 2 го́да.

   _____ на 2 го́да.
9. _____ 2-3 часа́.
   _____ на 2-3 часа́.

10. _____ мину́ту.
    _____ на мину́ту.

11. _____ себя́?
    _____ себе́?
    _____ собо́й?

12. _____ себя́.
    _____ себе́.
    _____ собо́й.

13. _____ себя́.
    _____ себе́.
    _____ собо́й.

14. _____ себя́.
    _____ себе́.
    _____ собо́й.

15. _____ себя́.
    _____ себе́.
    _____ собо́й.

Continue each dialog you hear by marking the appropriate space here.

16. _____ — Очень рад.
    _____ — Что с ва́ми?
    _____ — Нет, нельзя́.

17. _____ — Сейча́с осмотрю́ вас.
    _____ — Спаси́бо, я не курю́.
    _____ — Два ра́за.

18. ____ — Два дня.
____ — На два дня.
____ — Два ра́за в день.

19. ____ — Всего́ хоро́шего!
____ — Очень рад!
____ — Сейча́с осмотрю́ вас.

20. ____ — Всего́ хоро́шего!
____ — Наде́юсь, что нет.
____ — У меня́ температу́ра.

21. ____ — Споко́йной но́чи!
____ — Бою́сь, что ну́жно бу́дет.
____ — Что с ва́ми?

22. ____ — Всего́ хоро́шего!
____ — Спаси́бо, не курю́.
____ — У меня́ боля́т но́ги.

23. ____ — Пожа́луйста.
____ — Споко́йной но́чи!
____ — Тогда́ позвони́те врачу́.

24. ____ — Ду́маю, что нет.
____ — Тогда́ вам нельзя́ кури́ть.
____ — Всего́ хоро́шего!

25. ____ — Споко́йной но́чи!
____ — Нет, нельзя́.
____ — Тогда́ позвони́те от нас.

ПИСЬМЕННОЕ ЗАДАНИЕ

Образе́ц: Ни́на в шко́ле. — *Она́ ско́ро вернётся из шко́лы.*

1. Зи́на на ле́кции. _____
2. Макси́м в де́тском саду́. _____
3. А́нна Петро́вна у сосе́дки. _____
4. Вади́м на пля́же. _____
5. Де́ти у Васи́лия Никола́евича. _____
6. Ве́ра у врача́. _____
7. Никола́евы на конце́рте. _____
8. Ви́ктор в университе́те. _____
9. Ма́ша в па́рке. _____
10. Са́ша на заво́де. _____

Запо́лните про́пуски (идти́/пойти́ ~ ходи́ть).

11. — Отку́да вы_____?— Я_____ из поликли́ники от врача́.
12. Оле́г до́лго был бо́лен и ему́ нельзя́ бы́ло _____ .
13. — Где вы бы́ли у́тром? — Я _____ в поликли́нику к врачу́.
14. — Са́шенька совсе́м ма́ленький и ещё не _____ .
15. — Где де́ти? — Они́ _____ смотре́ть де́тский фильм. Они́ ско́ро приду́т.
16. Была́ хоро́шая пого́да, но вдруг _____ дождь.

17. Кири́лл Серге́евич о́чень не лю́бит _____ пешко́м.

18. Ива́н Ива́нович _____ на рабо́ту в во́семь часо́в и верну́лся домо́й в три часа́.

19. — Где вы бы́ли ве́чером?— Мы _____ смотре́ть но́вый неме́цкий фильм.

20. Но́ги у меня́ уже́ не боля́т, и врач сказа́л, что мне тепе́рь мо́жно _____ .

Add на *where necessary in the following sentences.*

21. На́ши друзья́ вчера́ бы́ли у нас _____ два часа́.

22. Сего́дня я _____ четы́ре часа́ был в консервато́рии.

23. Па́па уе́хал в Новосиби́рск _____ неде́лю, но он там был _____ две неде́ли.

24. Ва́ня, Васи́лий Никола́евич пришёл _____ мину́ту и хо́чет с тобо́й поговори́ть.

25. В про́шлом году́ мы _____ це́лый ме́сяц провели́ на Чёрном мо́ре.

Запо́лните про́пуски (есть, съесть, пое́сть).

26. — Хоти́те пойти́ в рестора́н обе́дать?— Спаси́бо, я уже́ _____ .

27. Макси́м _____ всё, что ему́ дала́ ма́ма.

28. Ма́ша, _____ суп и я дам тебе́ моро́женое.

29. Ни́на _____ суп и вы́пила ча́ю.

30. Пойдём в буфе́т. Я хоте́л бы _____ бутербро́д и вы́пить стака́н со́ка.

Запо́лните про́пуски (себя́).

31. Аня, тебе́ ну́жно купи́ть _____ но́вое пальто́.

32. Я сего́дня забы́л взять с _____ журна́л.

33. Вади́м всегда́ говори́т и ду́мает то́лько о _____ .

34. Как ты чу́вствуешь _____ сего́дня?

35. Ма́ша до́лго остава́лась у _____ в ко́мнате.

Переведи́те на ру́сский язы́к.

36. Unless you feel better tomorrow I advise you to go to the clinic. Although your temperature is normal, you've had a headache for two days. I'm afraid you have the flu.

_____

_____

_____

37. "Where are you coming from?" "From the philology department. I had to go there to see Professor Ivanov."

_____

_____

124

38. Valya called us up to tell us that her husband Misha has been sent to the hospital. The doctor thinks he has appendicitis and they'll have to operate. Probably he won't be allowed to work for 3-4 weeks.

_____

_____

_____

39. While you were gone Larisa came for a minute to see you to talk with you a bit about her vacation.

_____

_____

40. "Doctor, my legs hurt very much." "I'll examine you right away. Yes, you mustn't walk. You'll have to go to the hospital for a week or two." "I hope they won't have to operate on me." "I don't think so."

_____

_____

_____

_____

41. Mama suddenly felt bad and lay down to rest. Then she got up and went to the kitchen to get supper.

_____

42. Grandma was very happy that Seryozha ate up all the fish and vegetables she prepared for him.

_____

_____

WORKSHEET

Complete each statement you hear by checking the appropriate space here.

1. _____ ру́сский.
   _____ по-ру́сски.
   _____ на ру́сском языке́.

2. _____ ру́сский.
   _____ по-ру́сски.
   _____ ру́сский язы́к.

3. _____ ру́сский язы́к.
   _____ по-ру́сски.
   _____ на ру́сском языке́.

4. _____ ру́сский.
   _____ по-ру́сски.
   _____ на ру́сском языке́.

5. _____ ру́сский.
   _____ по-ру́сски.
   _____ на ру́сском языке́.

6. _____ к Макси́му.
   _____ с Макси́мом.
   _____ о Макси́ме.

7. _____ Вади́му.
   _____ Вади́мом.
   _____ Вади́ма.

8. _____ мать-геро́йню.
   _____ ма́тери-геро́йне.
   _____ с ма́терью-геро́йней.

9. _____ ру́чка.

   _____ с ру́чкой.
   _____ ру́чкой.

10. _____ ру́чки.
    _____ с ру́чкой.
    _____ ру́чкой.

11. _____ Ни́ну.
    _____ Ни́не.
    _____ с Ни́ной.

12. _____ па́пу.
    _____ па́пе.
    _____ с па́пой.

13. _____ откры́тки?
    _____ откры́тку?
    _____ откры́ткой?

14. _____ дочь.
    _____ внук.
    _____ вну́чка.

15. _____ он занима́лся в библиоте́ке.
    _____ он 3 го́да у́чит э́тот язы́к.
    _____ он из Аме́рики.

16. _____ занима́лась в библиоте́ке.
    _____ у́чится в университе́те.
    _____ ру́сская.

17. _____ учи́лся в те́хникуме.
    _____ занима́лся в библиоте́ке.

_____ изучáл рýсский язы́к.

18. _____ учи́лась.

_____ научи́лась говори́ть по-рýсски.

_____ рýсская.

19. _____ занимáлась у себя́ в кóмнате.

_____ онá рýсская.

_____ онá научи́лась говори́ть по-рýсски в Москвé.

ПИСЬМЕННОЕ ЗАДАНИЕ

Complete the sentences.

1. Лари́са чáсто бывáет в Пари́же и хорошó говори́т _____.

2. Роднóй язы́к Пáвла Николáевича рýсский. Он _____.

3. В Англии живýт _____.

4. Ви́ктор дóлго жил в Казáни, и емý чáсто пи́шут друзья́-_____.

5. Мари́ — францýженка. Её роднóй язы́к _____.

6. Джон понимáет рýсскую стюардéссу, потомý что он дóлго учи́л _____

_____.

7. Васи́лий Николáевич хорошó читáет по-англи́йски и чáсто покупáет кни́ги

_____.

Заполните прóпуски. (Use the words in parentheses in the required form.)

8. (Бори́с Пáвлович) Я иногдá игрáю в шáхматы с _____

_____.

9. (Лари́са) Мы живём ря́дом с _____.

10. (Юрий Сергéевич) Мы вчерá ходи́ли в теáтр с _____

_____.

11. (Мари́я Влади́мировна) Я чáсто разговáриваю с _____

_____.

12. (егó дочь Натáша) — Мы ужé познакóмились с _____

_____.

13. (америкáнец Джон) Ни́на перепи́сывается с _____

_____.

14. (консерватóрия) Ря́дом с _____ большóй парк.

15. (рýчка) Расписáться нýжно обязáтельно _____.

Запóлните прóпуски (друг дрýга).

16. Олéг и Кáтя чáсто звонят _____ .

17. Оля и Мúша ужé давнó любят _____ .

18. (с) Максúм и Мáша бóльше не хотят игрáть _____ .

19. (у) Максúм и Мáша чáсто бывáют _____ .

20. (о) Онú живýт в рáзных городáх и ужé давнó забыли _____ .

Запóлните прóпуски (изучáть/учúть ∼ учúться ∼ учúться/на-∼занимáться).

21. — Где вáши сёстры в э́том годý? — Онú _____ в Ленин-грáде.

22. — Где вы бы́ли всё ýтро? — Я _____ в библиотéке.

23. Нúна _____ англúйский язы́к и ужé немнóго говорúт по-англúйски.

24. Где вы так хорошó _____ говорúть по-армя́нски?

25. Нáша дочь ужé кóнчила шкóлу, и тепéрь онá _____ в Педа-гогúческом институ́те.

Переведúте на рýсский язы́к.

26. Victor was born in Kazan and speaks Tatar. He doesn't know who his parents were because he lost them during the war. He lived in an orphanage, and this was his home. He and his Tatar friends still write each other.

_____
_____
_____
_____

27. When Yura had to get his passport, he had to write (down) where and when he was born, and what his nationality was.

_____
_____
_____
_____
_____

28. "Where's Mama?" "She went to her sister's." "Why did she go there?" "To read a letter from her son." (i.e. son of her sister).

_____
_____
_____
_____

29. Neither Pyotr Alekseevich nor his wife speaks English. They have lived in America only 5 months.

_____

_____

30. Last night Larisa had supper with Vadim in the newest restaurant in Moscow.

_____

_____

31. Today I bought some beautiful new stamps for my collection. I also bought some post cards. You don't happen to know where my pen is? It seems I've lost it. What do you think, can one write post cards with a pencil?

_____

_____

_____

_____

WORKSHEET

Answer each question you hear by marking the appropriate space here.

1. _____ — Четвёртое ма́я.

    _____ — Четвёртого ма́я.

2. _____ — Двадца́тое а́вгуста.

    _____ — Двадца́того а́вгуста.

3. _____ — Восьмо́е декабря́.

    _____ — Восьмо́го декабря́.

4. _____ — Деся́тое ию́ля.

    _____ — Деся́того ию́ля.

5. _____ — Шесто́е января́.

    _____ — Шесто́го января́.

Continue each dialog you hear by marking the appropriate space here.

6. _____ До ве́чера.

    _____ К сча́стью, там был Ми́ша.

    _____ Я с ва́ми согла́сен.

7. _____ Я с ва́ми согла́сен.

    _____ Молоде́ц!

    _____ Что вы, э́то не Лари́са.

8. _____ Я с ва́ми согла́сен.

    _____ С больши́м удово́льствием.

    _____ Поздравля́ю!

9. _____ Что вы, э́то, коне́чно, Чайко́вский!

    _____ Я с ним уже́ знако́м.

    _____ Вам повезло́!

10. _____ Я согла́сен с ва́ми.

    _____ С больши́м удово́льствием.

    _____ Вам повезло́!

11. _____ Мы с Га́лей уже́ знако́мы.

    _____ Вам повезло́!

    _____ Молоде́ц!

ПИСЬМЕННОЕ ЗАДАНИЕ

Запо́лните про́пуски (Complete the sentences with appropriate forms of words given in parentheses.)

1. (э́тот спосо́бный ру́сский музыка́нт) Вы уже́ знако́мы с _____

_____ ?

2. (вся её семья́) Я вчера́ познако́мился со _____.

3. (э́та симпати́чная де́вушка) Кто там танцу́ет с _____
_____?

4. (своя́ ма́ленькая дочь) Вот идёт Татья́на Па́вловна со _____
_____.

5. («Вече́рняя Москва́») Ваш журна́л лежи́т там вме́сте с _____
_____.

6. (наш но́вый клуб) Ря́дом с _____
бу́дет парк.

7. (оди́н о́чень интере́сный челове́к) Я сейча́с разгова́ривал с _____
_____.

8. (бе́лый и чёрный хлеб) Ве́ра пошла́ в магази́н за _____
_____.

9. (прекра́сная балери́на) Тимофе́еву счита́ют _____
_____.

10. (хоро́ший врач) Никола́ев нам каза́лся о́чень _____.

11. (твой оте́ц) Кто там говори́т с _____?

12. (э́тот симпати́чный америка́нец) Лари́са уже́ знако́ма с _____
_____.

Запо́лните про́пуски (мочь/смочь).

13. Я наде́юсь, что вы _____ прийти́ к нам за́втра ве́чером.

14. Я бою́сь, что я не _____ пойти́ с ва́ми в похо́д. У меня́ боля́т но́ги.

15. Извини́те, я не _____ прийти́ к вам вчера́. У меня́ была́ температу́ра.

16. Как вы ду́маете, Оля и Ира _____ э́то прочита́ть до нача́ла ле́кции?

17. Я хоте́л откры́ть окно́, но не _____. Мо́жет быть, ты _____
_____?

Запо́лните про́пуски.

18. (3.02) Это но́вое кафе́ откры́ли _____
_____.

19. (22.06) — Како́го числа́ вы прие́хали в Москву́? — Мы прие́хали _____
_____.

20. (а́вгуст) — Когда́ вы отдыха́ли в э́том году́? — Мы отдыха́ли _____
_____.

21. (19.12) — Когда́ Ни́на написа́ла тебе́ э́то письмо́? — _____

_____ .

22. (янва́рь) В _____ мы провели́ неде́лю в Ки́еве.

23. (1.09) Заня́тия в шко́лах начина́ются _____

_____ .

24. (октя́брь, ноя́брь) Джон пи́шет, что он прие́дет в Москву́ _____
и́ли _____ .

25. (12.04) Сле́дующий конце́рт бу́дет _____

_____ .

Переведи́те с англи́йского языка́ на ру́сский.

26. "What's today, the 12th of January?" "Yes, yesterday was the 11th."

_____

_____

27. "When did he arrive, in August or September?" "In September, the 3rd of September."

_____

_____

28. "Larisa, where were you last night?" "I went with a girl friend to the amateur concert at our club."

_____

_____

_____

29. "You don't happen to have an extra ticket? I would very much like to hear Yevgeny Mravinsky's concert. I heard him once in Leningrad, and he made a very big impression on me." "You're in luck. It turns out I do have an extra ticket."

_____

_____

_____

_____

_____

30. "The young ballerina seemed very capable to me." "Yes, I agree with you. She's quite a girl! After all she's only 17."

_____

_____

_____

_____

31. "There's a good movie showing at our club tonight. Do you want to go with us? Admission's free." "With great pleasure."

_____

_____

_____

32. "What's that they're broadcasting. Tchaikovsky's concerto?" "What do you mean?! That's not Tchaikovsky but Rachmaninov."

_____

_____

_____

33. "Olya, who are you waiting for?" "For my girl friend Lena. Are you acquainted with her?"

_____

_____

34. Oh, I just remembered I have to go to the store for tea and white bread.

_____

_____

WORKSHEET

Complete each utterance you hear or answer each question you hear by marking the appropriate space here.

1. _____ мы ча́сто ходи́ли в теа́тр.
   _____ мы пошли́ в теа́тр.
   _____ мы идём в теа́тр.

2. _____ — Он ходи́л к дру́гу.
   _____ — Он пошёл к профе́ссору.
   _____ — Он хо́дит в де́тский са́д.

3. _____ — Мы ходи́ли на конце́рт.
   _____ — Мы пошли́ на конце́рт.
   _____ — Мы ча́сто хо́дим на конце́рты.

4. _____ хо́дит в шко́лу.
   _____ идёт в шко́лу.
   _____ ходи́ла в шко́лу.

5. _____ — Он е́здил в Эсто́нию.
   _____ — Он пое́хал в Эсто́нию.
   _____ — Он иногда́ е́здил в Эсто́нию.

6. _____ — Мы е́здили в Каза́нь.
   _____ — Мы пое́хали в Каза́нь.
   _____ — Мы ча́сто е́здили в Каза́нь.

7. _____ е́здим в дере́вню.
   _____ е́дем в дере́вню.
   _____ пое́хали в дере́вню.

8. _____ ходи́ть пешко́м.
   _____ идти́ пешко́м.
   _____ пойти́ пешко́м.

9. _____ хо́дите?

   _____ идёте?
   _____ е́здите?

10. _____ хо́дит.
    _____ идёт.
    _____ пойдёт.

11. _____ купи́ нам буты́лку молока́.
    _____ купи́л бы буты́лку молока́.

12. _____ я бы позвони́л вам.
    _____ я позвоню́ вам.

13. _____ е́сли у меня́ есть де́ньги.
    _____ е́сли бы у меня́ бы́ли де́ньги.

14. _____ е́сли бу́дет хоро́шая пого́да.
    _____ е́сли бы была́ хоро́шая пого́да.

15. _____ я бы забы́л об э́том.
    _____ я забу́ду об э́том.

16. _____ полови́на пе́рвого.
    _____ в полови́не пе́рвого.

17. _____ полови́на шесто́го.
    _____ в полови́не шесто́го.

18. _____ полови́на оди́ннадцатого.
    _____ в полови́не оди́ннадцатого.

19. _____ полови́на пя́того.
    _____ в полови́не пя́того.

20. _____ полови́на восьмо́го?
    _____ в полови́не восьмо́го?

Continue the dialogs you hear by marking the appropriate spaces here.

21. _____ — Вам повезло!
    _____ — Пожалуй, я так и сделаю.
    _____ — Садитесь, пожалуйста.

22. _____ — Будьте добры, чёрный.
    _____ — Я с вами согласен.
    _____ — Приятного аппетита!

23. _____ — Я с вами согласна.
    _____ — Я вам сейчас помогу.
    _____ — Свободны, садитесь, пожалуйста.

24. _____ — Я вам помогу!
    _____ — Молодец!
    _____ — Пожалуй, вы правы.

25. _____ — Будьте добры, чаю.
    _____ — Приятного аппетита!
    _____ — Я с вами согласен.

26. _____ — Молодец! Поздравляю!
    _____ — Пожалуй, я так и сделаю.
    _____ — Правда? Очень жаль.

27. _____ — Свободно, садитесь.
    _____ — Правда? Я очень рад.
    _____ — Я с вами согласен.

28. _____ — Пожалуй, мы так и сделаем.
    _____ — Вам повезло!
    _____ — Будьте добры, восьмой ряд.

29. _____ — Вам повезло!
    _____ — Будьте добры, чаю.
    _____ — Тогда пойдём в этот ресторан.

30. _____ — Молодец!
    _____ — Я с вами согласен.
    _____ — Приятного аппетита!

ПИСЬМЕННОЕ ЗАДАНИЕ

Заполните пропуски (идти/пойти ~ ходить).

1. Максиму уже семь лет, и осенью он _____ в школу.

2. Мы с мужем часто _____ в театр или на концерты.

3. — Куда Лариса сейчас _____ ? — Наверно, она _____ на работу. Она каждый день _____ на работу в Аэрофлот.

4. Сколько времени _____ отсюда в библиотеку?

5. Нина уже шесть лет _____ в школу.

6. — Где Кирилл Алексеевич? — Он _____ в киоск покупать спички.

7. — Где вы были вчера вечером? — Мы с сестрой _____ на новый балет.

8. Когда мы жили в Ленинграде, мы часто _____ в этот удивительный музей.

9. Вы любите _____ пешком?

10. Наш новый дом находится недалеко от школы, и дети _____ на занятия пешком.

Запо́лните про́пуски (е́хать/по- ~ е́здить).

11. Раз в ме́сяц па́па _____ в Ки́ев.

12. — Где дя́дя Серёжа? — Он _____ в Новосиби́рск на неде́лю.

13. Почти́ ка́ждый год мы _____ отдыха́ть в дом о́тдыха на се́вер.

14. — Куда́ вы сейча́с _____ ? — Мы _____ в Большо́й теа́тр на бале́т.

15. — Я вам звони́л ве́чером, но вас не́ было. — Да, мы _____ в дере́вню.

Запо́лните про́пуски (-то ~ -нибудь).

16. Кто- _____ уже́ был в за́ле, когда́ вы пришли́?

17. Тебе́ звони́л како́й- _____ молодо́й челове́к из институ́та.

18. Вы знако́мы с кем- _____ в Академгородке́?

19. — Где твоя́ ма́ма? — Она́ куда́- _____ пошла́ с мое́й сестро́й.

20. Вы куда́- _____ е́здили отдыха́ть в э́том году́?

21. Ни́на никогда́ не гуля́ет, она́ всегда́ что- _____ чита́ет.

22. Ма́ма всё у́тро провела́ в ку́хне. Наве́рно, что- _____ о́чень вку́сное пригото́вила.

23. Оля что- ____ сказа́ла бра́ту и бы́стро ушла́.

24. Ва́ля, е́сли ты бу́дешь в магази́не, купи́ нам каки́е- _____ фру́кты на у́жин.

Запо́лните про́пуски (сам ~ себя́).

25. Здра́вствуйте, Васи́лий Никола́евич. Как вы _____ чу́вствуете сего́дня?

26. _____ Васи́лий Никола́евич дал мне почита́ть э́ти кни́ги.

27. Посмотри́те, каку́ю хоро́шую кни́гу я купи́л _____ в букинисти́ческом магази́не!

28. Анто́н показа́л Ве́ре, как ну́жно чи́стить ры́бу, а _____ сел смотре́ть телеви́зор.

29. Я всегда́ беру́ с _____ лы́жи, когда́ иду́ в похо́д зимо́й.

30. _____ балери́на Плисе́цкая рассказа́ла нам о свое́й рабо́те в теа́тре.

Переведи́те с англи́йского языка́ на ру́сский.

31. "Olya, we're going out to see in the New Year! Yura and Ira invited us to their place." "But who will we leave the children with? My mother's going to see in the New Year in a restaurant with a friend and her husband." "We'll call the domestic service bureau, a girl will come with whom we can leave the children." "Excellent!"

_____

_____

_____

_____

_____

_____

_____

_____

32. "Look at Maxim. He's so sleepy!" "Of course it's boring for him to watch this broadcast. I'll put him to bed right away."

_____

_____

33. "Is this place free?" "Yes, sit down." "Bon appétit! I'm so hungry." "I suggest that you take borshch. It's especially tasty today." "Thank you. I'll order borshch."

_____

_____

_____

34. "Are the children asleep already? If they're asleep I'll open the bottle of champagne." "Yes, they've been asleep for a long time already." "Happy New Year!" "You too!"

_____

_____

35. Nobody could stay with our little daughter and we were seeing in the New Year at home. Instead of wine we drank juice and milk. Our daughter got sleepy very early and we put her to bed. But we were bored and went to bed early ourselves, at 10:30. If we had found a girl with whom we could leave Olechka we would have gone out to see in the New Year.

_____

_____

_____

_____

_____

36. "Look at the clock, please. What time is it?" "It's 12:30."

_____

_____

Упражнение № 7. *Переведи́те с англи́йского языка́ на ру́сский.*

1. This year Olya is studying at the university. She's a freshman and has to work a great deal. She hasn't gotten used to studying so much and therefore she gets very tired. She often goes to bed only at 1 a. m.

   _____

   _____

   _____

   _____

   _____

   _____

2. "Where did you learn to speak English so well?" "I studied English for five years in the philology department of a Moscow pedagogical institute. Now I'm working as a teacher of English in a school."

   _____

   _____

   _____

   _____

   _____

3. "If you hadn't lost your money you could have bought the ticket the young man was selling." "Yes, it's a great pity. I so wanted to hear Yevgeny Mravinsky's concert."

   _____

   _____

   _____

4. If you're planning on going on a ski hike tomorrow, I'll go with you unless the weather is too bad.

   _____

   _____

5. "Happy New Year, Katya!" "Yes, you too, Volodya!"

6. "Good night, Sasha. I hope you'll feel better tomorrow." "Thank you, my head no longer aches, and my temperature is almost normal, 36.9." "I'm very glad."

7. Papa always comes home from the factory at half past 5, but today he's late for some reason.

8. He seemed to us the most capable student in all the physics department.

9. Good morning, children! I congratulate you on the start of a new school year. Sit down.

10. Victor always arrives at the lecture on time, but today he was late.

11. I would like to buy this book about Leningrad, but I haven't money just now.

12. "If I hadn't lost Nina's address, I'd write her." "But I have her address."

13. Do you drink coffee with milk or without milk?

14. Our children always eat ice cream with great pleasure.

15. We're planning to go to the hospital to see Vadim, who's been there for four weeks already. They operated on him, but he still feels not particularly well.

16. Be so kind as to give me a glass of juice, a sandwich and a pastry.

17. Larisa called and said all her friends would meet at her place to see in the New Year.

18. "It's so warm here. I wanted to open the window, but couldn't. Maybe you can open it." "No, I can't either. Maybe Vadim will help us."

19. Last night we went to Boris and Anya's. We really enjoyed ourselves and returned home very late, only at 11:30.

20. "I'm so sleepy. I'll go to bed right now." "The children have long been asleep."

21. "May one smoke here?" "No, it's forbidden."

22. Zina dreams of visiting the home town of her Tatar (girl) friend.

WORKSHEET

Complete each utterance you hear by marking the appropriate space here.

1. _____ депута́т Верхо́вного Сове́та!
   _____ депута́том Верхо́вного Сове́та!

2. _____ крановщи́ца.
   _____ крановщи́цей.

3. _____ компози́тор.
   _____ компози́тором.

4. _____ учи́тельница.
   _____ учи́тельницей.

5. _____ ру́сский.
   _____ ру́сским.

6. _____ строи́тель.
   _____ строи́телем.

7. _____ ди́ктор.
   _____ ди́ктором.

8. _____ инжне́р-строи́тель.
   _____ инжене́ром-строи́телем.

9. _____ профе́ссор.
   _____ профе́ссором.

10. _____ арти́стка.
    _____ арти́сткой.

11. _____ — Нет, у меня́ мно́го рабо́ты.
    _____ — С больши́м удово́льствием!
    _____ — Что но́вого?

12. _____ — Впро́чем, она́ всегда́ мечта́ла там рабо́тать.

_____ — Да нет, мы ещё не реши́ли.

_____ — Пожа́луйста, бу́ду о́чень рад вам помо́чь.

13. _____ — Что но́вого?
    _____ — Кто вы по специа́льности?
    _____ — Благодарю́ вас.

14. _____ — Сейча́с, мину́точку.
    _____ — Благодарю́ вас.
    _____ — Поду́мать то́лько! Тако́й молодо́й!

15. _____ — Поду́мать то́лько! Така́я молода́я!
    _____ — Что но́вого?
    _____ — У меня́ к вам про́сьба.

16. _____ — Благодарю́ вас.
    _____ — Нет, мы сейча́с за́няты.
    _____ — Впро́чем, он всегда́ люби́л фи́зику.

17. _____ — Сейча́с, мину́точку.
    _____ — Переда́йте ей, что звони́ла Ма́ша.
    _____ — Что но́вого?

18. _____ — Что но́вого?
    _____ — Да нет, мы ещё не реши́ли.
    _____ — Я рабо́таю монтёром.

19. _____ — Нет, мне ещё нужна́ ру́чка.   20. _____ — У Ве́ры роди́лся сын!

_____ — Как то́лько ко́нчится ле́кция.   _____ — Как то́лько я получу́ де́ньги.

_____ — У меня́ к вам про́сьба.   _____ — Переда́йте, что я опозда́ю сего́дня.

ПИСЬМЕННОЕ ЗАДАНИЕ

Образе́ц: Ива́н Ива́нович — шофёр. Он хо́чет, чтобы его́ сын то́же *стал шофёром.*

1. А́нна Петро́вна — учи́тельница. Она́ хо́чет, чтобы её дочь то́же _____
   _____ .

2. Анто́н Никола́евич — врач. Он хо́чет, чтобы его́ сын то́же _____
   _____ .

3. Ве́ра — гео́лог. Она́ хо́чет, чтобы её сын то́же _____ .

4. Лари́са — стюарде́сса. Она́ хо́чет, чтобы её подру́га то́же _____
   _____ .

5. Пётр Васи́льевич — матема́тик. Он хо́чет, чтобы его́ вну́чка то́же _____
   _____ .

Complete the sentences.

6. Ми́ша у́чится в консервато́рии, потому́ что он мечта́ет быть _____
   _____ .

7. Оля у́чится в педагоги́ческом институ́те, потому́ что она́ мечта́ет быть _____
   _____ .

8. А́ня у́чится в театра́льном институ́те, потому́ что она́ мечта́ет быть _____
   _____ .

9. Са́ша у́чится в строи́тельном институ́те, потому́ что он мечта́ет быть_____
   _____ .

10. Ка́тя у́чится на математи́ческом факульте́те, потому́ что она́ мечта́ет быть
    _____ .

Запо́лните про́пуски. (Use the words in parentheses in the required forms.)

11. (ра́зные города́) Ви́ктор и Курт тепе́рь живу́т в _____ .

12. (ва́ши друзья́) Расскажи́те, пожа́луйста, о _____ на Да́льнем Восто́ке.

13. (заня́тия) Почему́ тебя́ вчера́ не́ было на _____ по ру́сскому языку́?

142

14. (де́ти) Ни́на Никола́евна, мать-герои́ня, всё вре́мя говори́т о _____ .

15. (свои́ мла́дшие бра́тья и сёстры) Вади́м о́чень лю́бит говори́ть о _____
_____ .

16. (э́ти неприя́тные разгово́ры) Прошу́ вас забы́ть об _____
_____ .

17. (свои́ друзья́ и знако́мые) Джон ча́сто вспомина́ет о _____
_____ в СССР.

18. (люби́мые увлече́ния) Учи́тельница попроси́ла дете́й написа́ть о _____
_____ .

19. (холо́дные дни) Ле́том, когда́ о́чень жа́рко, я люблю́ вспомина́ть _____
_____ .

20. (люби́мые профессора́) Мы ча́сто вспомина́ем _____
_____ университе́та.

Запо́лните про́пуски (∧ = ходи́ть ~ идти́/пойти́, ☉ = е́здить ~ е́хать/по-).

21. Утром я всегда́ ☉ _____ на рабо́ту на трамва́е, а ве́чером ☉
_____ домо́й на авто́бусе.

22. — Где ты была́ всё у́тро? — Я ∧ _____ в библиоте́ку зани-
ма́ться. За́втра ведь начина́ются экза́мены.

23. — Где Анто́н Никола́евич? — Он ∧ _____ к Ива́ну Ива́но-
вичу игра́ть в ша́хматы.

24. — Макси́м уже́ ∧ _____ в шко́лу? — Нет, но о́сенью он ∧
_____ в шко́лу. Ему́ ведь 7 лет.

25. В воскресе́нье мы с жено́й ☉ _____ в лес гуля́ть.

26. Утром мы обы́чно ☉ _____ на рабо́ту на тролле́йбусе, но е́сли
мы опа́здываем, мы ☉ _____ на такси́.

27. Ка́ждый день кро́ме суббо́ты и воскресе́нья Са́ша ∧ _____
на рабо́ту на заво́д.

28. Вади́м купи́л маши́ну, и тепе́рь он никуда́ не ∧ _____ пешко́м.

29. Любо́вь Ива́новна о́чень лю́бит ∧ _____ и ре́дко ☉ _____
_____ на рабо́ту на маши́не.

30. — Где ма́ма? — Она́ ∧ _____ в магази́н за хле́бом и молоко́м.

Переведйте с английского языкá на рýсский.

31. Anya's been working as a geologist in the Far East for 5 years already. Her parents wanted her to become a physicist, but she said she wanted to know one's own country.

32. I'm afraid we'll be late to the station. I ordered tickets for the 8 p. m. train, and it's already 7:30.

33. What do the young people who complete this vocational school become?

34. "What's new, Anton?" "My younger brother is coming visiting from the Far East where he has been working as a construction engineer at various construction projects."

35. "Have you ever seen this ballerina dance?" "Yes, she makes a tremendous impression."

36. We listened with great interest to Klava telling about her work in the Far East and asked her for a long time about her impressions.

37. I have a request to make of you. Buy a certain book for me when you're in the capital. However, I'll be there next week myself, and you probably will have no free time anyway.

144

_____

_____

38. As soon as I finish reading this book I'll go to the library and check out another.

_____

_____

39. "You owe 6 roubles 5 kopecks." "Here's 6 roubles 20 kopecks. "Here's your change, 15 kopecks."

_____

_____

_____

WORKSHEET

Complete each utterance by marking the appropriate space in each case.

1. _____ пятьдеся́т седьмо́го го́да.
   _____ в пятьдеся́т седьмо́м году́.

2. _____ шестьдеся́т тре́тьего го́да.
   _____ в шестьдеся́т тре́тьем году́.

3. _____ со́рок пя́того го́да.
   _____ в со́рок пя́том году́.

4. _____ восьмидеся́того го́да.
   _____ в восьмидеся́том году́.

5. _____ ты́сяча семьсо́т девяно́сто
   девя́того го́да.
   _____ в ты́сяча семьсо́т девяно́сто
   девя́том году́.

6. _____ Ни́ны Никола́евны Серге́евой.
   _____ Ни́не Никола́евне Серге́евой.
   _____ Ни́ну Никола́евну Серге́еву.

7. _____ Ни́ны Петро́вой.
   _____ Ни́не Петро́вой.
   _____ Ни́ной Петро́вой.

8. _____ Серге́я Анто́новича Фроло́ва.
   _____ Серге́ю Анто́новичу Фроло́ву.
   _____ Серге́ем Анто́новичем Фроло́вым.

9. _____ Юрия Гага́рина.
   _____ Юрии Гага́рине.
   _____ Юрием Гага́риным.

10. _____ Анне Па́вловой.

_____ Анну Па́влову.
_____ Анне Па́вловой.

11. _____ Юрия Гага́рина.
    _____ Юрии Гага́рине.
    _____ Юрием Гага́риным.

12. _____ Алёшу Фёдорова.
    _____ Алёше Фёдорову.
    _____ Алёшей Фёдоровым.

13. _____ Зи́ну Соколо́ву.
    _____ Зи́ны Соколо́вой.
    _____ Зи́не Соколо́вой.

14. _____ Серге́я Миха́йловича Ка́рпова.
    _____ Серге́ю Миха́йловичу Ка́рпову.
    _____ Серге́ем Миха́йловичем
    Ка́рповым.

15. _____ Ни́ну Никола́евну Серге́еву.
    _____ Ни́ны Никола́евны Серге́евой.
    _____ Ни́ной Никола́евной Серге́евой.

16. _____ интере́сно.
    _____ интере́сное.

17. _____ краси́во.
    _____ краси́вые.

18. _____ хорошо́!
    _____ хоро́шее!

19. _____ необыкнове́нно!
    _____ необыкнове́нные!

20. _____ норма́льно.
    _____ норма́льное.

ПИСЬМЕННОЕ ЗАДАНИЕ

Запо́лните про́пуски.

1. (свои́ кни́ги) Положи́ ру́чку вме́сте с _____,
   а то забу́дешь её.

2. (мно́гие на́ши студе́нты) Вади́м знако́м со _____
   _____ .

3. (други́е ма́ленькие де́вочки) Ма́ша сиде́ла вме́сте с _____
   _____ .

4. (симпати́чные де́ти) Ма́ша и Макси́м нам показа́лись о́чень _____
   _____

5. (на́ши са́мые спосо́бные бу́дущие балери́ны) Этих де́вочек счита́ют _____
   _____ .

Complete the sentences with appropriate forms of words given in parentheses.

6. (1971) Юра на́чал выпи́сывать «Огонёк» _____
   _____ .

7. (1.09.85) Ма́ша пойдёт в шко́лу _____
   _____ .

8. (3.04.79) Мэ́ри пе́рвый раз прие́хала в Москву́ _____
   _____ .

9. (4.10.57) Пе́рвый спу́тник был в ко́смосе _____
   _____ .

10. (12.02.1913) Ба́бушка Вади́ма родила́сь _____
    _____ .

11. (1983) Кла́ва ста́ла депута́том Верхо́вного Сове́та СССР _____
    _____ .

12. (31.08.81) Этот музе́й откры́ли _____
    _____ .

13. (17.05.56) А́нна Петро́вна родила́сь _____
    _____ .

Запо́лните про́пуски.

14. (Юрий Ива́нович Па́влов) Вади́м говори́т, что он знако́м с профе́ссором _____

_____ .

15. (Анна Петро́вна Петро́ва) Мы ча́сто вспомина́ем свою́ учи́тельницу _____

_____ .

16. (Кири́лл Миха́йлович Серге́ев) Ви́ктор до́лжен позвони́ть _____

_____ .

17. (Алекса́ндр Серге́евич Пу́шкин) Сего́дня бу́дет ле́кция об _____

_____ .

18. (Ната́лья Ви́кторовна Никола́ева) Кто там разгова́ривает с _____

_____ ?

19. (Анна Па́влова) Ни́на чита́ет кни́гу о балери́не_____

_____ .

20. (Михаи́л Серге́евич Ивано́в) Ра́зве вы зна́ете _____

_____ ?

21. (Ни́на Никола́евна Серге́ева) Это де́ти _____

_____ .

22. (Никола́й Дени́сович Ка́рпов) Это биле́ты для _____

_____ .

Запо́лните про́пуски (приня́ть).

23. — Ира, ты уже́ _____ лека́рство? — Нет, сейча́с _____

_____ .

24. Наде́юсь, что профессора́ _____ мой прое́кт.

Запо́лните про́пуски (посла́ть).

25. — Юра, ты уже́ _____ телегра́мму ма́ме? — Нет, сейча́с _____

_____ .

26. Ни́на, _____ , пожа́луйста, э́ти ма́рки Джо́ну для его́ колле́кции.

Переведи́те с англи́йского языка́ на ру́сский.

27. Dear Oleg, we all — Mama, Papa and I — wish you Happy New Year. We often
remember you. How are things there in Novosibirsk? We wish you happiness and
continued success in your work. Love, Zina.

_____

_____

_____

_____

28. Dear Sergei Antonovich! We thank you for your telegram to the Academy of Sciences in which you write that you received the signals of the Sputnik from outer space. We congratulate you and wish you further success. Sincerely yours,

_____

_____

_____

_____

_____

29. Everything in our life used to be ordinary. But suddenly my elder brother became a cosmonaut. Now he's become a well-known person. We're proud there's such an unusual person in our family.

_____

_____

_____

_____

30. "What's the matter?" "It's just that you're our millionth visitor. Please accept from us this small souvenir."

_____

_____

_____

31. When I was only six I went with my parents for the first time to the Exhibition of the Achievements of the National Economy. Everything was interesting, but I particularly liked the pavilion with the toys.

_____

_____

_____

_____

УРОК **28**

WORKSHEET

Complete each utterance you hear by marking the appropriate space here

1. _____ де́вушка.
   _____ де́вушки.
   _____ де́вушек.
2. _____ студе́нт.
   _____ студе́нта.
   _____ студе́нтов.
3. _____ студе́нтка.
   _____ студе́нтки.
   _____ студе́нток.
4. _____ студе́нт.
   _____ студе́нта.
   _____ студе́нтов.
5. _____ крова́ть.
   _____ крова́ти.
   _____ крова́тей.
6. _____ ма́рка.
   _____ ма́рки.
   _____ ма́рок.
7. _____ врач.
   _____ врача́.
   _____ враче́й.
8. _____ я́блоко.
   _____ я́блока.
   _____ я́блок.
9. _____ музе́й.

   _____ музе́я.
   _____ музе́ев.
10. _____ ру́чка.
    _____ ру́чки.
    _____ ру́чек.
11. _____ люде́й.
    _____ челове́к.
    _____ наро́ду.
12. _____ люде́й.
    _____ челове́к.
    _____ наро́ду.
13. _____ люде́й.
    _____ челове́к.
    _____ наро́ду.
14. _____ люде́й.
    _____ челове́к.
    _____ наро́ду.
15. _____ люде́й.
    _____ челове́к.
    _____ наро́ду.
16. _____ пригото́вить у́жин.
    _____ пригото́вила у́жин.
17. _____ купи́ть ему́ самолёт.
    _____ купи́ла ему́ самолёт.

18. _____ позвони́ть ему́.

_____ позвони́ла ему́.

19. _____ помо́чь мне.

_____ помогли́ мне.

20. _____ прийти́ к нему́.

_____ пришли́ к нему́.

ПИСЬМЕННОЕ ЗАДАНИЕ

Complete the sentences with appropriate forms of words given in parentheses.

1. (врач) На конгре́сс прие́хала 1.000 _____ .

2. (брат, сестра́) У Шу́ры 5 _____ и 6 _____ .

3. (де́ти, сын, дочь) Ни́на Никола́евна мать-геройня. У неё 10 _____ , 6 _____ и 4 _____ .

4. (но́вый, студе́нт) У нас мно́го _____ _____ .

5. (фру́кты, я́блоко) В магази́не бы́ло мно́го _____ , но ____ _____ не́ было.

6. (челове́к; челове́к) — Ско́лько _____ бы́ло на конгре́ссе? На конгре́ссе бы́ло 2.585 _____ .

7. (общежи́тие, студе́нт) У нас ма́ло _____ , потому́ что мно́гие _____ живу́т до́ма.

8. (аудито́рия, лаборато́рия, хоро́ший, библиоте́ка) В на́шем университе́те мно́го _____ и _____ и не́сколько _____ _____ .

9. (эта́ж, кварти́ра) В э́том но́вом до́ме 17 _____ и 68 _____ .

10. (письмо́, откры́тка; газе́та) Сего́дня я получи́л по по́чте 7 _____ , 6 _____ и не́сколько _____ .

11. (рубль, копе́йка) Это пальто́ сто́ит 57 _____ 75 _____ .

12. (наш, де́ти, игру́шка, кни́га) У _____ _____ мно́го _____ и _____ .

13. (год; год, ме́сяц) — Ско́лько _____ вы живёте в Москве́? — 21 _____ и 10 _____ .

14. (день) Лари́са то́лько что провела́ 6 _____ в Пари́же.

15. (америка́нец, францу́з, англича́нин) В на́шем институ́те у́чится мно́го _____ _____ , _____ и не́сколько _____ .

16. (де́ньги; рубль, копе́йка) — Ско́лько у тебя́ _____ ? — У меня́ 4 _____ и 81 _____ .

17. (брюки, рубашки) Антон положил в чемодан всё, что нужно, кроме _____

     и _____ .

18. (гость) Вчера у Оли было очень много _____ , и всем было очень
     весело.

19. (весь, мальчик, девочка) Учительница купила для _____ _____

     и _____ мороженое.

20. (наш, дети, старый, журнал) Ира оставила здесь для _____ _____

     много _____ _____ .

     Заполните пропуски (много ~ многие).

21. (преподаватель) В нашем университете работает очень _____

     _____ . _____ из них живут около университета, на
     Ленинских горах.

22. (иностранец) В этом году в Москву приехало учиться очень _____

     _____ . _____ приехали из Америки.

23. _____ не любят отдыхать на севере, а мне север очень понравился.

24. (иностранный, марка) У Коли в коллекции _____ _____

     _____ .

25. (пассажир) В поезде было _____ _____ .

     Переведите с английского языка на русский.

26. It's a pity you have so few acquaintances in Moscow. Come to our institute and
     I'll introduce you to my friends. Many of them are from other cities.

     _____

     _____

     _____

     _____

27. Many consider that Lena's one of our most talented young ballerinas.

     _____

     _____

28. Why are you laying your books on the table? Mama asked you to stand them on
     the shelf.

     _____

     _____

29. Nina sings very well and already knows many Russian songs.

     _____

     _____

30. "How long does it take to get to the Lenin Library?" "20 minutes on the subway."

_____

_____

31. "What do young people become when they finish this institute?" "Many become civil engineers."

_____

_____

32. Masha, sit here until you drink all of your milk.

_____

33. John came to Moscow for 5 weeks.

_____

34. Pyotr Sergeevich paced around the room for a long time. At last he began to write.

_____

35. "Wouldn't you like to go to this concert? Admission is free." "Contemporary music doesn't interest me."

_____

_____

36. "Can you tell me how to get to the hotel Rossiya? I'd like to stay there." "I heard that hotel has no free rooms. I suggest you to go to the Ukraina hotel."

_____

_____

_____

_____

WORKSHEET

Complete each utterance you hear by marking the appropriate space here.

1. _____ э́ти де́вушки.
   _____ э́тих де́вушек.
   _____ э́тим де́вушкам.
2. _____ сове́тские космона́вты.
   _____ сове́тских космона́втов.
   _____ сове́тским космона́втам.
3. _____ свои́ роди́тели.
   _____ свои́х роди́телей.
   _____ свои́х роди́телях.
4. _____ молоды́е арти́сты.
   _____ молоды́х арти́стов.
   _____ молоды́м арти́стам.
5. _____ свои́ подру́ги.
   _____ свои́х подру́г.
   _____ свои́м подру́гам.
6. _____ чудаки́.
   _____ чудако́в.
   _____ чудака́ми.
7. _____ все э́ти ма́льчики.
   _____ всех э́тих ма́льчиков.
   _____ всем э́тим ма́льчикам.
8. _____ э́ти балери́ны.
   _____ э́тих балери́н.

_____ э́тим балери́нам.
9. _____ на́ши но́вые сосе́ди.
   _____ на́ших но́вых сосе́дей.
   _____ на́шими но́выми сосе́дями.
10. _____ э́ти иностра́нные учёные?
    _____ э́тих иностра́нных учёных?
    _____ э́тим иностра́нным учёным?
11. _____ дешéвле.
    _____ доро́же.
    _____ да́льше.
12. _____ жа́рче.
    _____ лéгче.
    _____ ча́ще.
13. _____ лу́чше.
    _____ ме́ньше.
    _____ дешéвле.
14. _____ ме́ньше.
    _____ быстре́е.
    _____ ху́же.
15. _____ бо́льше.
    _____ ме́ньше.
    _____ доро́же.

ПИСЬМЕННОЕ ЗАДАНИЕ

Complete the sentences with appropriate forms of words given in parentheses.

1. (эти молоды́е балери́ны) Мы ви́дели _____
_____, когда́ они́ выступа́ли в на́шем клу́бе.

2. (все мои́ бра́тья и сёстры) Вы, наве́рно, уже́ зна́ете _____
_____ .

3. (все профессора́) Мы ча́сто вспомина́ем _____
на́шего университе́та.

4. (свои́ роди́тели) Я счита́ю, что Шу́ра совсе́м не похо́ж на _____
_____ .

5. (эти краси́вые де́вушки) Я вчера́ встре́тил _____
_____ в библиоте́ке.

6. (на́ши жёны) _____ ску́чно смотре́ть футбо́л и
хокке́й.

7. (все иностра́нные го́сти) _____
_____ бы́ло интере́сно на вы́ставке.

8. (эти молоды́е лю́ди) _____
о́чень повезло́. Они́ посмотре́ли но́вый бале́т «Анна Каре́нина».

9. (свои́ знако́мые и друзья́) Васи́лий Никола́евич сове́тует_____
_____ каки́е кни́ги чита́ть.

Образе́ц: — Фильм «Война́ и мир» тако́й интере́сный! — А кни́га ещё
интере́снее.

10. — Валенти́на Фёдоровна краси́вая! — А Ве́ра гора́здо_____ .

11. — В Москве́ так хо́лодно! — А в Новосиби́рске сего́дня ещё_____ .

12. — Мы живём дово́льно далеко́ от шко́лы.— А Ко́ля и Ира живу́т ещё
_____ .

13. — Этот костю́м тако́й дорого́й! — А тот костю́м ещё_____ .

14. — У нас хоро́ший телеви́зор.— А у на́ших роди́телей телеви́зор ещё _____
_____ .

15. — Васи́лий Никола́евич ста́рый.— А Алексе́й Фёдорович намно́го_____
____ .

16. — У меня́ оста́лось ма́ло де́нег. — А у меня́ оста́лось ещё_____ .

17. — Этот дива́н дово́льно дешёвый.— А э́тот дива́н ещё_____ .

18. — Ма́ма вку́сно гото́вит.— А ба́бушка гото́вит ещё_____ .

11*

19. — Вáся так бы́стро бéгает! — А Сáша бéгает ещё_____.

20. — Максúм ещё плóхо катáется на конькáх.— А Мáша катáется ещё_____
   _____.

21. — Двáдцать девя́тый урóк óчень трýдный! — А двáдцать восьмóй намнóго
   _____.

22. — Сегóдня так жáрко! — Вчерá бы́ло горáздо_____.

23. — Мой брат ещё óчень молодóй.— А мой брат ещё_____.

24. — Сегóдня на ýлице óчень теплó.— Говоря́т, что зáвтра бýдет ещё_____
   _____.

25. — Оля рéдко опáздывает на заня́тия.— А Вúктор опáздывает ещё_____
   _____.

26. — В моéй коллéкции мнóго мáрок. — А у меня́ горáздо_____.

27. — Я вчерá пóздно пришёл домóй. — А сегóдня, навéрно, придёшь ещё_____
   _____.

Переведúте с англúйского языкá на рýсский.

28. "What's the matter? Why did Kolya come home so upset?" "The problem
   is the doctor told him to engage in sports, or he's going to be ill often."
   "The doctor's right, of course. If I were he I'd run or play tennis." "But
   Kolya doesn't agree with the doctor and said he would play only chess!"

   _____

   _____

   _____

   _____

   _____

   _____

   _____

29. "What's your favorite sport?" "I'm mad about hockey."

   _____

   _____

   _____

30. In the winter I ski and skate, and in the summer I ride a bicycle or swim in
   the university pool. That's why I feel better and look younger than before. I consider
   sport the best medicine.

   _____

   _____

   _____

   _____

31. Larisa's six years younger than her elder sister. But she's much older than her brother.

32. Everybody immediately called our new neighbors eccentrics because they saw them swimming in the Moscow River when the temperature was 20 below Celsius.

33. "I'm at the airport for the first time. Can you tell me where the ticket office is?" "To the left and then straight ahead." "When will there be a flight for Kiev?" "Flight No. 16 will be at 10:30. You can proceed for boarding already, go to the right."

34. Igor used to do calisthenics in the yard, but some considered that that's indecent.

35. Bon voyage, Maria Vladimirovna! Come to Moscow more often.

WORKSHEET

Complete each utterance you hear by marking the appropriate space.

1. _____ Ивано́вы?
   _____ Ивано́вых?
   _____ Ивано́вым?

2. _____ Соколо́вы.
   _____ Соколо́вых.
   _____ Соколо́вым.

3. _____ Черно́вых.
   _____ Черно́вым.
   _____ Черно́выми.

4. _____ Виногра́довы.
   _____ Виногра́довых.
   _____ Виногра́довыми.

5. _____ Петро́вы.
   _____ Петро́вых.
   _____ Петро́выми.

6. _____ Москвины́.
   _____ Москвины́х.
   _____ Москвины́м.

7. _____ Серге́евым?
   _____ Серге́евыми?
   _____ Серге́евых?

8. _____ Фёдоровы.
   _____ Фёдоровым.
   _____ Фёдоровыми.

9. _____ Ка́рповым.

   _____ Ка́рповыми.
   _____ Ка́рповых.

10. _____ Фроло́вы.
    _____ Фроло́вых.
    _____ Фроло́вым.

11. _____ — Я могу́ разменя́ть вам де́ньги.
    _____ — Плати́те в ка́ссу 5 копе́ек.

12. _____ — Биле́т в авто́бус сто́ит 5 копе́ек.
    _____ — Пожа́луйста, сади́тесь.

13. _____ — Спаси́бо, нева́жно. А вы?
    _____ — Это я купи́л на па́мять о Па́лехе.

14. _____ — Плати́те в ка́ссу 25 рубле́й.
    _____ — На́до пересе́сть на тролле́йбус № 15.

15. _____ — Счастли́вого пути́!
    _____ — Да, но Оля танцу́ет гора́здо лу́чше.

16. _____ — Я ничего́ не понима́ю в хи́мии.
    _____ — Вот почему́ ты пло́хо вы́глядишь.

17. _____ — Это потому́ что я
          занима́юсь   спо́ртом.

    _____ — Счастли́вого пути́!

18. _____ — Вот почему́ вы вы́-
          глядите моло́же меня́.

    _____ — У меня́ сейча́с экза́-
          мен по исто́рии.

19. _____ — Нева́жно. У меня́ бо-
          ля́т но́ги.

    _____ — На ва́шем ме́сте я
          купи́л бы ва́зу.

20. _____ — Плати́те в ка́ссу
          5 рубле́й.

    _____ — Счастли́вого пути́!

ПИСЬМЕННОЕ ЗАДАНИЕ

Complete the sentences with past passive participles.

1. (потеря́ть) Объяви́те, пожа́луйста, что _____ ключ от но́мера.

2. (приня́ть) Не волну́йтесь! Коне́чно, Лена бу́дет _____ в университе́т.

3. (прочита́ть) Эта кни́га должна́ быть _____ до экза́мена.

4. (основа́ть) Ленингра́д был _____ в 1703 году́ Петро́м Пе́рвым.

5. (закры́ть) Когда́ я пришёл в кинотеа́тр, две́ри в зал бы́ли уже́ _____ .

6. (отпра́вить) Де́нежный перево́д уже́ давно́ _____ Оле́гу.

7. (купи́ть) Наконе́ц, биле́ты _____ .

8. (написа́ть) Когда́ бы́ло _____ письмо́, кото́рое ты то́лько что получи́л?

9. (заня́ть) — Эти места́ свобо́дны? — Нет, они́ _____ .

10. (нача́ть) Когда́ бу́дет _____ рабо́та на э́той но́вой стро́йке?

11. (сде́лать) Я пое́ду на юг отдыха́ть, как то́лько э́та рабо́та бу́дет _____ .

12. (откры́ть) Мы о́чень ра́ды, что на́ша но́вая шко́ла наконе́ц _____ .

13. (постро́ить) Кем была́ _____ э́та замеча́тельная но́вая библиоте́ка?

14. (прода́ть) К сожале́нию, все биле́ты на э́тот сеа́нс уже́ _____ .

15. (получи́ть) Я наде́юсь, что де́нежный перево́д уже́ _____ Лари́сой.

16. (посла́ть) Это письмо́ бу́дет _____ за́втра у́тром.

17. (переда́ть) Ни́на говори́т, что все ве́щи уже́ _____ Васи́лию Никола́е-
вичу.

Запо́лните про́пуски.

18. (Ивано́вы) Я чуть не забы́л пригласи́ть _____ к нам в пя́тницу
ве́чером.

19. (Москвины́) Вы чита́ли, что пи́шут сего́дня газе́ты о _____ ?

20. (Соколо́вы) На конце́рте мы сиде́ли ря́дом с _____ .

21. (Фёдоровы) Это дети наших новых соседей, _____ .

22. (Петровы) Мы очень завидуем _____ — они только что получили новую квартиру.

Переведите с английского языка на русский.

23. "Yura, can you explain this to me? I have a physics test tomorrow." "Unfortunately I don't know the first thing about physics and therefore can't help you."

_____

_____

_____

_____

24. I wanted to go to GUM to buy some souvenirs as remembrances of Moscow. But I got on the wrong bus and some passenger explained to me that I must change to the metro in order to get to Red Square, where GUM is.

_____

_____

_____

_____

_____

25. For my birthday my parents gave me a beautiful Palekh box that had been bought by them in the U.S.S.R. when they were there last year, in the fall.

_____

_____

_____

_____

26. At every metro station there are machines which change money. On a bus you can ask other passengers to change money so that you'll have change to buy a ticket.

_____

_____

_____

_____

27. They say Professor Chernov lectures very well. I'd like to take his English literature course.

_____

_____

_____

_____

28. I'm in a bad mood today. I have an English test tomorrow and I'm not ready for it. I still have to learn all of these new words.

_____

_____

29. There were many cheerful young people on the bus. It was noisy and everybody was having a good time.

_____

_____

30. An elderly man got on the bus and a young man in glasses gave up his seat to him.

_____

_____

31. I'm afraid Nina's taken the wrong textbook. Her textbook is here on the table.

_____

_____

Упражнéние № 6. *Переведúте с англúйского языкá на рýсский.*

1. Everybody was having a good time at the Ivanovs', but Valerka got sleepy and his parents had to go home. Vera put him to bed and now he's asleep already.

_____

_____

_____

_____

2. "Did anyone come while we were out?" "Yes, some young man came for a book he left here. We couldn't find it and he said he would come again tomorrow."

_____

_____

_____

_____

3. "On what date did you come to Moscow?" "On May 3, 1979." "So we came before you, we came on September 29, 1978."

_____

_____

_____

4. "Does anyone know whose book this is? It seems I've taken somebody else's book?" "It's not mine. I wonder whose book it is. Here comes Valya. Let's ask if she knows whose book it is."

_____

_____

5. I saw Olya put some sort of book on the shelf. Then she left the room.

_____

6. As soon as I've sent these letters we'll go to the airport. Our flight will be at 10:30 a.m. and it's already 9:30.

_____

7. "Do you have any change? Can you change a rouble for me?" "No, unfortunately I have no change at all."

8. There were several pencils and three red pens lying on the table.

9. "Have you ever been in Leningrad? Many consider it one of the most beautiful cities in the world." "Yes. But I consider, it's more interesting in Moscow than in Leningrad."

10. Vera's a geologist by occupation. She's three years older than her younger sister, but she's much younger than her brothers.

11. Have you already bought everything you need for gifts for your friends and acquaintances as remembrances of Moscow?

12. "I've just learned that Alexei Fedorovich swims in the Moscow River in the winter, when it's 20 below!" "Ah, now I understand! That's why everyone calls him an eccentric." "Yes. Drive there to see him swim."

13. "What did Mama request of Nina?" "She asked her to put the cups on the table."

14. There were a lot of people at the exhibition today. I heard there were almost 15,000 people. Many of the visitors were tourists from various countries.

_____

_____

_____

_____

15. "Vitya, would you like to go to the new ballet tonight? I have a ticket." "Unfortunately I can't go. I have a history exam tomorrow that I'm not ready for and I must study."

_____

_____

_____

16. Dear Anya, I'm writing from the Black Sea, where I'm vacationing with my family. Everything here is so beautiful and interesting, and we're enjoying ourselves very much. In the afternoon we swim and sunbathe and in the evening we dance at the café. We'll be here for 3 weeks. Love, Tanya.

_____

_____

_____

_____

_____

_____

17. Dear Igor Petrovich: We thank you for your telegram to the Academy of Sciences. We congratulate you and wish you continued success in your work. Sincerely yours,

_____

_____

_____

_____

_____

18. You're driving the wrong direction. Drive to the right. The (train) station's on the next street.

_____

_____

19. "How many rooms does your new apartment have?" "Three rooms, kitchen, bath and toilet. My room has two big windows."

_____

_____

20. It seems we've gotten on the wrong trolleybus. We'll transfer to trolleybus No. 17 at the next stop.

_____

_____

21. "You don't happen to know what nationality his parents were?" "They say his father was Russian and his mother.Tatar."

_____

_____

22. "Why did Vadim go to Kiev?" "He went there for a week because his mother's in the hospital. She's very ill, but he hopes they won't have to operate on her."

_____

_____

_____

23. "Why did you go to the store?" "We'd run out of sugar and I also needed matches."

_____

24. "What happened?" "The lights went out. But fortunately Misha was at home. I called him and he came right away. In 10 minutes everything was OK."

_____

_____

25. "Bon appétit! What's that you're eating?" "Fish. It's very tasty."

_____

26. What delicious tea! Give me another cup, please.

_____

27. Masha, sit here until you eat everything I gave you.

_____

28. "Let Kolya do what he wants." "You're right."

_____

_____

_____

29. Where did you learn to swim so well?

_____

30. The children listened to his lecture with great interest. Then they asked him several questions about his life in the Far East.

_____

_____

_____

31. I rarely drink tea and even more rarely drink coffee.

_____

Making a Success of Your Food Garden

Raymond Browne

MEMBER, BEDFORD FARMERS CLUB

DOUBLEDAY & COMPANY, INC.

Garden City, New York

1976

Library of Congress Cataloging in Publication Data

Browne, Raymond.
   Making a success of your food garden.

   Includes index.
   1. Vegetable gardening.   I. Title.
SB321.B873   635
ISBN 0-385-09877-4
Library of Congress Catalog Card Number 75–3641

Contents

PART III *Cornucopia*

Making a Success
of Your
Food Garden

Come into the Garden
And See What You're
Getting Into

Anyone with even a small plot of ground can raise top-quality vegetables if that plot gets sunlight. The work is not hard, just healthy exercise. Expenses are minimal. Savings, when compared with food-store prices, make food gardening a blue-chip investment. A six-month growing season can reduce the household budget literally by $200 or even more, year after year.

But your greatest gain from your home garden is a fresh, true taste you cannot buy at retail, no matter how high the prices. Your vegetables are far more tender than the commercial varieties, which must be more fibrous to hold water that enables them to withstand shipping; often from out of state.

An ear of corn is a classic example. Held in transit or in a display bin for even an hour, the sugar in the corn changes chemically into starch. Or take strawberries. In June, when for the third week in a row you rise from your knees in the strawberry bed with six full quarts of Fairfax or Sure Crop or Sparkle beauties ready for cream and powdered sugar or for quick freezing for next winter's desserts, just try to wrap your mind around the price the grocer is charging for one tiny pint box of berries of unknown breed, probably nowhere near as rich in strawberry flavor.

Vegetables, as you probably know, contain no cholesterol but do provide a wealth of vitamins. Casimir Funk first named them. That was back in 1912. Sometimes they were spelled vita*mines* . . . the scientific view being that these food factors, essential to nutrition, were amines. You see it all now, of course. V*ita*, the Latin for "life," merged with *amines*. And you've always known that vitamins come in sizes A, B, C, D, E, G, H, K, P and double P, and various odd widths. A lot of them come from garden vegetables. Carrots are famous for their orange-yellow carotene, a substance that converts to Vitamin A when it meets one's intestines. Said to do wonders for night vision. Leafy vegetables are long on Vitamin C, in case one is the scurvy type. All in all, vitamins from your own fresh vegetables make your food garden a family spa. Healthier than a swimming pool or a sauna, at that.

You can make your food garden an outdoors hobby or an amateur scientific research project or a domestic economy measure. For me personally, one object of the exercise is to cut down on the exercise. I go out beagling all winter, and running after a pack of beagle hounds in full cry is a lot more breath-taking than is gardening. But it is not for the heat of summer.

Whatever your gardening purpose, the most important element in your success is not so much what *you* do but what plants do . . . and knowing why they do it. Instructions *qua* instructions come on every packet of seeds you buy. A real understanding of why those instructions work comes with actually cultivating the soil and growing the seeds. "How to" is not enough for today's gardener and not as enlightening as the "whys" of vegetable culture. Once the pages of Nature's own book are open to you, you are bound to make a success of your food garden.

RAYMOND BROWNE

PART I

Starting Out

Seed Catalogues and Plot Planning

It may be down to freezing temperatures outside, with frost in the ground and snowdrifts on top of it, yet you will find this is the best time for planning your food garden. For it is in January or even December that the prominent seed houses begin advertising their seed catalogues. Send away for one or more, and when the mail service delivers them, lose yourself in dreams.

A single, typical seedsman's catalogue these days offers you 64 different vegetables, 24 different kinds of tomatoes you can order by number, 15 sorts of corn plus 2 popcorns, 12 varieties of cucumbers, 16 kinds of lettuce, covering crisp heading, Boston, loose leaf, and cos or romaine types, etc.

Each year the catalogues also offer a number of new varieties. The new varieties they present do not propose change for the sake of change. A new cucumber or a new string bean or a new hybrid corn possesses, according to carefully conducted tests and trials, certain distinct advantages. It may come into bearing earlier or it may be resistant to some disease or insect pest or it may just taste better to you and your family. It may replace your old favorite, Kentucky Wonder Pole Beans, or that other old standby, the Rutgers tomato, or it may simply add a hybrid newcomer to your garden.

A hybrid is the offspring of a tame sow and a wild boar. But that was long, long ago in old Latin. In modern horticulture, it is the cross of 2 different plant varieties, by artificial non-bee pollination, crossbreeding, or other hybridization. To you, reading the new seed catalogues, "hybrid" means a new variety showing marked improvement due either to breeding out some vulnerability or to increasing cropability or other desirable attribute, such as earlier maturity.

Since 1932, the All-America Selections Committee (headquartered at

Gardenville, Pennsylvania) has functioned to conduct trials and tests of entry samples of seeds and to rate them officially, designating its choices as "All-America Award" winners. A council of unpaid judges, some 30 of them, resident at all official A.A.S. trial stations (mostly co-operating member-seedsmen), are given 2 years to grow and try numbered lots of seed samples (without any entrants' names attached thereto). After thorough field trials conducted according to exacting and expert criteria, they report their independent rating for each anonymous sample. The coveted awards are made according to the combined numerical ratings achieved by the respective entries. Awards are gold, silver, or bronze medals.

What is rewarding to you as a vegetable gardener is that A.A.S. selections are deliberately concerned with vegetables for home gardens and local markets. The standards of quality and characteristics (as, for example, vine-ripened fruits) differ somewhat from those acceptable for commercial crops. The latter types of vegetables have their own merits, but they are intended for mechanical harvesting and for much handling throughout such steps as grading, packing, shipping, and market distribution. Since they must appear fresh at the point of sale, they are necessarily picked at varying stages of ripeness, including green. In commercial cropping, too, the harvesting machines destroy the plants. The growing acreage is gone over only once, whether the crops are to be shipped, canned, or frozen.

For such crops, the commercial growers need varieties maturing uniformly at one time. You, for your garden, would prefer varieties that produce over a longer season. You want your vegetables to be fully ripe, tender and juicy, and full of "fruit sugars," ready for picking just in time for the preparation of a meal.

In addition to new varieties that have been designated for "All-America" Awards, many leading suppliers of seeds for the home garden also present certain recommendations of their own. These are varieties, old or new, that seem especially suited to the home gardener's requirements. They are offered for outstanding quality and flavor, for early and abundant yield, for uniform vigor and dependable growth performance under most conditions. Or, they may be unique and therefore especially interesting sorts.

I really don't see how any vitamin gardener can hope to get through a hard winter without refreshing his outlook with a good seed catalogue or two.

From the catalogues, you and your family can select the vegetables you most enjoy eating. Settle on a dozen or more different kinds, with an eye on saving over local food store prices. For each vegetable, the catalogue(s) will show several varieties, telling how long they will take to mature and how much seed of each you need (usually a single packet will do) and how much it costs this season. Write up the order on the form, enclose a check to cover the costs and mail. Now begins the pleasure of anticipation.

TYPICAL GARDEN LAYOUT
(25' x 50')

Dimensions across top (columns): 8' | 12½' | 12½' | 8' | 8' | 8'

Garden plan rows (north-oriented, with NORTH arrow pointing up):

- **POLE BEANS** 2nd planting | **POLE BEANS** 1st planting | **CUCUMBERS** 2nd planting | **CUCUMBERS** 1st planting
- LETTUCE replaced by SPINACH — 1', 1½'
- BEETS (½ row) replaced by LETTUCE — 2'
- LETTUCE to be replaced by PEA PODS followed by CAULIFLOWER — 2'
- RADISHES to be replaced by CABBAGE transplants — 2'
- PEPPERS (transplants) ½ row | BRUSSELS SPROUTS ½ row — 2'
- CELERY (transplants) ½ row | RUTABAGAS ½ row — 2'
- PARSNIPS ½ row | BASIL ¼ row | DILL ¼ row — 2'
- This row for seedlings of cabbage, peppers, celery to be used as transplants in above rows and 3 sorts of tomatoes (below left) — ½'

- **TOMATOES** from transplants (Early, midseason, and late varieties, staked) — 8'
- **STRAWBERRIES** from crowns (Early, midseason, and late varieties in permanent bed)

- **ASPARAGUS** (Permanent bed) — 25'

Bottom dimensions: 19' | 22'

NORTH →

NOTE: Outside east edge of main garden are hills of ZUCCHINI and free-ranging BUTTERNUT SQUASH.
NOTE: CORN, and ONIONS . . . SCALLIONS are in a separate bed, approx. 15' x 12'.

Just to show you how really easy the basic arrangement can be made, here is my main garden for a recent year, presented as a simple sketch with notations of first and second plantings.

Incidentally, one receives one's vegetable seeds packaged in labeled envelopes. This practice stems from the ingenuity of the religious sect known as Shakers. In 1881, they began to cull seeds from carefully nurtured vegetable plants and to sell them in paper packets. They were notable peddlers from their horse-drawn wagons and, despite the eccentricity of their religious practices, were widely respected for their honesty and for the quality of their seeds.

While waiting for your seeds to arrive is a convenient time to put down on ruled paper a simple diagram of your planting area. You can draw it to scale, either exactly or approximately. It will definitely prove a helpful guide when you are standing in the middle of the proposed plot, trying to get all the rows properly placed and spaced. It looks so different out of doors from the paper plan indoors.

Producing your first crop of family vegetables is such a chest-inflating achievement that it deserves careful planning and preparing for. Besides, your very first steps can directly affect the success of that crop . . . and subsequent ones. Yet actually beginning is so simple. You just step outdoors some sunny morning and pick a *site* for your food garden. The optimum location is one where:

(a) the sun shines at least 5 or 6 hours each day.
(b) the ground is level or slopes only just enough for heavy rains to run off without either eroding or puddling.
(c) the plot is entirely outside the branch tips (i.e., "drip line") of any nearby tree, so that its roots, which grow as far out from the trunk as do the branches, will not be competing with your vegetables for nutrients and moisture.
(d) drills or rows of plants can run north and south, so that the sun's rays will reach more of each plant's surface. Still, vegetables do quite nicely in rows running east and west or even, as the cowboys say, slanchwise. After all, whose life is all sunshine?

What size should your food garden be? Any size. A single row can be as short as 6 feet or as long as 50 feet or even longer. You can plan as many rows side by side as you have room for, allowing at least 2-foot aisles or "middles" between rows or drills, a carry-over from farming practice.

Look to the Top 4 Inches
For It Is the Soil That Is
the Garden

With the season's seeds on order and the proposed food garden sketched to scale, your next concern is with the *soil* on your chosen growing site. Veteran gardeners have found—and you will too—that they can grow almost anything, and grow it bountifully, to precisely the extent they have studied and cultivated and fortified and nourished with abundant humus their garden *soil*. You raise good soil and it will in turn raise good crops for you.

Autumn is a good time to dig up your garden area, for then you can mix into your soil either commercial fertilizers or waste vegetative matter like fallen leaves, spoiled hay, and similar humus-making materials. Animal manures, until recently the mainstay of farming, are no longer readily available but fortunately not at all necessary to successful food gardening, especially in the home garden.

If, however, your vegetable garden was just a gleam in your eye last fall, you can start from scratch during the first balmy days in spring or even summer.

Four or more stakes, driven upright into the ground and connected by a string, will mark the measured bounds of that food garden you diagramed on your planning paper. Now, within your staked-out garden plot, what kind of soil do you have to work with?

Soils are either sandy, clayey, or loamy. In addition to these three basic types of soil and the 120 various mixtures or combinations thereof, you often hear knowledgeable gardening folk describe the land in their area as muck soil, shale soil, hardpan, desert soil, and in other colloquial terms.

George Washington was an obsessive buyer-up of promising land and often kept an agent on the go seeking "rich bottoms" for bumper crops. As he was himself a licensed surveyor, he usually saved the fees for having his acquisitions measured. He did not propose to lose these valuable possessions either to the French (against whom he led troops, not very brilliantly) or to the British (who led troops against him, even less brilliantly).

In those days, agriculture consisted mainly of letting crops extract the nutrients from the virgin soil. Little heed was taken of the need for replacing them by restorative cultivation. Ultimately and inevitably, the soil began to show signs of exhaustion. As its structure was altered by man's exploitation, millions of tons of topsoil, accumulated through the ages, were washed away from the denuded surface of the land by heavy rains on defenseless fields and were lost to the nation's ecology and economy as silt in the rivers. Other starved soils were simply blown away by high winds with no windbreaks to stop them. Result? Dust bowls. The Father of his Country undoubtedly would have been a determined conservationist could he have foreseen the nation's profligate expenditure of its irreplaceable land treasure. Citizens, including presidents, of far more recent birth than his failed to perceive our present rate of population growth or the closely related need for food crops. The problem also affects every home food garden. Millions of American home gardeners producing food crops can significantly contribute to the food stocks available to the population as a whole.

WHEN YOU EXAMINE YOUR SOIL, WHAT SHOULD YOU LOOK FOR?

Good garden soil is often described as "friable." The word is derived from the Latin *friare,* which means to crumble. Crumbly soil (literally looking and feeling like crumbs of earth) has the right structure for vegetable roots; it is porous, ventilated, and permeable (more of that convenient Latin) by water.

Worms like it. But then they tunnel through almost any soil structure and gradually make its texture more friable. Matter of fact, you get a lot of other help, too, from those fast-breeding worms. They digest rotting vegetation, carry it down into the soil, replace it by bringing up subsoil for processing. The procedure is not as fast as a Waring Blendor, but it's continuous. Worms' tunnels aerate and also drain the garden for you. They are your wiggle-plows. Be glad of worms and speak kindly to them. For when they die, their bodies feed your plants.

Whatever the type of soil in your garden, you can largely "remake" it to have the desired crumb structure. The soil *dans le jardin de ma tante* is often benefited by the addition of materials that affect its *structure* rather than its nutrient content. Examples of natural substances are clean builder's sand (not the highway department's calcium chloride mixture for sanding icy roads) and hardwood ashes, particularly at the charcoal stage. You can introduce decayed vegetable matter (which is called "humus") into loose, sandy soil and bind it together. You can add the same decomposing material into clayey soil and loosen it up. You can scarcely add too much humus to any soil, since it is a source of plant food and thus of soil fertility. Limestone, added to soil to alter its alkalinity-acidity balance, also usefully affects its structure, but it is a very "slow release," so it is often applied in fall for effect in spring. Peat moss is not much in favor, especially on the soil surface. Here it holds water instead of passing it through to the roots. Also, it hardens, cakes, and actually sheds the water.

In recent years, increased use is being made in gardening of *commercial* substances called "soil conditioners." The most readily recognized of these is "exploded" mica, or vermiculite. It is sold at retail garden departments in big paper bags and little paper bags, under several different brand names. Trade names are used to prevent vermiculite from becoming or appearing a bulk or staple commodity, like sand, and selling at a lower price.

By any other name, it smells as sweet (it's odorless) and soaks up moisture, thus acting as water boy to vegetable roots. Likewise, it admits air (carrying indispensable oxygen) into the soil via the interstices it forms. During spring seeding time, one sprinkles it plentifully between index finger and thumb straight along the drill, in the manner of a Navajo chanter or "medicine man" drawing a religious sand painting in some Arizona hohrahn. I believe the gods approve.

You discover as you garden that conditioning (virtually "remaking") soil adds, year after year, new treasures of fertility to your garden. You find increasingly that your soil is incomparably more successful in producing good growth. It is becoming spongier, more resilient, to step upon. It may be darker in color. And the enriched topsoil is no longer 4 inches or 6 inches but 8, 10, 12 inches in depth before your shovel reaches the subsoil underneath. It is pleasantly moist, too.

You can't expect to find the soil in your brand new garden mellow, easily worked, and fully productive when you first stake it out and put in your first seeds or seedling transplants. But after just a few seasons, you'll be proud of your land, repaid for the care you took in building it up. It absorbs and holds water for the plants' roots. Air penetrates it. Worms traverse it.

You can count on such extra dividends from your labor, especially if you faithfully add vegetable humus-making materials. This is why it pays you handsomely to salvage the daily plate waste from family meals. Dumped into a standby garbage can just outside the kitchen door and, perhaps once a week, emptied into a 10-inch-deep hole or trench in the aisles or slipped under the mulch already there, these ecological raw materials lastingly enrich and endow the food garden. You don't even need to compost them . . . just mix them into the soil where the bacteria will rapidly convert them all to plant food.

Especially valuable for this purpose are all your crop residues. The stems, foliage, and root systems of the plants you have raised all contain nutrients for your next crop. Just "reinvest" them. Tomato vines help you raise better tomatoes next season because they absorbed and contain the very soil chemicals that make tomatoes. Similarly, carrot, cabbage, or Brussels sprouts provide in their residues appropriate fertilizing elements for growing future generations of their kind.

The rule of life is: return to the soil all that it grew for you except what you eat.

DIGGING, TURNING, RAKING

The three ordinary methods of breaking ground are (1) plowing with a team or tractor, (2) roto-tilling, (3) hand-digging with a four-tined fork or long-handled shovel. If the land which you will be using has been fallow and overgrown with weeds or if it has been kept in sod (for a lawn, perhaps), the first step may be hard work. Usually it is best performed mechanically. One can rent a roto-tiller for several hours for a few dollars or hire a man to operate it. I have often hand-forked my entire garden in spring and fall but only in soil that had been cultivated previously and was therefore relatively easy to work.

You'll be raking up some stones after the soil-breaking, but don't discard them. Pile or spread them under a tree, for they often come in handy. Under a tree, they actually serve as a stone mulch and help the tree conserve soil moisture. If only one had access to some stone-crushing machinery, one's garden rocks would be quickly transformed into a mineral additive of lasting value to the soil. But with only a hammer and one's arm, this is too much like work.

Speaking of raking, one does this for two reasons. The first is simply to level the planting area and render it moderately smooth and free of lumps and stones. The second is to prepare the bed for seeds, particularly in the rows or drills your paper diagram calls for. What you actually do is thoroughly re-rake your rows into finer soil particles minutes before you seed them.

YOU ARE RAISING INVISIBLE VEGETABLES, TOO

The famous Pasteur, when he demonstrated that definite diseases could be produced by bacteria, indirectly opened the gate to spreading knowledge about soil and about growing vegetables.

Bacteria are all one-celled creatures and were at first regarded as animals. They have since come to be classified as plants. Bacteria are found universally . . . in the air, water, and soil around us as well as on our persons and even within our bodies. Their eating habits give flavor to Edam cheese, cause milk to sour, and turn one apple rotten in every barrel. They are markedly fond of ice cream, all twenty-eight assorted flavors.

Without bacteria, there would be no other living thing in the world. This is because every plant and animal owe their lives to the fertility of the soil. In turn, this depends upon the activity of the bacterial microorganisms that inhabit our soil in inconceivable billions. We owe to bacteria, even more than to worms, the fertility of our garden soil.

Brag, if you will, that you have a green thumb, but remember the while that it is our bacterial colleagues whose labors are breaking down all the remains of plants and plant mulch into simpler substances to be used as food by our crops. Further, when these benign bacteria die, the chemical constituents of their tiny corpses, too small to be seen by the unaided human eye but often identifiable under a microscope, become both food and growth hormones for humans' vegetables.

Knowing that these invisible creatures are themselves plants, you can readily understand that they need the same sort of food and fertilizer as the edible vegetables they nourish. They particularly require nitrogen and divert to their own consumption a small portion of it from any nitrogenous fertilizer you spread on your garden.

In fact, when you see plants turning from gorgeous green to sickly yellow, it is a sign that active bacteria, failing to find enough nitrogen in fertilizer, are taking it from the soil and robbing your vegetable plants in doing so. You can quickly correct this jaundiced abnormality by applying a solution of nitrate of soda or ammonium sulfate or any balanced fertilizer with a fair amount of N in its formula.

Routinely, you can supply the bacteria in your garden with dried blood, urea, fish oil emulsion, or manufactured "balanced" fertilizers (like 10-5-5 or 8-8-8, etc.). Equally effective and much more valuable, since they are humus-producing materials, are dug-in grass clippings, kitchen garbage (vegetative only, please—no meats or fats to attract digging animals), spoiled hay, autumn leaves, or composted matter if you go to the bother of composting.

It was Xenophon, the Greek historian, who taught as early as 400 B.C.

the benefits of restoring to the farmer's soil field weeds and unused crops. The idea was then, as now, that such substances restored the soil's fertility in the same way as the dung commonly spread on the fields. He did not, of course, mention bacteria: they had not been discovered yet.

THERE'S NO ONE RX FOR PH

You can learn, if you fancy yourself as a psychologist, a good deal about human nature from a study of gardeners. For example, their tendency to let their angry passions rise when they debate soil acidity vis-à-vis soil alkalinity is fearful and wonderful to behold. Arguments degenerate into disputes over the precise degree of either that some particular vegetable "likes" best.

True, there exists a sort of scale for describing the relative acidity of your garden soil. Readings on this scale run from 1.0 (most acid) through 7.0 (neutral) to 14.0 (most alkaline). The numbers on this scale are not so much measurements (cf. inches or degrees or light years) as indicators or indices.

Gardeners talk about it as the pH scale or just the pH of the soil. This arcane symbol stands for "potential for hydrogen" or just "hydrogen index."

Many are the diagrams, dissertations, and decretals dealing with the degree of acidity or alkalinity deemed desirable for garden vegetables. These various systems all have one thing in common. And that is, they all give you for any one vegetable a *range*, and not just a single figure, as its pH index.

Most of the vegetables commonly grown in home gardens have a pH that falls somewhere between 5.0 and 7.0 on the scale. That gives, in my kindergarten arithmetic, a span of 2 degrees out of 14. It is therefore impossible to conclude that it makes much difference to any vegetable precisely which scale position is assigned to it, just so it is not *excessively* acid or alkaline.

Snap beans or peppers or radishes or squashes can be expected to grow best in the range 5.5 through 6.5. (Strawberries, 5.25–6.5.) The scientifically accepted range for limas, cucumbers, parsnips, or tomatoes is 5.5 through 6.75. (Corn, 5.5–7.0.) Membership in the cabbage family or the carrot club means a rating of 5.75–7.0. Exception: broccoli is notably indifferent to the pH of the soil it grows in. Asparagus, lettuce, peas, spinach, among the least acid group, respond gratefully to soil in the range of 6.0 through 7.0. (Onions prefer a narrower 6.0–6.6.)

So there it is. If your garden soil pH is anywhere from 5.0 to 7.0, vegetables will probably grow there for you. In other words, the gardener's rule of thumb is, build your soil to a pH level that is neutral or just slightly below, on the acid side. Optimum would be 6.0 to 6.9. That's the theory. Scientific, too.

Two practical questions remain. One, how do you adjust the pH of your garden soil to a given vegetable? Two, how do you know when your soil has reached a predetermined pH?

Logically, in order to modify your soil to conform with the pH requirements of a given vegetable, you must first know the soil's present pH level. So equip yourself with an inexpensive soil-testing chemicals kit, collect a soil sample, and make a color-matching test according to directions on the package. This part is so easy that, even if you flunked your high school chemistry course, you can pass this one.

If the soil is more acid than the books call for, sprinkle a little ground limestone to "sweeten" it. Contrariwise, if it isn't acid enough, potatoes or strawberries won't "like" it, so you mix in a little ammonium sulfate for increased acidity. Now, I will concede that directions like "a little limestone" or a "light sprinkling of ammonium sulfate" are not sufficiently precise to be a practical guide to you. Further, lime is "slow-releasing" and does not alkalize the soil in just a few days.

But that's not the worst of it. When you start out to gather a tablespoonful of soil that will serve as a sample of your garden plot, you immediately face the fact that the pH at one end is not likely to be identical with the pH at the opposite end. Acidity and/or alkalinity may vary in a dozen spots. If your spoonful sample is taken from a mixture of soils from different parts of the garden, all you have achieved is an "average." And that's like statements about "the average man."

Ideally, all the planting rows or drills in the vegetable garden should test between 6.0 and 6.9 or 7.0. Starting from such a base, you can lime or sulfur particular vegetables "to taste." A little of the latter for tomatoes; a little of the former for lettuce or beans. Real exactitude for each row of each planting is virtually unattainable.

Even water (theoretically neutral at pH 7.0) will itself differ in pH reading according to whether it is well water, chlorinated water, city pipe water, or rain water. Anyway, any given vegetable you want to grow can find happiness in a *range* of pH numbers.

Actually, the whole pH business is only worth knowing about, not worth worrying about. Soil that is enriched with humus has no serious pH problems, anyway.

How much more informative are the vegetables themselves! They come up with smiling faces and grow into flourishing, edible produce. That is the real pH "test," is it not?

YOUR GARDEN DOESN'T NEED ANIMAL MANURES

You might think, from paeans sounded by some home gardeners, that the endless bushels of manure (horse, cow, chicken, pig, goat) that they lug into their gardens were the stuff of the sacred rites of spring.

Actually their practice is an innocent carry-over from the routine of farming. Animal husbandry yields animal excreta for which the farmer has no other use than to dress the land with it. This has been going on for centuries. Today, however, we know that the passage of fodder through the digestive tracts of kine and swine adds no values benefiting home garden soil. Indeed, unless it is applied in a "well-rotted" condition, it may even do some harm. Farmers *must* dispose of accumulating manure; home gardeners don't need to (unless they, too, own animals).

The hay that the farmer feeds his plow horses in stall or the ensilage he bestows upon his milkers in their cow-barn stanchions could just as well go directly to the garden soil as grass or other vegetative matter. Spread upon its surface or dug into the top 4 inches of the soil (preferably in spring or, better, fall), its nutrients are converted into the finest plant food, namely, *humus.*

If you like to start off with a dictionary definition, humus is vegetable mold, the dark-brown or black substance resulting from the slow decomposition of organic matter. It is a valuable constituent of soils. Unquote.

Now, if we shut the book and walk out into the vegetable garden, humus is what our growing crops are feeding on. The nutrients in humus are made available to our plants by bacteria, which have fed on dead plant material, have digested it, and have released it into the soil. What the dictionary terms "slow decomposition" we know less formally as well-rotted vegetative matter. In any case, the more we give our garden of this "natural" plant food, the more our plants can produce for us.

Since it is clear that humus comes from decaying forms of plant life, gardeners can manufacture a supply of humus by assembling a quantity of dead plant materials and exposing them to the action of soil bacteria. In practice, this is usually done in one of two ways. One is by composting leaves, grass clippings, kitchen garbage, and similar plentiful dainties. The other is by allowing mulch to remain in the aisles between rows of our vegetables long enough to compost itself there and be carried by worms into the soil. Hay thus used as "sheet composting" keeps down weeds. With or without the addition of manure, vegetative matter can be converted to humus by composting in a pit in the ground or a pile above ground.

A compost pile usually covers an area 6' by 6' and consists of alternate layers of vegetable matter and loam to a height of 4'. It is kept moist but not flooded with water. It is completely forked over two or three times in the growing season. When finished, it can be screened (for easier application) or it can be used "in the rough" as needed. Either way it will continue to decay after being mixed into the garden soil. To speed the production of humus, one can also sprinkle a little nitrogenous fertilizer on compost to encourage the bacteria that, in six months or less, make it a pile of composted humus. Composting, properly done, is a hefty job of work. I'm glad it's not necessary.

But unless a compost heap is a convenience, a handy scrap pile on which to toss casual corn shucks, carrot and radish tops, and overblown cucumbers, these materials can just as well be put right on top of or into the soil.

Composting *by mulching* the garden soil requires nothing more muscular than adding more and more hay or whatever you're using on top of prior applications. Garbage can be dumped right out of the can *under* the covering mulch, where it will rot promptly and unobtrusively. Without odor. Or the garbage can be buried in a series of holes dug down to the subsoil and then covered with the soil thus dug out of the holes.

With humus mixed into it, soil can be looked upon as a living thing. It is structured like a well-baked cake; that is, a series of crumbs is connected by a film of moisture, with air spaces in between them. A microscope or even the naked eye reveals in this mélange minuscule particles. Each of these soil particles holds a thin film from which a root hair can absorb water and minerals in solution.

COMMERCIAL FERTILIZERS

So as not to get mixed up in terminology, let's note that anything that feeds plant life is a fertilizer. This includes decayed vegetative matter, animal manures, and also includes bone meal, dried blood, nitrate of soda, wood ashes and many others; also the commercial "complete" fertilizers (complete because they contain nitrogen, phosphate, and potassium plus, sometimes, manganese, boron, and other "trace" elements). In common usage, the word "fertilizer" indicates, not animal manures or humus, but one of the many mixtures or "balances" of commercial plant foods.

Commercial fertilizers are usually bagged or otherwise packaged and labeled as to their chemical constituents. These are often indicated to you by a conspicuous triple-number formula. A typical formula would be 10-6-4. The first number stands for nitrogen content, the second for phosphate content, the third for potassium (i.e., potash) content. Some experts favor a potassium content that is at least half of the nitrogen in the formula.

In broad terms, nitrogen promotes growth, especially green growth (leaves, for instance). Phosphate promotes root growth, primarily. Potassium promotes production (the actual beans, tomatoes, squashes, etc.). This categorization is oversimplified but underscores that you choose a numbered "complete" formula with a specified purpose in mind. Thus, if you apply excessive nitrogen to tomato or strawberry plants, you're likely to get foliage rather than fruits. But a heavy application of nitrogen in spring to asparagus increases the crop of spears.

Commercial fertilizers (but not animal manures or humus, which are always organic) may be either organic or inorganic. Both types are, in the scientific sense, chemicals. In that same sense, plants feed on chemicals. Their root systems will absorb a solution of horse droppings with as much facility as they will a solution of ammonium sulfate. One comes out of a factory; the other comes out of a colon. Among commercial fertilizers cottonseed meal is organic; nitrate of soda is inorganic. All manures are fertilizers but not all fertilizers are manures.

In these days of high prices, one does not scatter increasingly scarce commercial fertilizer over one's garden by broadcasting. Instead, one sprinkles it along the row where seeds are to be sown, and then gently rakes it under the soil surface. Better still, one fertilizes the seedlings after they are 4 inches high.

Any fertilizer you add while your vegetables are making their growth is called "side dressing." You dribble it between thumb and forefinger at a distance of 3 to 4 inches from the base of the plants in a row or in a circle around plants in "hills" (which aren't hills at all, just foot-wide circular areas). It is important that you scratch the fertilizer in just a little way, so as to preclude its crusting and thus slowing its absorption into the soil to feed the roots. By all means, gently water-in the fertilizer to start at once nourishing the plants with nutrient solution.

Remember as you spike the soil with extra fertilizer that nitrogen promotes foliage, so you might want to dose lettuce with a little but not tomatoes from which you want, not leafy growth, but big red fruits.

In recent years you may have heard about something called "organic" gardening. From conviction, I am *not* an "organic" gardener. This term has an established meaning (as does the word "inorganic") in the chemistry of hydrocarbons. However, it has caused some ambiguity, even controversy, when applied to gardening. In the latter context, it apparently refers both to fertilizing plants and to pesticides. If you care to inform yourself objectively, the matter is definitively and scientifically disposed of by the United States Department of Agriculture, in Bulletin No. 299, available for 15 cents from the Superintendent of Documents, Government Printing Office in Washington, D.C.

Seed-Planting Time

In America the Beautiful, the vegetable garden was at first the little brother to the farm. The beans, the tomatoes, the cabbages, and corn dished out upon the farm family's dinner table came, more often than not, from their regular field crops grown for the market. Some items, such as rhubarb and parsley and horseradish and a few herbs for drying, might be grown in a small patch called the "kitchen garden." As a consequence of farming and gardening simultaneously, farm households tended to carry their farm-field techniques over into their smaller-scale cropping.

And why not? The same farm horse and plow turned over the garden soil after the fall pumpkins were harvested and the rutabagas stored in the root cellar. And the spring harrowing was done just when and as it was being done in the farm fields.

Equally, those town dwellers who had sizable gardens near the carriage shed and other outbuildings also managed their plots as if farming them.

Those were the best days of my boyhood. I loved milking the Guernseys, gathering the new-laid eggs from under the proudly indignant Rhode Island Reds or, out in the fields, dropping a young tomato plant, fresh-pulled from the hotbeds, on each cross-furrowed hill. A man coming along behind me and using a pointed dibble, would stick the transplant into the soft earth. And behind him another boy would soak it in with a stoup of water, brought in wooden barrels from a nearby pond.

Farm methods, practical enough for the gardens of those times, do not necessarily possess the same validity in the gardens of today. Then, the width of the aisles between the planting rows was determined, obviously, by the girth of the draft horse drawing the cultivator and the span of his iron-shod hoofs. That width had nothing to do with the space needed by the plants for growth, for air, for sunlight. You can see proof of this in the fact that onions, for example, can be planted four or five inches apart in the row (closer if some are to be pulled young for eating as scallions) and really do not need more than that same distance between rows.

You can, then, determine how far apart the rows in your garden should be by deciding how much width your feet will require when you weed or cultivate (if, indeed, you're insistent upon weeding or cultivating at all, instead of simply mulching).

The planting directions given in today's seed catalogues and on seed packets continue to specify the old-fashioned and largely obsolete widths of between-the-rows aisles, but they are just a carry-over from the good old days. This practice does no perceptible harm except that it cuts down somewhat on the amount and variety of vegetables you can raise in a given garden area.

The simple, observable fact is that your plant (be it radish, lettuce, or summer squash) needs only the room required for the normal spread of roots and/or foliage. That can be your common-sense criterion today.

Although the word "row" or "drill" is commonly used to describe the prevailing system of arranging seeds or transplant seedlings, there is another word (denoting a slightly different method) that is worth mentioning. It's the word "band." It could be "strip." For certain vegetables, especially quick-growing ones, the seeds can be distributed within a wider area than a linear row. Thus, if you mark off with sticks-and-strings a strip of soil that is 4 or 6 or even 8 inches broad, you can get more radishes or carrots or lettuces out of the same distance simply by scattering your seeds within such a band. You can readily see that such a band system lets you pull things like scallions and beets and other vegetables that you want to eat young or must thin out anyway. True, you may find it harder to suppress weeds in a band or strip, but the extra crop yield is likely to be worth the trouble.

For greater ease of planting, you might try the relatively new *seed tapes*. Many vegetables can now be planted at predetermined intervals of space by buying a gelatinous plastic strip containing specific seeds. Covering them with soil per directions and watering them constitute, conveniently, the entire seeding operation. Tapes are not absolutely novel, but their paper predecessors did not always facilitate germination and, unlike today's tapes, contained no plant nutrients to nourish seedlings.

Measure off rows according to your paper plan or diagram, say, 2 feet or 3 feet apart, and drive in a small stake (perhaps 2 feet long) at each end. Running a string from one of these stakes to the one at the other end of the same row will enable you to place your seeds in straight parallel rows. This makes it easier later to weed them or hoe them or water them or mulch them.

Let's say you have stretched a string over a row to help you seed in a straight line. How *deep* should you plant your seeds in that line? The seed packet will tell you. Most people tend at first to bury the seeds too deep. The rule of green thumb is: cover seeds with soil to a depth about equal to their own thickness. Another thumb rule, for all but the tiniest seeds, is to

Lettuce is a good example of how to sow, especially small-seed food plants. That is, one first rakes the seed bed into fine particles, then uses a string between stakes to guide a shallow furrow made with a pointed stick or one's finger, or the track of a tooth of your rake will serve. The tiny seeds are carefully sprinkled into the furrow, then covered either with some soil or some vermiculite, so lightly that they are barely out of sight.

Strings between sticks mark a row for each crop.

Next, gently treading with one foot, as shown, all down the row will put the seeds in close contact with the soil. Watering with a misty spray nozzle, if you have one for your hose, or just a good sprinkle with your watering can completes the simple operation.

From this point on, plants are hungry for the sun. So you can position mulch alongside the seeded furrow or drill, but not cover or shade the planted seeds.

cover them with a quarter-inch to half-inch of fine sifted soil. Modern vermiculite can serve this same purpose: just be sure to wet it thoroughly and at once. It is important, too, to press the soil gently to put the seeds in contact with it. Easiest way to place seeds in a row is to make a shallow "furrow" with a stiff index finger, guided by the string or its shadow on the ground, should the sun be shining at the moment. If you are planting in summer in a hot climate, put the seeds in a little deeper to keep them dark and moist.

In any case, water your row of seeds lightly to snug the soil around them. After they sprout, keep them moistened . . . but not soaked. All you are trying to do is prevent their drying out at the roots. Later, when the roots have lengthened downward, you can water to a greater depth: say 4 inches or more.

If you are like most food gardeners, you are eager to be first in your neighborhood with early peas or red, ripe tomatoes or sweet corn. Especially corn. Tomatoes, at least, and certain other crops can be given a

There are two basic methods for starting vegetables in the house. One is a planter box, which is watered from underneath through a slot. Water moves up slowly, roots move down to reach it. The other is with peat pots, shown in the foreground. They perform exactly the same starting function, but each seedling can be transplanted intact; the pot is simply set in the soil, where the seedling's roots grow right through it and it becomes simply peat moss in the soil itself. Both methods employ exploded mica or vermiculite, thoroughly wetted, as the growing medium. The seeds live on their own nutrient content but after a week should be fed by a weak solution of 10-5-5 "balanced" fertilizer. Vermiculite contains no plant food but can prevent "damping off," a fungus disease that causes the collapse of baby seedlings at their base.

head start by seeding them in planting boxes or "flats" indoors. In your seed catalogue, you will find several aids expediting your early garden, among them special planting soil including a few nutrients. Newer are the compressed lumps or shapes of fertile growing medium, sometimes including sterile sphagnum moss, in which you can plant your seed. If you use soil from your garden, you'll protect sprouting seeds from damping off and dying before your horrified eyes if you spread a 1-inch layer of vermiculite or "perlite" on top before seeding. The shallow box or flat should be well moistened, and a bag or sheet of thin, clear plastic should be in readiness, together with some kind of temporary labels identifying the varieties you are raising. Your vegetable seeds can be scattered in each soil box, or they can be dropped into tiny furrows, easily made by pressing the soil with a stick. It works better to keep these furrows 2 inches apart, at least, across the area of the box. Just as in outdoor seeding, you barely cover the seeds. The important thing is to place your plastic bag or sheet over them and tuck it in under the box. This gives a hothouse effect or, more plainly, the humidity that plants need. Seeds live their first few days on their self-contained nutrients. After that, a very dilute solution of commercial plant food will nourish them, applied every week . . . or oftener if their soil is drying out. This fertilizer might well be a 10-5-5 "balanced" formula in water.

Most seeds, if kept in their flats or metal planters at a temperature above 54° F. and out of a draft, will respond to window sunlight in about 5 days. One week after germination or when they show their first "true" leaves, thin them enough to give each tiny seedling room to grow without touching another. Shade or darkness will cause them to grow "leggy" or spindly and they may collapse. In that case, you will want to reseed immediately to make up for lost time. Generally one starts indoor seeding about 1 month before one would seed the same vegetables outdoors. In other words, about the time the garden is expected to be frost-free, you are ready to set out house-raised young plants. This is your head start.

As soon as you see that you have sturdy little seedlings (perhaps at age 3 weeks), wet them thoroughly and prepare to transplant them. This first transplanting simply means transferring them to another box of soil, exactly like the first, although the need for vermiculite, etc., is not so great. A small spoon can be used to "dig" the seedlings out and keep a lump of damp soil clinging to the roots. Space them out to twice as far apart, cover them with plastic, and put them back in the sunshine of the window. If at any time you notice that the plastic undersurface is condensing large drops instead of a delicate mist, ventilate by lifting up one edge of the plastic. These drops of condensation are too hot for the baby foliage.

At a later stage (tomatoes, for instance, might be 5 inches high) choose fair and windless spring days and put the whole flat outdoors for a few

A cold frame with protective plastic cover gets baby plants ready for life in the soil.

When the sunshine is too strong for the tender seedlings, give them partial shade.

hours. Here occurs what is called "hardening" of the young plant, preparing it for the day when it is moved outdoors permanently and is either protected by a cold frame or a wax-paper tent, so that the hardening is continued but gradual. Tomatoes' stems are turned purple by "hardening." Until the nights are warm, the baby seedlings are brought back into the warm house every night. A cold frame is so called because it is unheated. "Hotbed" is the name of the equivalent heated by fresh horse manure. A modern hotbed can be achieved by an electric heating cable arranged under 6 to 8 inches of soil. In either case, the frame (which is simply a bottomless wooden box, usually 6′ by 3′ and 10″ high) is kept covered by a glass sash or a clear or translucent plastic sheet. This covering is carefully raised several inches on warm sunny days in order to prevent overheating and the drip of harmful, hot condensation. Plants will grow indefinitely in a cold frame but are transplanted to rows for more space.

Any transplanting should be done most gently so as not to break off roots and thus give the seedlings a setback. Prior wetting down of the cold frame's seedbed, like the indoor flat, helps ensure safe transfer.

Any seedling, but especially tomatoes, should be set into its new site just a little deeper than it had been growing. All transplants should be further protected by shielding them from the sun's direct rays. A cloudy or overcast day is a good time to perform this delicate operation.

When you consider it the time to set out your seedlings in new soil, it is useful to mark each variety with wooden stick markers or otherwise. A grease pencil is used to avoid fading. The label or marker can tell the name of the vegetable, its catalogue number, and the date of transplanting.

Seed catalogues and seed packets almost always warn against seeding your vegetable garden "until all danger of frost is past." But who ever knows when that is going to be? Spring always comes on the day and at the minute when the earth's orbit brings it into the right astronomic relation with the sun's rays. Astronomers can scientifically predict the exact instant of the change of *seasons*. But spring *weather* and its attendant frost are not so precisely predictable. For the first several days and sometimes weeks of spring you may get cloudy, rainy days and chilly nights, down around 40° F. or even closer to freezing. What's the use of putting in seeds if they are only going to rot in the ground?

This is why it makes little sense to tell a gardener what tasks to perform week by week or month by month including planting. In one part of the United States the spring season may arrive much sooner or much later than it does where you live and garden. You manage a garden according to your thermometer, not according to the calendar.

Exactly when the daily temperature will consistently rise above the 30°–40° mark up into the 40°–50° mark or higher will depend on the normal climate of the country you live in, plus the vagaries of your local weather conditions.

Numerous charts are published in various media, as well as government bulletins, which purport to tell you when to expect "last frost" in spring and "first frost" in autumn. They can be indicative but are not sufficiently reliable to plant by. Somehow, Jack Frost slips one over on us with a below-32° day or night that does not conform with the chart. Fact is, frost varies too greatly by locality to be usefully charted in "average" terms.

If you can derive from government figures anything that tells you when to plant *your* garden, in *your* geographical neck of the woods, you are an abler gardener than myself or more clairvoyant.

What you and I both need to know are successive night temperatures, not the warmer noontime temperatures. A maximum-minimum thermometer, hung outside a north window, will reveal both. And when we find the weather settling to the low fifties, we can feel pretty safe in planting our seeds outdoors.

Meantime, the United States Department of Agriculture's isothermal charts, showing average dates of first and last killing frosts, are available free if you'd like to see them, in the Home and Garden Bulletin No. 9, entitled "Suburban and Farm Vegetable Gardens." Write to the Publications Division of Information, U.S.D.A., Washington, D.C. 20250. Send no money but do give your zip code in your address.

Frost starts at 32° F. As we all know, that is the point at which water changes its physical form from liquid to solid (ice) and starts expanding, thus rupturing plant tissues and killing them. Even slightly warmer weather, say, 33°, 34°, 35° or higher, may not be conducive to vegetables' growth. In general, low temperatures retard, even when they do not kill. This is not so important in the fall, when some of your mature crops will survive a moderate overnight drop and continue ripening. But in the spring, sprouting seeds and tender seedlings react to chilling and make slower progress. On balance, it is worth curbing one's natural impatience on a balmy spring day and waiting for consistently warm weather.

Correctly timing your plantings at the outset of a new spring is a skill that you acquire bit by bit. At first, maybe, the calendar is your guide. Then, with the greening of your gardener's thumb to a deeper and deeper hue, there comes a homely wisdom from simple observation of all the growing life around you. For you discover in due course that your vegetable garden has become an integral part and portion of surrounding vegetation. The planting of your vegetables is then seen to fit in, so to speak, with the growth phases of certain nearby shrubbery and perennial flowers and even trees.

For instance, it is a pretty concept and a useful bit of growers' working knowledge that when your forsythia bushes are shaking their full bells in the springtime zephyrs, you are likely to be quite safe in putting down seed for beets and cabbages and other earlier crops, notably lettuce and peas.

Over the years, you somehow catch on also to the idea that, when your tulips or your neighbor's lilacs are rioting with their color and perfume, that's the time to slip your zucchini into the humus hills and only barely cover them. Corn goes in, too, and is likewise pressed firmly but not deeply into the damp soil.

This fellowship that you find between horticultural contemporaries strengthens your growing sense of season. Your observations become very personal to you in your locality. Your seeding dates are not always necessarily identical with those of another garden three miles down the road, especially if the road is downhill, where late frosts linger longer.

The main thing to remember about planting seeds is: *nothing is gained by rushing the season.* Cold or wet weather, even when frost doesn't actually kill the young seedlings, slows their growth. Thus seeds planted later will catch up as soon as the weather does warm a bit.

Old-timers in raising vegetables start with early varieties . . . wrinkle-seeded peas, onion sets, early beets, carrots, and, soon after, lettuce and radishes. A month or so later is safer for seeding beans and cucumbers and corn. Vegetables you start indoors or buy as young plants from nurseries and florists with hothouses (tomatoes, peppers, for example) are held back for steady warm weather. Of course, the common-sense way to pick your planting time is to take a gamble on settled weather and merely re-seed if germination proves slow or scanty.

This is particularly the case if you live in a "short season" area. Then when-to-plant is affected by the number of days of growing weather you can expect. Let us suppose you have made your selection of the vegetables you'll grow this season. Your seed packets tell you the variety of broccoli you chose takes 55 days from planting to harvesting, the muskmelon requires 87 days for maturity, the beets 58 days, and your corn needs 82 days. You can check the maturing dates for all your vegetables and then calculate your planting dates by working backwards from the harvesting dates. Hopefully you will have chosen vegetables that mature within the time you can reasonably expect to enjoy amenable growing weather.

It will occur to you that the same kind of figuring is done when one practices succession seeding. If you are planning more than one planting of some strain of Chinese cabbage that requires 50 to 60 days, then the maturity date must not take you into frost. The practical advantages of succession plantings are pretty obvious. Instead of all your lettuces or beans or cucumbers coming to maturity and flooding you for a period of plenty, followed by a dearth, you can by succession or replacement seeding keep up a continuous supply all season long.

You can accomplish much the same result by planting simultaneously one early and one late variety of, say, beets or sweet corn. For any vegetable, all it takes for full production is calculating backwards from maturity dates.

Similarly, if your children are going to demand jack-o'-lanterns to light up on Halloween, and the pumpkin seeds you bought are going to need over a hundred days to mature, you plant them at least a hundred days before the festival date.

Water, Water Everywhere

A water "table" lies somewhere under your garden land. In some areas, this level is but a few feet beneath the surface. There is water vapor hanging in the air, too, breathed out by all growing plants and trees as they "transpire." In winter, there is water in its solid forms as ice and snow. And all year, of course, there is rain water. Like the quality of mercy, it droppeth on the place beneath. As it droppeth, it bringeth down ammonia, a compound including nitrogen, one of the three essential fertilizers. If, in dropping, it should be struck by lightning, the effect is the formation of nitrites which, in turn, upon their descent into the soil structure, are transformed by bacterial action into nitrates, a prime plant food. Finally, for dry periods, there are hose and sprinkler.

Water is important to the gardener as a means of getting nutrients into his plants' growth systems. In order to nourish your various vegetables, all plant food, with the exception of carbon and oxygen gases, *must* be dissolved in water. The molecules of the resultant fluid are then absorbed by the plant's roots and literally (and marvelously) transported upward, finally reaching even the topmost leaves and being there evaporated by transpiration.

It is the plant's filament-like root hairs that open the channels for the absorption of food-fluid and start the complex chemical-physical process of growth. The walls of root-hair cells are thin membranes designed by Dame Nature to enable the passing of liquids from outside into the plant and through its inner structure. This is the well-known phenomenon of *osmosis,* the principle by which liquid from a less dense solution may pass into a denser solution through a permeable film or skin, in this case the cell wall itself.

Since the protoplasm inside the root-hair cells is denser than the food-water outside them, they absorb that food-water. They become swollen, in fact, from their increasing fluid content. The *pressure* of such swelling irresistibly forces that fluid upwards and into the plant's stem. This inner "root pressure" will raise the fluid an inch or two off the ground but is not strong enough to push it farther. Additional upward pull is provided by the exhalation or transpiration (by the leaves above ground) of plant moisture in the form of the gas oxygen. The suction is slight but sufficient.

Plants breathe out any excess water as evaporation through the microscopic mouths or stomata all over the underside of their leaves. In very humid weather, when evaporation is difficult, water is forced out by "guttation." If you turn over a melon leaf, let's say, you can actually see this effect in infinitesimal droplets. On a hot, dry day these same stomata close to conserve the vital moisture.

Supplies of water are necessarily related to the amount of food the plants can manufacture in their leaves. And this amount is, in turn, directly proportional to the hours of sunlight the leaves receive. There's not much point in furnishing your vegetable garden with fertilizers unless the plants are getting enough sunlight to use that fertilizer.

The chemical process by which your vegetables manufacture food in their leaves is called "photosynthesis," meaning "putting together by the action of the energy of sunlight."

Photosynthesis takes place *only* in the leaves and *only* in sunlight. The food that is made is glucose, a simple sugar ($C_6H_{12}O_6$). The chemical equation for this operation of Nature is $6\ CO_2 = 6\ H_2O$ *energy from the sun* $C_6H_{12}O = 6\ O_2$.

Such sugar is converted into a starch and stored in the plant. Some of the starch is in turn transmuted into proteins, but chemists are not yet quite sure how a simple plant does this complicated trick. Come sunset, it is tuckered out and shuts down for the night.

Not at all incidentally, the foregoing chemistry is possible only because the green coloring matter in the plant leaves acts as a catalyst and permits and promotes it. Somebody once put that coloring material in chewing gum, but it has never displaced Wrigley's Spearmint.

Put differently, vegetables live on a liquid diet. When you wish to feed your vegetables and expedite their growth, water is the *vehicle* by which you furnish nutrients to your growing plants. Ideally, enough water should be encountered in the soil by the tiny hair roots or "feeder" roots, so that they are in contact with a continuous film of moisture. If the film should be broken, through lack of water, it must be reconnected up, so to speak, which is an undesirable interruption to the feeding process.

Rain is free, of course, but you cannot count on regular deliveries from the Supplier. The meteorology people speak of an annual "norm" for a given region, say 42.03 inches of rain per year. But see how the actual rainfall may vary in two successive years. The figures are real, not fictional:

ONE YEAR　　　NEXT YEAR
43.42 inches　　48.54 inches

This is a variation, obviously, of 5.12 inches or as much as 10 per cent in those two successive years in the very same area. As a fun item you may wish to place a simple plastic water measure in your food garden and read the rainfall or hose water in inches on its scale. This does not tell you exactly what depth the water is reaching, obviously, since some of it is held by the soil, humus, etc.

In reverse, lack of reasonable water supplies can impair growth of vegetables, sometimes with unlovely visual effects. Tomatoes for example, if allowed to become parched, will draw vital water back through the stems and stalks from the tomato fruits themselves. This leaves an ugly black deformity at the bottom of each tomato affected. It is called "blossom end rot" (because it occurs at the blossom end rather than the stem end of the tomato fruit). This disease is a good argument for watering your tomato plants regularly and plentifully.

The best water for vegetable gardens is, of course, rain water. This is simply because it brings with it from the heavens the extra gift of trace-ammonia (Nature's water softener). The ammonia breaks down into components including nitrogen, the growth-producing chemical in the soil.

One can have, in some years, too much of a good thing in rainfall. The year 1972 in the Northeast was a record breaker in this respect. Not only did some rain fall on each of 188 days or 51 per cent of the 365, but they added up to 67.05 inches. Some gardens suffered because so much water cut off the equally needed supply of oxygen, thereby "drowning" the plants.

When rains do not come with sufficient frequency or adequacy, one irrigates, hoses or sprays, or sprinkles the growing rows with a watering can or a rotating or oscillating sprinkler. These artificial substitutes for natural showers have one advantage; that is, you can control the rate of application. The optimum is one in which the water is supplied in sufficient quantity to seep down about 4 inches for maturing plants or a third or quarter of that depth for seedlings and young transplants. A canvas soaker gently oozing water on the ground alongside a row is one good technique. A mist-forming nozzle is excellent, too. In any case, the painstaking gardener waters his plot slowly enough for the soil to absorb it. In other words, you don't want puddles in the aisles.

If scientific theory holds interest for you, you may wish to add to your gardening miscellany that root systems are naturally hydrotropic. That erudite term translates literally into "water seeking." Attracted to water, roots reach toward the underground water table. Thus, watering vegetables *deeply* encourages their roots to grow downward, whereas too light application of water tends to keep them lingering too near the surface.

In hot, dry weather, fifteen or twenty minutes of sprinkling every morning will produce visible results in growth and ripening of vegetables. Also, when their foliage has wilted in the heat of noon (rhubarb is a typical example), a prompt soaking will often restore stems and leaves to crispness within an hour. (Flower gardeners are familiar with this effect in the case of *Impatiens*.) Covering it with a light plastic bag will often revive a failing plant by inducing humidity.

A potent form of dietary liquid is what gardeners know, delicately, as "barn tea." This is commonly made in a large barrel or steel drum by soaking a burlap bag filled with horse manure in water. After ripening for three weeks or so, this foul-smelling decoction can be diluted in your watering can and sprinkled along the rows near the plants. You keep adding water to the barrel. Chanel No. 5 it is not, but growing plants respond notably to its allure. One suspects they would do the same for plain water. Anyway, it's optional, as merely one way of lightly feeding the growing things. The scarcity of horse manure in so many areas these days also makes it dubious to recommend this procedure over solutions of commercial fertilizers.

Mulch Ado About Nothing

If you describe yourself as a "mulch gardener," you have not really set yourself apart.

Everyone who runs a successful garden necessarily mulches. Some do it with a hoe; others with hay. The principle is the same, but some mulching methods are more comprehensive than others.

Mulching is done for the primary purpose of retaining moisture where the vegetable's roots (more precisely, the vegetable's hair roots) can reach it and absorb it.

In any garden soil, a certain amount of moisture is found at some depth within a zone of influence upon roots. It gets there by reason of rains or of sprinkling. But it does not stay put; it leaches out of reach or it evaporates into the upper air. This dynamic process is continuous.

When a good, heavy rain shower pours down upon your soil, the wetted surface dries out and forms a crust that is punctured by innumerable holes, like open ends of tiny pipes going down into the soil below. Unless the crust is broken up by a hoe and these pipes disrupted and sealed, the moisture evaporates through them into the atmosphere. So hoeing is one form of mulching. Indeed, it is sometimes referred to as making a "dust mulch" and usually must be done after every rain or hosing.

Mulching with hay and/or other decayable vegetable matter also prevents or retards the evaporation of soil moisture. It offers you several advantages over hoeing, apart from the obvious one, namely, the physical work of wielding a garden implement. Hay and grass clippings and others of that ilk let water seep down through their porous bulk without themselves absorbing and holding much of that water. These vegetative mulches can be spread two, four, or more inches thick to blanket the soil against rapid evaporation. Then, too, they begin to rot where they come in contact with the ground and, subjected to the action of worms and bacteria, are transformed into humus, on which your crop feeds.

Vegetative mulches also tend to maintain an even temperature in the soil beneath, and this in turn tends to create a conducive environment for soil bacteria to work in. They like it warm, moist, and comfy down there in the dark.

That same darkness (i.e., impenetrable by sunlight) prevents unwanted weeds from sprouting, whereas hoeing and similar "cultivating" merely cut off their tops, leaving the roots intact, exasperated, hostile, and all ready to try another vengeful sortie.

Not all vegetable matter serves equally well as mulch. Take peat (what my Irish ancestors dug up in blocks as "turf" for the fireplace). It will hold unbelievable amounts of water per cubic unit of peat. But that's all it does; hold it. If you use peat moss as a mulch, you're not getting water through to your vegetables. Peat moss just won't share the wealth. Unless it is absolutely soppy with water, it's as ungenerous as a politician's family foundation.

Even worse, peat moss will often form a hard upper crust in the heat. Then it will actually resist the water you pour on it. All things considered, you do better mixing peat moss right into the vegetable garden soil than merely spreading it on the surface. Then, with a mulch of hay or something of the sort on top of that, peat moss will permit plant roots to penetrate the mixture's interstices and share the vital fluid it is holding onto.

Vegetative mulch confers on you another benefit, too; it keeps the soil soft and friable under it. Even in ground-freezing, winter temperatures, it minimizes the inch depth of the frost. If applied after the soil has frozen hard, a mulch helps to hold any given temperature stable, i.e., less subject to the heaving of successive thawings and freezings, which can damage the roots of overwintering plants.

By layering vegetative mulch stratum by stratum, you are building up mulch on top and humus on bottom. If leaves are used for this purpose, mulch gourmets prefer leaves from nut trees. This is because all those nutty leaves curl up as they dry out and do not pack down into a wet blanket like maple or oak or other leaves. The soil itself is nowhere near as fussy.

If overwintering mulch is left on the soil into early spring, it will keep the soil cold after the weather starts to warm up and thus may retard seed germination and even cause seeds to rot. For this reason, many knowledgeable gardeners pull back the mulch from the ground so the sun can warm it up for planting.

The *new* thing in mulches for your vegetable garden is sheet plastic. It comes in rolls about a yard wide and in clear "white" (used as a substitute for fragile glass on cold frames, mainly), translucent green, and opaque black. Mulching plastic can be purchased at any up-to-the-minute garden center at a few pennies per yard. You will do well to roll it up on a pole or stick for easier handling at the garden bedside. On farms it is sheeted onto the land from a large reel and the edges weighted down by a few inches of soil turned over upon it by mold boards fastened on the tractor that pulls the whole rig. This matter of anchoring the edges in the garden is worth noting, too, because without stones or wooden strips, the tough but flimsy plastic flutters and billows away like a loose-footed jib at the start of a yacht race.

Obviously, an impermeable and virtually imperishable material like mulching plastic cannot deteriorate and add fertility to your garden soil. But it is a quickly applied method of warming up the soil and shutting the daylight out from newly planted seeds until they germinate.

Skull and Crossbones

That convenient symbol for "POISON" seems more useful in the bathroom medicine chest than in the family garden. Yet a lot of scare talk about pesticides has proliferated, which can be very disconcerting to people starting food gardens. We elder dirt daubers have learned to discount it.

Much of the rumor and gossip about "poison" has focused on insecticides and fungicides. Both these types of control are disdained as "chemicals," usually by people who ignore the fact that every living thing and many inanimate objects are composed of chemicals. Certain it is that soils and rocks and plants, not to mention the human body, are varying complexes of recognized chemicals, organic or inorganic.

Principally to reduce damage to crops from chewing and sucking insects and also from various fungus afflictions, America's agricultural chemical manufacturers have developed a wide range of products for farmers and gardeners. These are dusted on the plant foliage or the "wettable" (soluble) ones are sprayed on when there's not much wind to carry either the powder or the mist away. The United States Government passes on and permits the sale and use of these chemicals under stated, restrictive conditions. This authority also often advises avoiding their use for, say, two days or a week before picking the vegetables, to avoid ingestion by humans. Few of them carry any skull and crossbones; they are not seriously debilitating.

Insecticides are successfully employed against insects and fungicides against mildew, rust, and similar afflictions of foliage. Unlike so many "organic" crops (itself a palpable misnomer, since all plants grow and can only grow organically) chemically protected crops are nearly uniformly clean, clear of blemishes and free from the brown threads that are traces of excrement left within the vegetable by insects' thoroughfare.

Gardeners have other "controls" at their disposal in addition to chemicals. Birds, snakes, toads, and certain "beneficial" insects all further the normal cycle or balance of nature by devouring insect pests. Some plants are also effective "controls" for others. Thus, the pungent odor of marigold plants nearby is an effective deterrent to Japanese beetles.

Other gardeners may prefer an immediate physical attack when they discover the presence of such intruders. Now, it happens that the slow-moving Japanese beetle must drop off the vegetation to take flight. Therefore, one arms oneself with a small stick and simply knocks them downward into a coffee can partially filled with water. They shortly drown there.

Here is a simple summary of insecticides and fungicides you can use if your vegetables show signs of marauders. They are all available through your regular seed supplier or garden center.

They are all you need, if indeed you need any. They can be used on all vegetables against all pests (i.e., both chewing and sucking). They are often combined in "general" dusts and sprays.

> *Captan* is a fungicide and is safe. Dusted or sprayed on vegetables, it protects against scab, leaf blight, and damping off where the stem touches the soil.
>
> *Rotenone* is not poisonous to either humans or "lesser" animals. It discourages cabbage worms, bean beetles, etc. You can use it to advantage on vine crops like cucumbers, melons, and squash. Either dusting or spraying according to package directions will work.
>
> *Sevin* is generally approved as doing in corn-ear worms, vine borers, and bean beetles, Japanese beetles, leaf hoppers, and many other nuisances. This comes handily packaged for dusting from the container. Generic name, Carbaryl.
>
> *Maneb* is to be sprayed on tomatoes, carrots, and peppers. If the package label on any pesticide reads "wettable," you can use it as a spray.

Now you are prepared to fight back, should you ever discover holes in foliage, wilted vine leaves, or signs of other visitations. Most garden pests come with warm weather and in successive hatches. The warmer the weather, the worse the infestation is likely to be. One tries to avoid spraying blossoms so as not to interfere with pollination or the bees that do this indispensable work.

Mexican beetles, which concentrate on bean foliage, are quicker on take-off than the Japanese but can be largely eliminated by crushing their yellow egg masses on the underside of the bean vine's leaves.

Corn borers, if discovered in ripening ears by pulling back the sheaths an inch or so, can be tweezered out or scissored where they pursue their nefarious trade. They can be controlled, too, by a little mineral oil inserted at ear ends with a medicine dropper.

Borers into the large-diameter, fluid-filled stems of squash plants can sometimes be intercepted with a bent wire inserted into the same hole they entered the stalk. The vine can then be buried in the soil at that point to regrow itself. But prevention is surer than cure. Spray and dust before the squash blossoms start showing their pollen-bearing stamens.

For a broader background on insect pests, you can write to the same Superintendent of Documents cited on page 18 for your free copy of "Safe Use of Pesticides in the Home, in the Garden" (1964). Ask for PA No. 589 and be sure to give them your zip code. *Sine qua non.* Also, all gardeners have access to county agents for consultation on specific problems they may be encountering.

What Implements *Does Experience Suggest?*

In thinking about your garden work you will want to consider which tools, accessories, and supplies you are likely to need. In an initial overview such as this, it seems sensible to reassure the food gardener that he will not need to go to great expense, even if he does not now own much gardening equipment. Something to dig with, something to rake with, these are basic and indispensable.

Thus you can list as primary a long-handled shovel, a four-tined spading (not haying) fork, a strong metal rake. Secondary items might include a sturdy trowel, a watering can (and/or a sprinkler with hose), light wooden stakes (scrap will do as well as new), and twine for marking the rows. For washing root crops, you will find it handy to have what seamen call a "bucket" and landsmen call a "pail."

All garden implements, like any tools used out-of-doors, should be reconditioned every winter. Cutting edges can easily be sharpened with a rough file and the metal surfaces protected with antirust paint or even discarded crank case oil.

Wooden parts of garden tools can be painted to preserve them from weathering and from splintering. Leftover house paint will serve admirably. Green, brown, yellow, or gray is a good serviceable color.

Tools were invented to make manual labor easier. In the garden, certain farming techniques can make it easier still. For instance, take any task involving digging . . . with fork or spade. Insert the tool straight down, press with the foot to the required depth (say, four inches to spade depth). Then pull the handle straight back. In other words, use the tool to dislodge the load. Don't bother to lift its weight but let leverage take the strain. Only in moving residual bits of loose stuff need you lift. And that is best done by putting one leg, bent at the knee, under the shovel handle and pushing down on the end of the handle. If you have much of this sort of "spring plowing" to do, such a simple laborsaving technique can spare you fatigue today and an aching back tomorrow.

Somewhat similarly, raking can most easily be accomplished by lazily pulling and pushing on the rake handle and thus letting the rake itself rake. Sparing your muscles doesn't add to the time of the operation, yet the result is the same.

As for hoeing, it is not often done in a vegetable garden where ample mulch is keeping the weeds down. If you have no mulching materials at the moment, hoe to improvise a dust mulch. This is done by scuffling the blade of the hoe flat and lightly on the surface of the soil. In fact, there is an implement called a "Dutch hoe" or "scuffle hoe" designed for this very purpose. For work other than "scuffling" to cut off worm holes and other vents into the soil, thus sealing in moisture, a hoe should be lifted high enough so that gravity sinks the blade; not just your muscles.

Foresight suggests fencing your food garden to protect it during growth and ripening stages from invaders. Chicken wire can keep out trespassing dogs and children. Rustic fencing with closely spaced poles will also protect crops from excessively strong winds if positioned against the direction from which they usually blow . . . but it may also throw unwanted shade.

One most effective form of fencing has been borrowed from the modern cow pasture. It is a simplified *electric* fence. This is easy to erect with iron garden stakes or two-by-fours and the circuit is readily insulated with metal or ceramic clamps. It will operate all season long on either house current or one 6-volt battery with controller. Save current by turning it on, usually, only at night. Nothing else seems to save your sweet corn from nocturnal raiding by raccoons. The six volts are not strong enough to shock you more than your automobile spark plugs will. But when a deer, dog, or other intruding animal touches the bare wire with an inquisitive wet nose, the effect is, shall we say, electric.

If you use 3 strands (of No. 5 wire), the bottom one should be only 2 inches from the ground (for squirrels and field mice and chipmunks) . . . and the next one 4 inches above that . . . and the top one 6 or 8 inches above the middle one. Height is not the most important consideration in interception.

Curiously, white-tailed deer have been seen to turn away from an electric fence without actually touching the wire. Suspicious, no doubt instinctively.

Under the Hunter's Moon

What must I do *now?*" asks the food gardener in autumn. The harvest home is over; the soil has yielded him the bounty of its crops. Plants are withering at the finish of their life cycle. The nights are cool as they were in early spring. A fortnight after the autumnal equinox (September 22, 23) a full moon will rise not as Luna but as Diana, her "huntress name," as Shakespeare put it.

Now among other things you can prepare your food garden for next year's "spring plowing" and planting. Pull up the tomato vines and all the other crop residues and scissor off any remaining old strawberry leaves, and then bury them in a hole or a series of holes or a trench. This hole-digging can go down into the subsoil, if you like, although 8 inches is usually deep enough. Leave a few holes or a few feet of trench for the vegetative waste from the household during the months ahead, as it proves far easier to dig the soil now than after it becomes frozen hard. If, later, you find orange peels and banana skins in your garden area, you'll know that hungry little animals have dug them up from under the frost and snow. Simply covering the new-buried garbage with a heavy board or two will end that.

As an aid to permanent soil improvement, you can dust lime over the surface of the entire garden before digging. A reason for choosing this time of year to apply limestone is that this mineral is "slow release" (i.e., dissolves gradually). And the effect of autumn liming is not complete until spring, anyway. One limes the soil of a food garden sparingly, either by sprinkling the lime from a coffee can with a dozen eighth-inch holes punched in the bottom or by casting the talcum-like stuff in wide arcs from such a can. You'd put more sugar on a saucer of strawberries.

From its outward appearance, it is hard to believe, but it is nevertheless quite true, that your vegetable garden does not really come to a full stop. Low temperatures, cold nights, do slow down the busy bacteria, but they still do the same work, at least part time, down there out of the wind chill.

If you have added a little nitrogenous fertilizer to your buried garbage, you have helped feed these invaluable, invisible workers in the vineyard. However, such fertilizing is not strictly necessary and may be too expensive. Better, then, to save your "boughten" fertilizer till the spring and summer growing season.

Winter activity in the food garden includes, eminently, the storage in the frosted soil of root crops like carrots, parsnips, salsify, winter beets, and some varieties of turnips such as rutabaga. These and winter cabbages can be dug up, piled in a pit or sunken box, and covered with soil as an outdoor "root cellar." A 2-foot-square piece of wood or galvanized tin roofing can be utilized as a door to make stored vegetables available as wanted in the kitchen all during the winter. Somewhat similarly, winter cabbage can be piled on the ground and covered with soil till a head or two are needed.

Also, if you have raised kale in your food garden, you can just leave it. It will survive rough weather, ice and snow and still show green. In fact, it can be picked in small amounts whenever the weather lets up and you can find the kale row. If not thus used, it will at least show up early among your spring crops and renew itself. Of course, you have to like kale.

The labor involving holes, pits, trenches, and storage piles of earth will raise in your mind the broader question of whether to dig up the top 4 inches or more of your entire garden. You have seen farmers get out their tractors and till their acres in what is called "fall plowing." But this is done largely to plow under cereal crop residues or to permit seeding some of the land to vetch and other "green manures," which they like to plow under in the springtime when the rotting root systems will help feed their next crops. You don't have the same need to turn over your garden, although it always benefits your soil by aerating it, letting in oxygen, and, if you'll leave it rough, by catching rain and snow and by avoiding erosion if your garden is on a slant. After you have built up the humus content in your garden soil for several years, by adding vegetative matter from the kitchen and returning plant residues to it, you can, if you wish, raise good crops without doing much more than raking the soil each spring. You see, you are accumulating the riches of fertility year after year. For the first few seasons, however, you might be wise to invest some time in autumn cultivation.

The work of turning over the soil can be done by hand, with a sharpened spade, shovel, or spading fork. Many gardeners own or rent locally a gasoline-powered roto-tiller, which cuts down the time of the operation and also allows one to crisscross his tracks, breaking up the soil particles even finer. The roto-tiller is particularly useful if you want to add leaves, grass clippings, garbage, etc., to the soil in autumn so they can decompose into humus by spring planting time.

Before you perform the digging or turning or roto-tilling, it is suggested that you bring into the house a box, bag, or bushel of your best soil, carefully sifted and screened, plus a peck or so of builder's sand if you have it. Store these materials in a dry place. The object is to make it easier next spring to start your own seeds in flats before you can do any "on site" seeding outdoors. If, at the time you're ready to start tomatoes, peppers, cabbages, *et al.* in the warmth of your house, you have to get garden soil from a frozen-hard ground, you'll wish you had forehandedly stored some planting soil ahead of time. A plastic bag will hold it.

For the very reason that your food garden is dormant or quiescent instead of being completely at a halt, you may wish to sheet-compost all or some of your garden plot. Let's suppose you have acquired some bales of spoiled hay (or a load of "barn dressing" if you use manure). You can scatter it over the soil liberally. It may blanket the garden with a 6-inch cover, or even more. Just leave it to heaven. It will weather and slowly decompose. When springtime, sweet springtime, comes around again, such sheet-composting, because it constitutes insulation to some extent, will hold back the normal warming up of the soil unless you rake it back from the rows and drills you have planned in your garden diagram. Or unless you now "plow" it under by hand or machine.

If, in the course of your autumn restoration work, you face a heavy leaf fall and want to remove it from your lawn before it rots the grass beneath, you can dump bushels of it between rows of raspberry canes to settle down under the snow and become a permanent soil. In the same way you can pile leaves on top of rhubarb clumps as deep as you like; they'll find their way up in the spring. Alternatively, you simply make a massive leaf pile somewhere out of the way, like under a maple tree or in the lee of a privet hedge, and let it all decompose in the course of the year to black leaf mold. This mold you can either screen for your vegetable furrows (example: garden peas) or apply in the rough to the sites you plan for tomatoes, squashes, and Brussels sprouts. Making leaf mold can be hastened by covering the decaying mass with a tarpaulin and by forking over the entire bulk every 4 months. Keeping the stuff moist is easily done by now and then sticking a hose under the tarpaulin for 20 minutes.

Otherwise, your annual leaf harvest can serve you by being dug or rototilled directly into the top 4 inches of your garden soil to enrich it for next year's crops. Undoubtedly, renting a gasoline-powered shredding machine for a few hours and chopping the leaves (an easier process while they're dry) facilitate spreading them just where you want to dig. They rot faster, too, being in small pieces. Since the rental charge for a shredder adds to the cost of your year's food garden, you may prefer to accomplish shredding with the power mower you now use to cut the grass on your lawn. In that case, you need only pile the leaves and aim the discharge vent of your mower downwind, blowing the shreddings right onto the garden.

Leaves from your trees supply carbon as an ingredient in soil nutrients. So do sawdust and wood chips. On the other hand, grass clippings add to the soil's nitrogen, as do vegetative crop residues and uncooked kitchen waste.

Every gardener knows better than to burn leaves. However, if you plan to burn other materials, like storm-downed dead branches and discarded pieces of lumber, why not plan to reduce them only to charcoal, not to fine ashes? The charcoal, in almost any size pieces, can go right onto or into the soil. It has a desirable "sweetening" effect. Ashes from your fireplace can be collected in the spring, if you like, and scattered over the soil for their slight potassium content.

Should Madame desire to keep a pot of parsley or chives or other small herb on the kitchen window ledge, autumn is, of course, the time to accommodate her. One selects some of the younger plants to lift out of the row for this estimable culinary purpose. By moistening them deeply a few hours ahead of time, one can trowel them out without injuring their roots unduly. After potting in some of your most friable soil, water them gently but thoroughly again. Those plants remaining in the garden can be kept during winter by placing a portable wooden cold frame over them and giving them the protection of 4 inches of mulch plus a glass or plastic sash.

While late winter/early spring is a preferred time for dividing any rhubarb clumps you may have growing, in order to help a neighbor start his own source of rhubarb pies, this can be done in autumn. Simply wait until the big leaves and thick stalks die down and the plants start to go dormant. Tell him rhubarb is not very demanding as to soil quality but does prefer slightly acid conditions. Therefore, if he can get hold of some sawdust from a nearby lumberyard or sawmill, it will give him a more suitable mulch. To help rhubarb to a good start in spring, he should apply some nitrogen (especially with a sawdust mulch) and provide frequent watering. Incidentally, you can renew your own rhubarb plantation at this time of year (or next spring, when there's likely to be more rainfall) by dividing the old, mature root clump into three or even four pieces.

Some food gardeners like to treat their asparagus beds before spring with an application of rock salt (table salt will do, too, but may prove rather expensive). The purpose of salting asparagus, which one may never do to any other plant in any other part of one's garden, is to kill weeds. And why doesn't salt kill the asparagus, too? Because the original, wild asparagus grew in Mediterranean salt-water marshes and your cultivated asparagus of today has inherited an atavistic salt compatibility. Salting becomes unnecessary where the asparagus bed is heavily, watchfully and repeatedly mulched from earliest spring all during the summer. Ordinarily, salt will kill and suppress vegetation, edible or not, and the immunity of asparagus makes it an extraordinary exception.

And so, when the curtain has been rung down on this year's growing season in your food garden, you immediately begin to set the stage for next spring's opening performance. New seed life waits in the wings. Below ground the bacteria are still at work. For the soil is only resting, never asleep. As winter comes, you find yourself thinking about a new cast of characters, about which vegetables shall be given leading roles next spring when once again the spotlight is the sun.

PART II

Crop Choices

Tomatoes—Your Own Love Apples

Y ou are lucky to be living in modern times when nobody any longer believes that the tomato (dubbed "love apple" by our forebears) is poisonous.

It's lucky, too, that plant breeders have so developed and refined this vegetable that you can choose from sixteen or seventeen kinds and strains. There are more heavy-yielding hybrids than ever. Yet there are older varieties that have never been surpassed. One example of the latter is the "Rutgers," a late bearer with a distinctive flavor commanding a loyal following each year.

Commercially, tomatoes are big business (with commensurately rising prices), but the home-grown product still excels. Almost any variety you choose is likely to bear a prolific crop.

Although commercial tomato growers raise "field" tomatoes (that is, flat on the ground without staking), the home gardener can get a better result in quality by staking or fencing his home-grown plants. Also, pruning them by limiting them to a single stem apiece will mean the strength of the plant is directed into production of its fruits. Do this by pinching out the little branches that start new foliage in the axillas or "armpits" of the growing branches.

You will probably turn out to be possessed of the same frenzy as your neighbors who want to be the first to report red, ripe tomatoes in their gardens. And you stand just as good a chance as they do, provided Lady Luck gardens with you.

With this in mind, your best bet (for a family of four, say) is to buy a dozen young plants from a florist or garden center if they sell the variety you want. Next best is raising your own seedlings in the warmth of your house. In the latter case, the transplants should go through a finishing

period outdoors, protected by a covered cold frame to "harden off." They thus acquire a purplish tinge up and down their stem. Whenever you transplant tomato seedlings of any size, either from indoor flats or from the soil in the cold frame, they should be set in their new location inches deeper than the level at which they were growing.

Tomato vines start life rather tender and readily susceptible to the slowing-up effect of cool, especially wet weather. Later, you'll marvel at their fibrous toughness and, in fact, at the ability of some tomato seeds to over-winter in freezing temperatures and then show up in the warm sun of spring (usually in a part of your garden where you don't want them) as "volunteers."

This particular year, staking was a little different, in that the 4-foot "rot-resistant" wooden stakes used were positioned and ready before transplants themselves were fully hardened for setting out. However, the usual practice was followed by which stakes were staggered in the rows, giving a minimum distance between any 2 plants of 3 feet. (A useful device in a small garden plot.) Stakes set 12 inches or so into the soil will normally support the plant's weight. Even before the actual planting, a heavy mulch of 6 inches of hay was spread to stabilize temperature and any rainfall. The young plants, about 7 inches tall, were brought out of the house in flats, separated gingerly, and placed in troweled holes almost up to their leaves. In this transplanting process, each stem was loosely "bandaged" with a 1-inch strip of aluminum foil to foil the wicked cutworms, always ready to

chew them through at ground level. Purely as an improvisation (but one that worked) the little fellows were given warmth and humidity by inverting over each one a discarded plastic ice cream container for its first week. Tomatoes originated in a tropical climate, hence their happy response to high humidity. A grease pencil was used to mark the plastic "hothouses" with the names of the varieties being grown and with the planting date. This is only one of the ways in which transplants can be helped by humidity. Thin, clear plastic from the dry cleaner's or food store is very practical as temporary protection.

Staking entails tying. You won't favor string or binder twine for staking once you observe how they cut into the tomato plant. Yet you need a strong tie, capable of supporting the growing weight of clusters of tomatoes being produced all along the stem. Nothing has ever proved much better than an old bed sheet or shirt torn into strips. The strip is tied to the stake first, then looped around the stem and square knotted. Ties are added along the stake, to keep up with the increasing height of the tomato plant, which often reaches and exceeds 4 feet.

What a satisfaction to watch your plants come along, thrifty and luxuri-
ant, even at half stage. If you are ambitious to be the first food gardener on
your block to brag of ripe tomatoes, you can help win the race by *consis-
tent* watering. This means using a fine spray from your hose or sprinkler for
the same length of time (say 10 minutes in the forenoon) every single day
the sun shines. On cloudy days, less water is needed and on rainy days, obviously, none. Scanty, irregular water supplies can cause blackening at the
base of the fruits, called "blossom-end rot" when the plant, lacking water,
withdraws moisture from its own fruits to preserve its own life. It's quite
unnecessary to lose tomatoes this way.

Tomatoes develop in green clusters that turn to greenish "white," then redden as they ripen. You wind up the season with small, immature tomatoes and larger green ones which would ripen on the vine if Nature would only hold back Jack Frost. If you can outguess the date of his arrival (usually at night) you can pick the larger of the green tomatoes and ripen them indoors, each wrapped in a thickness of newspaper. A better method is to pull up the entire plant, shake off a little soil, and suspend it, roots uppermost, in a cool, dry cellar. The tomatoes ripen to a slightly deeper red and have more "tomato taste." Your seedsman's catalogue has told you in how many days from setting out in your garden your particular variety can be expected to produce ripe tomatoes. However, unlike strawberries or string beans, your tomatoes are unlikely to overwhelm you by coming in a flood. You really won't need to pick every day. After all, some members of your family may prefer their fresh tomatoes riper than do others. A tomato may ripen on the vine for a week after it's red without becoming too ripe to enjoy. Ultimately, if left much longer, they will of course turn overripe.

Onions—You Can Eat Your Crop and Have It, Too!

Onions may draw tears from your eye and render your breath asocial, but, cooked or raw, they delight the palate in many dishes, especially salads.

Even in the chill of early spring, it is safe to plant onion "sets" long before you'd risk other crops. Few veteran food gardeners and almost no novices plant onion seed, but instead buy a more convenient pound or two of small half-grown onions known as onion "sets." They are available only in spring, but every seedsman's catalogue shows them and your neighborhood garden center or even hardware store may have them. Stuck in the soil with only their dry "necks" showing, they come to life from their dormant state in about two weeks, showing tightly rolled green tips.

You can arrange your sets in a single or double row or in a rectangular plot as long as they are not closer than, say, 2 inches together. You are going to thin them to 4 inches apart by eating the "thinlings" as scallions. The remainder, left unpulled, will mature into full-sized onions good for cooking and salads, and these will keep for months in a cool, dry, dark place if hung up or stored in a mesh bag that gives them air. Scallions are ready in less than a month, and you judge them by the size of the new bulblets they form in the soil. Pick a mess for the table every few days.

All onions like a moist soil and as many hours of sun as your garden design will provide. As your onions approach maturity, you can plant other crops between rows. Above sweet corn has just been planted and watered. To help preserve moisture, these rows have been mulched with grass clippings, but any type of mulch will serve the same purpose.

The sign of ripeness of the mature crop is the natural falling over of their slender green "leaves." At this point, use the back of your rake to bend down those that have not done so fully. Now they will dry for several days in the summer sun and be ready for pulling and clipping.

Shorn of their green "leaves" down to their necks, they are shown drying on a screen, which allows air to circulate under them. This is not the only drying method. Dry mulch or the ground itself will do the trick, thanks to the onion's impervious skin. Various factors—such as temperature, humidity, etc.—influence the length of drying time. It's wise to examine them every few days.

Don't Lose Your Cool, Cucumber!

You can allot a big share of your garden space, if you have it to spare, to allow cucumber vines to spread out flat. Or you can save most of that area by training them to climb up some fencing.

Your cucumbers are up! These 4-day-old youngsters are part of the first section growing from seeds stuck half an inch deep into soft, rich soil. The simple fencing is sturdy enough to take their weight even when they've reached a height 4 or 5 feet and are laden with cucumbers. This particular fence material was lath lattice supported by sapling poles. But practically any fencing will do. Common sense is worth more in a food garden than doctrine.

Quite early in life, say in 10 days, the vines show a yellow blossom or two. (See color page 74.) Some of the flowers are male, some female. The cucumbers form, naturally, in the latter. Long before the vines have attained the top horizontal slat of their fencing, many of their flowers will have turned into inch-long "pickles." Watch for these babies. You'll hardly believe that they're going to be 8 inches long within 2 weeks, ready for slicing.

You can trust fenced cucumbers to reach out, grasp their supporters, and hold on tight. Their tendrils are sensitive in locating nearby security and are tough enough to curl around it without tearing under the strain of wind and weather.

Help! They're running away! Humus-rich soil, near daily watering at the base of the vines, and the sun's bright, warming rays combine to promote prolific growth of foliage, flowers, and fruits. And it's not yet the 62 days which the seed catalogue specified! Let's go looking for the first cucumbers under the massive greenery.

Cucumber vines are beautiful to watch as they mature. Also, they provide plenty of hiding places for their fruits to grow in. That is why you have to look carefully, sometimes, to find where they are lurking. (Cucumbers are definitely sneaky.) These are almost ready to pick. (See color page 74.) You may be surprised to find that a fresh cucumber has prickly spines. Commercial cucumbers are usually waxed to help preserve their freshness.

"Cukes" yield plentifully all summer long—cool and delicious to eat. Always more coming if you just keep picking them. And this will go right on up until frost. After that, they and their parent vines can go into a hole or trench in the soil to be converted by bacteria to plant food for next year.

Fresh Garden Peas
in Cool Spring Weather

The several varieties of peas offered in the seed catalogues are all pre-eminently early spring contributions to your family dinner table. All it takes is a little empathy with pea nature to win a lavish yield. For instance, you will learn to sympathize with the fact that this vegetable is particularly partial to cool growing conditions. Similarly, you are willing to lavish nitrogen feeding on your pea vines once you learn of their remarkable capacity for "fixing" nitrogen in the soil by means of characteristic nodules in their root systems. This growth habit results in your getting back at the end of the season all the nitrogen you put in and more. This is why you always bury the vines in your garden soil after harvesting the crop.

Peas from one's own garden will keep in the pod for days. They are best shelled just before cooking and the empty pods returned to the soil for humus. Family preference may be for a little harder or a little mushier cooked peas, but that fresh garden flavor will be very different from store-bought, either way. They really need only butter and a very little salt, if anything, as a separate side dish, yet it must be admitted they combine admirably with boiled onions and other ingredients.

Peas are planted in rows or drills, but much deeper than most other vegetables. In fact, your furrow becomes a trench 4 inches deep or so. In it you plant your peas. They are large enough between thumb and forefinger so you can readily space them out 13 to the foot. (They will not require thinning.) They can be watered gently in their open trench.

Then some of the soil is shoved back to cover the seeds about half an inch to an inch deep. The back of a hoe or rake will tamp this soil down firmly. More soil is moved back as the plants grow up to 5 inches, so they get support. At 10 inches, they get the rest of the loose stuff that came from the trench. This step-by-step practice keeps the peas' roots cooler as oncoming summer warms up your food garden. Mulching helps too, but you needn't worry about weeds once your crop is fully started; the peas are by then getting their nutrients at a deeper level than, say, chickweed or other aliens. Since you usually pull the ripening peas all the while the vines are bearing and since, unlike beans and broccoli, Brussels sprouts and cucumbers, *et al.*, they do not renew themselves as you pick them, it is all the more advisable to practice succession planting with garden peas.

Different strains of garden peas grow to different heights. Some exceed 24 inches at maturity. These call for "brushing." In other words, they should have support to keep them upright and off the ground. You can use actual brush cut from hedges or wild shrubbery, or else netting. Wire may get too hot in the sun and scorch the green foliage. You won't need to tie up the vines; just place the "brushing" near enough to them for their tendrils to reach out and take hold.

You are likely to find both blossoms and well-formed pods on the same vine at the same time. The temptation is to pick your peas according to the apparent size of the pod. Open one or two, however, and they'll soon teach you how to judge their ripeness by the fatness of the 5 or 6 or more peas inside. A delicate tactile touch will thereafter tell you. Incidentally, the pea pod is often hard to discern amid the vine's foliage. Pole beans are like that too.

Farmers know that, using a pickax or a crowbar, they can often break through a late-winter crust of frost and get their seed peas into the soft ground beneath, with an excellent chance of making a crop for the early market, with its higher prices. A "smooth" variety is traditionally planted first because it is considered more cold resistant than the "wrinkled" sorts. You can do the same.

Whatever Became
of the Beanbag?

Your seed beans . . . green, wax, horticultural, lima and pole . . . are big seeds and should germinate easily under warm, moist conditions. They all take the same culture, except that pole beans grow on poles or fences. Pole beans produce somewhat bigger yields than bush types, and besides they save a lot of space, which you can allot to other rows, other crops. This is because you can circle a pole with them or plant them in a drill along a fence or stretched netting. Just don't try to beat the season. They respond to warm weather. They'll try to make a crop for you in almost any soil, although, being legumes, they will repay a little nitrogenous fertilizer when their blossoms commence to show.

They will grow 10 feet tall and bear beauteous little blossoms. And you can hardly pick them often enough.

The standard variety known as Kentucky Wonder Pole Beans brings you (like the Rutgers tomato) a distinctive, characteristic flavor. Boiled till barely tender with a ham hock or slice of lean bacon, Kentucky Wonder is lowly but Lucullan.

Some 4 to 6 inches from the base of any fence or netting you are using, in a straight line guided by a stretched string (like your other seedlings) push the seed beans an inch down into soft soil, tamp the soil firmly to enclose it, and water gently. You will not be thinning them, so plant beans 2 or 3 inches apart to keep them from competing for food. Here they are just breaking through the crumb-like soil, reaching for the sun.

Assuming you plant successive 6-foot sections along your fence, the first one can be 3 or even 4 feet high before you need seed your second section in succession. At this rate, your bean crop will provide your family with a plentiful and continuous supply right into early autumn. The extra warmth and humidity of a temporary (3-day) mulch of black plastic helps achieve a more uniform germination of seeds. (This particular fence was easily erected, using saplings and slats.)

This is what a satisfactory germination looks like after about a week of warm, moist weather. The first true leaves have spread themselves to the sun. Under 3 or 4 inches of hay mulch, the roots are busily feeding on the nutrients supplied by humus in the soil. In no danger of drying out under such culture, they nevertheless were watered in the late morning nearly every day. In your food garden, vegetable plants tell you by their fresh, un-wilting look that they are doing well and have every expectation of making a crop for you.

Another planting, for a succession crop. These beans are a little older, but the main thing to note is that they have been mulched with a couple of inches of green grass clippings spread right over hay. The grass has been heavily fertilized and treated with pesticides, so the bean crop will benefit in both feeding and of protection. If we can keep the Mexican bean beetle off the maturing foliage (by seeking and crushing their egg clusters on the undersides of the leaves) we'll have plenty of tasty beans.

Like many another vegetable in your garden, the pole bean can be beautiful, with delicate flavors. (See color page 76.) Children can be shown how the tiny bean, like a fairy saber, emerges from the end of the bloom. Easy lesson in basic botany! As the vines rise out of convenient reach, you can pinch them near the upper ends. This helps stop unwanted growth and encourages production of beans lower down the vine. Otherwise, what's to stop the vines from reaching the Wicked Giant's Castle above Jack's Beanstalk?

Your harvest will almost certainly be prolific, and you can decide whether to eat your pole beans at a young, svelte, and tender stage (say, 6 inches long) or at a more mature and flavorful stage (up to 10 inches long with fat, clearly visible beans inside the pod).

New asparagus spears as they appear shortly after pushing up out of the ground.

Uncut asparagus grows into a lovely fern-like plant reaching 4 feet or more. Your asparagus bed will have both male and female plants and the ladies will end the growing season with a striking show of these bright red seed berries.

Early in the growing season cucumber vines develop small yellow blossoms such as this one, harbingers of the fruit to come.

These cucumbers are almost ready to pick. Notice the prickly spines formed on fresh cucumbers and not often seen on the ones from the store.

The exquisite, pale yellow blossom of a Butternut squash, one of the most beautiful in your vegetable garden.

Butternut squash full grown but not yet ready to pick. When truly ripe they will have changed from this yellow/green shade to a definite tan.

Early rhubarb whose stalks have just begun to turn pink. Notice the foliage, yellow at this stage, which is beginning to unfurl.

Mature rhubarb plants have enormous leaves like these.

Pole beans develop lovely, delicate flowers. Children can be shown how the tiny bean, like a fairy saber, emerges from the end of the bloom.

A typically prolific harvest of pole beans.

Another favorite bean is the lima bean. Some varieties of limas are grown as "bush" beans in rows, while others can be grown on poles and fences like the regular pole snap beans shown in the other pictures. The culture is the same for pole-grown limas. Shelling is a nuisance, but home-grown limas are rewarding in both tenderness and deflationary cost.

Your Own "Sweet Corn" Is Bound to Taste Sweet

If you want to put corn on the cob on the family table, you have to grow your own. That is, if you also want it to taste like corn at its prime. Nobody can ship it to you or serve it to you in a restaurant, for corn on the ear is changeable. Once it ripens and especially after it is picked, its sugar turns to starch within two hours or less. That changes its sweetness—radically. So in starting your own food garden (unless it is very small indeed) count on corn you grow yourself.

Also plan succession plantings (meaning about 6 feet of row every 2 weeks) so you can keep picking it half-a-dozen ears at a time, at their best stage, knowing that more stalks, bearing more ears, are coming along. You can either plant the same variety of seed corn at 2-week intervals, or you can plant early, midseason, and late corn all at the same time. Seed catalogues and seed packets tell you which is which.

Incidentally, the new hybrid varieties of seed corn are beyond the fondest dreams of our forefathers. So butter yourself an ear and taste real corn!

Young corn mulched with grass clippings to maintain soil moisture. Throughout its life, from tiny green spear to brown-tasseled ear, corn is a distinctly pretty plant. It is shown here seeded closely enough in a block to permit and promote fertilization by the pollen of neighboring plants. In each row, a seed was dropped into a 2 inch deep hole, spaced one foot apart.

Corn grows faster if the sun is hot and the nights are warm. Like the rest of your garden, your corn can take almost daily watering in sunny, especially windy, drying weather. Here each separate planting in succession was arranged in 3 rows 3 feet apart. You can see the difference in growth stage.

At first, you wonder where the ears of corn are going to show themselves. But the pollen must ripen first. "Sacred pollen" is much used in Navajo religious exercises and often sprinkled on the sand paintings in their hohrahns (cabins). You just let it ripen; you don't have to do anything about it. Pollen disperses itself in due time. The pollen capsules hang down when they are ready to be breeze borne. By this time, immature ears are putting out their "silk" filaments to catch the tiny pollen grains. This is a good time to scratch in some fertilizer with high nitrate number (6 or higher) along the rows, at a distance of 6 to 8 inches.

Any day now, the stalks will send out surface roots as seen here, spread wide for bracing against winds.

As the pollen stalks start to wither, you can watch the ears fatten from day to day. When the silks are fully dry, you can enjoy corn on the cob for dinner. Have a big pot boiling and ready *before* you pull the ears. They'll cook in 6 minutes or less (preferably 3). Later, you can return the husks to the garden soil . . . like all other crop residues.

Lettuce for the
Salad Gourmet

In one's garden soil, one plants either seeds or young transplants. Lettuce does not transplant readily without shock and temporary arrest of its growth. Since one is seeking rapid harvesting of this salad crop, one usually seeds directly onto the soil. This cool-weather food plant takes a little understanding of its needs but is then very responsive to simple culture. The Buttercrunch shown growing here is only one of half-a-dozen varieties of lettuce. It is really a leaf lettuce rather than a head lettuce, although it does form a rosette while young and, thinned to 4 inches apart in the rows, will head up loosely. For family use, 6 to 10 feet of seeds are planted every three weeks.

Shading is helpful after lettuce sprouts because even Buttercrunch (the variety pictured in all the photographs), which tends to go through the summer without "bolting" to stalks, blossoms, and seeds, does not thrive at its best in a hot sun. Watering every morning, stopping short of puddling, should get you 4-inch growth, and you can start thinning to 2 inches between plants, then later to 4 inches apart. Thinning is highly important for lettuce and many other plants in your garden. Besides, it enables you to start enjoying the thinlings in your first salads of the season. At age 3 weeks, you should be enjoying good-sized lettuces.

In very early spring, your rows of lettuce can be seeded directly on the soil within a readily moveable cold frame.

As the days turn milder, you can dispense with the cold frame in extending your lettuce rows.

Better start bringing your lettuces into the house as soon as they rosette to the size shown above. That way, you can have crisp, succulent salads early in the season and, since you plan to extend your lettuce rows every three weeks, you won't end up with more fully mature heads than you can eat. As with so many of your fresh garden vegetables, you just "keep 'em coming".

Continuous Performers—
Broccoli, Parsley, and Sprouts

You keep on picking . . . They keep on producing.

By the time you have reached this page, you will undoubtedly have digested and mastered the simple instructions and techniques of planting even small-seeded vegetables like Brussels sprouts, broccoli, and parsley. The following paragraphs are oriented to their culture because the more they are picked, the more all three produce.

For several weeks right into autumn's first light frosts, Brussels sprouts will continue to "sprout" upwards along its tough, fibrous, swaying stem as you keep cutting them off, starting at the bottom of the plant. As the buds form and grow to, say, 1-inch diameter at the point where a leaf stalk joins the main stem, the leaf stalk dries up and you break it off in order to reach the little cabbage. An upward slice with a sharp and sturdy-bladed kitchen knife does the trick. You don't cut into the main stem, just parallel to it. In effect, you are pruning off the Brussels sprouts, taking a dozen or so from each plant and leaving the smaller, tight-wrapped buds to ripen in the next few days. Six Brussels sprouts plants yield amply for a family of three or four. Like big cabbages, they are cooked to the degree of "doneness" preferred. Sometimes people who say they "can't stand" cooked cabbage get a pleasant surprise from freshly cut Brussels sprouts . . . cabbage taste without cabbage aftertaste. Cook lightly to retain garden freshness.

Broccoli, a connoisseur's vegetable, is another one of those continuous performers . . . in a slightly different way. That is to say, after the main head and its thick stem are cut from the plant, a few smaller heads appear farther down. These, too, are a great delicacy. You'd better watch your broccoli crop as it matures its heads; otherwise all those tight little budlets which constitute the head will soon blossom into hundreds of tiny florets. Exquisite to look at, they are a trifle past the point for gourmet eating.

As soon as you harvest broccoli, bring it into the house and submerge it for an hour or two in cool water. If any unwelcome cabbage worm is lurking within, this simple treatment brings him out in the open.

Again, your little row of parsley, after its slow germination, produces a lovely, tender foliage . . . and it will continue to do so all season if you just keep picking or cutting it. And why not? It flavors or garnishes so many family dishes. It is a biennial and overwinters with just a little frost protection to come up in the spring to make a second crop.

Garden Zucchini–You Can Pick at Any Size

Generally, the larger a vegetable is allowed to grow, the less tender it becomes. That is substantially less true of home-grown zucchini. Perhaps it is because you have built a mellow soil with lots of vegetative matter converted to humus. At any rate, you can pick your young zucchini when they are only 6 to 10 inches long, maybe 3 days old or not much older. Or you can wait till they grow to twice that length and weigh pounds instead of ounces. They can remain on the vine till you're ready to use them. Your own home-grown zucchini, even the bigger ones, will be tender without too big seeds and, of course, the bigger they grow, the more you are getting for your seed money. The younger ones are often sliced and eaten raw in salads. The bigger ones are cut up for simmering without added water, especially à l'onion, or they lend themselves to baking, stuffed. The point is, any squash is a *bland* vegetable and often gains from blending with a stronger flavor such as tomatoes and/or Cheddar cheese. So-called "summer squash" is grown just like zucchini, cocozelle, *et al.*, but are usually picked younger . . . say 6 to 8 inches long.

Squash is a "gross feeder" (as are tomatoes) and will utilize all the leaf mold or other humus you give them in the garden soil in which they are planted. Make "hills" as shown, above, mixing in the rich humus material with the topsoil. An occasional dusting with limestone will sweeten their nature. The big seeds are not planted in rows, but 4 or 5 are stuck in the soil in 10-inch circles 3 feet or more apart, pressed in and watered. On germination they are thinned to 3 seeds per circle (called a "hill" even though flat). Stakes as pictured simply serve to make neater spacing and can be withdrawn after planting or after sprouting.

All squashes start off quicker under the warm, humid conditions provided by wax-paper tents or caps. Seeds sprout in approximately 5 days and soon show their first true leaves. The wax-paper caps can be slit on one side to allow air in on the seedlings after they have grown 3 inches or more. In another week, you can remove the caps altogether.

This is what your zucchini plants will look like a week or so after sprouting. (Above.) All that mulch will keep their root-level temperature even and preserve moisture. Like all vegetables, zucchini grows better, in flavor especially, when it is grown fast. Morning hosings on days that promise to be hot and sunny or windy help squash make the most of the nutrients in their bed. Spraying for 15 minutes with a rotating or oscillating sprinkler is enough, 5 minutes of steady but gentle watering from a hose suffices.

Within 3 weeks your thriving zucchini should look like the ones below. By the way, don't be surprised if your layer of mulch shows signs of disappearing rapidly in warm weather. This just proves that the bacteria and the earthworms are doing their damnedest. Just keep building up mulch around the plants. Piling it on to a thickness of 4 inches is not too much mulch.

At this elephant's-ear stage, you wonder if your zucchini is ever going to stop growing. But you now see why so much distance between "hills" is desirable. At this point, part of the fun of growing your own zucchini is watching these speedy plants produce their striking yellow blossoms. (Is it any wonder young Hopi maidens tuck one behind an ear to signal "I'm marriageable" to the young men of her tribe?) They'll turn right before your eyes into edible young fruits at the base of each gorgeous flower.

You can start picking zucchini when its fruit has reached a length of 6 inches or even less. From there on, it just gets bigger until it is 12 or 14 or 16 inches long. And zucchini is a notably prolific vegetable. Like snap beans or cucumbers, it is so generous in output that the more you pick the more the plant produces. This goes right on into fall and frost. So you may want to get rid of surplus zucchini among nongardening friends, neighbors, and fellow-workers in the office. Tell them that thin slices of fresh zucchini (rind and all) when lightly salted, show a gratifying taste affinity for dry vodka martinis.

"Butternut," Your Own
Prime Winter Squash

Many squashes are good "keepers." That is, they will store well. Depending on how rapidly you consume Butternut squash, they will often last you all winter and right into spring, when you're already planting peas and onion sets. Their durability is due to their tough, smooth rind, which ripens to a handsome tan.

They spread pretty far, so you won't want them in the middle of your garden but along one edge, where you can distract and direct the venturesome vines.

Cooking Butternut squash can be simple. Remove the seed pulp and put it back into the soil. Pare off the rinds. They go back to the garden too. Cut the rest of the squash into 2-inch cubes. Then boil up the chunks till reasonably soft and proceed to casserole them in the oven with a generous sprinkling of brown sugar on top. Anyway, that's one way. Hearty, wholesome, and addictively good.

Blue Hubbard squash has a blue-green rind as wrinkled and hard as an elephant's hide. But the flesh makes the best "pumpkin" pie in America.

Acorn squash is smaller and, naturally, more or less acorn-shaped. It is not as good a winter keeper as the others. Usually it is halved, baked and served with a lump of butter dropped in each hollow half and salted and peppered.

All winter squashes' culture is virtually the same. Plant your Butternut squash much as you do your zucchini. Then one fine morning, there appears in an axilla (a vegetable vine's "armpit") a pale yellow blossom. (Above and color page 75.) Looking closely at the base of the female blossom, you can detect the infant fruit forming beneath it.

The blossom soon withers and drops away, but before it goes, behold, you find a perfectly formed, if miniature, Butternut squash on the vine.

Farther along the same vine you discover a second young squash. And in the next two weeks you discover on that vine more Butternuts growing, as it were, in series. Other vines in the squash patch are doing the same thing, one "dumbbell"-looking squash following another. The first squash to arrive is making growth all the while the younger ones farther along on the vine are shedding their flowers and emerging as squash like the first one.

Longer and larger they get, but the initial difference in relative size between the first and the last is leveling off as they all approach their normal maximum. Butternut squash can stay on the vine till the latter dries up, if you like, but when you finally pick them, weighing several pounds apiece and looking totally unlike the Butternuts offered in most food stores, you do best to store them in a cool, dry place in the cellar with plenty of air around them. This supply of deliciously flavored garden squash will not readily rot, so you may be enjoying it with a meal until late winter or even until early spring.

Children Like to Learn
Gardening by Raising Radishes

R adishes in early spring! Every family loves them. They are easy to grow
. . . but they do not thrive on neglect. By this sage observation is meant
that radishes are not fussy about soil, although, like any other root crop,
they need a bed lightly enough textured to expand in. Thus, mixing in
sand or vermiculite is good. They do insist on thinning once, twice, or
thrice until they are at least 2 inches apart.

They will grow in a drill (row) or in a swath or in a double row as
shown. A row is more readily weeded; a swath or band gives you more
radishes per linear foot. They teach simple fundamentals to children just
beginning as gardeners, because the large seeds are easily handled and
spread, they germinate gratifyingly soon, and they are ready to eat in a few
weeks.

Extending your radish rows every 2 weeks keeps the table supplied. Frequent watering helps rapid growth, especially during their first week. The photo illustrates successive plantings in a double row, from 5-day-old seedlings to 2-week-old maturing plants to 3-week-old ripening radishes, some of which have been pulled.

What you want, of course, are radish *roots*, not excessive foliage. Successive thinnings every few days until the plants have about 2 inches of growing space helps this, and so does mulching. Above all, give plenty of water a day or two before the tops of the roots above the ground show they're getting nice and fat. This makes them crisp for eating. M-m-m!

Beets Come in Dark Red, White, and Golden

This root crop insists on a place in your food garden. It is delicious boiled and served piping hot enough to melt cold butter. Or, after being cooked and cooled (and vinegared), it adds greatly to most salads or majors as a salad itself.

The odd-colored varieties are novel but unlikely to replace the old standby, rich, red shade. Coming out of a garden, your beets are choicer and sweeter than the store-bought kind, although almost any beet is a good bet.

Beet seeds are odd creatures. They come in small, cork-like spheres, each containing 2 or 3 of the seeds. Because of their relatively large size (bigger than radish seeds, not as big as peas), these ball-like seed holders can easily be spaced an inch or more apart in a furrow 1 inch deep. The first signs of sprouting (which may take 10 days, despite careful daily watering) are so tiny they are hard to see, but, being red-stemmed beneath their narrow

leaves, they are unmistakable once you spot them. In another 5 days, they are about to put forth their second or "true" leaves and like these are now ready for thinning to 2 or 3 inches apart. Like any young growing things, they should be watered gently, often enough to ensure their not drying up. Every day is not too often unless they've had rain. Yet not so much at any one time that puddles form on the soil surface.

At this 3-week-old stage the foliage is tender enough for boiling as a separate dish. Personally, I'd rather wait for the delicious round roots, and I try to speed up their growth rate by watering in a weak potassium fertilizer solution.

Here it is easy to discern the respective sizes of beets seeded 3 weeks apart. Even older garden beets are surprisingly tender. This circumstance makes it all the easier to keep up a continuous supply for the family table.

Beets are a naturally "sweet" vegetable. (You've heard about beet sugar.) During favorable weather (i.e., warm and humid) most beets mature in 60 days. The beets in front are about ready for eating. But there's no hurry. They'll grow bigger and bigger and still remain tender, because they are home-garden raised. Mulched in autumn, they'll stand a little cool weather.

You Dig Roots?

That's the worst pun yet.

But something had to be done to call attention to the root crops you can raise. They all store well for winter meals and save food money when most vegetables are out of season.

Rutabaga can serve as an example of garden-grown roots. It happens to be too little known, considering its simple culture and perk-up taste. It is more like turnips than carrots or parsnips but has its own, almost spicy flavor. Very wholesome, too.

Like most roots, it's small-seeded, slow to germinate, and rewards you with substantial food value. You can help it along by "side dressing" with potash and phosphate (not nitrogen). Like most roots, also, it can be protected from an intrusion of a root crop's enemy, maggots, by sprinkling coffee grounds in the seed row and alongside the growing plants.

The same general culture applies to other garden root crops, which include turnips (kin to rutabaga), carrots, parsnips, salsify, et al. And, of course, that old standby radishes. The main attention they require is deep-dug soil (full spade depth or more) of a light, friable, and well-pulverized structure. This plus rigorous thinning allows them room to grow and grow straight downward. Stiff clay tends to distort roots, but mixing in sand and/or vermiculite will help correct it.

For the rutabaga, a 40-foot row of soil was prepared to a depth of about 10 inches. Although reasonably rich in humus, it was improved in texture by the addition of clean builder's sand so that the soil would not compact around the roots and cause them to be stunted or twisted. The tiny seeds of rutabaga were dribbled between thumb and forefinger into a straight furrow only half an inch deep. Then a sprinkling of soil was applied, barely covering the seeds. As in the planting of other garden seeds, the soil was firmed down along the row and gently watered with a watering can.

Incidentally, this "root row" was kept moistened every day until after germination had taken place and the seedlings were well up. The photograph shows a mulch of fine grass clippings from nearby golf greens.

The foliage of most root crops develops to relatively large size. This is taken into consideration in diagraming the dimensions of your food garden and allowing adequate space for the aisles. As shown, the plants are only a few weeks old. They will grow to much larger size and will occupy the site right into winter.

When your root crops, in this case parsnips, reach this mature stage in their growth, a foot or more in height, visitors to your garden will be impressed by the decorative effect of the rich-looking rows.

Even after foliage dies down in winter, parsnips continue to show a little green around the tops of the buried roots. The tiny leaves grow under the bales of hay placed on top of them for frost protection. Actually, most food gardeners swear that parsnips taste better (i.e., have a stronger characteristic parsnip flavor) after frost than before it. As I myself have a parsnip palate, I'll eat them any way.

These parsnips were dug up one winter's day in time for family dinner. You see how straight they grow and how far down in the soil when soil texture permits them to. Only one was stunted or thickened at the top and one other was deformed by stiff soil at one place in the row. Parsnips are naturally more wrinkled than, say, carrots but can be grown large enough for an ample dish. These have been washed with the tops left on prior to brushing with a stiff vegetable brush in the kitchen, where they will be further prepared for baking.

Carrot foliage gets quite big; over a foot high sometimes before the roots have developed beyond fingerling stage. But the plants are hard at work all the time. Often you detect the root tops above ground as they are reaching maturity.

The different strains of carrots vary somewhat in shape. This doesn't really matter much except in cooking time. Carrots can be kept in good supply all winter long. A heavy layer of snow will protect the fat and flavorful roots against frost.

Rhubarb? Well, It's Good *for You!*

Not many generations ago, our families set great store by rhubarb as their "spring tonic." They often could hardly wait to tug its red tinged stalks free from the buried crown and stew them or make pies with them. Indeed, even today many folks serve a dish of rhubarb as a wholesome dessert, sometimes cooked with strawberries. Its sour taste often prompts the cook to add so much sugar that rhubarb's nutritional value may be offset by all that carbohydrate. But it's the custom of the country.

One good thing can be said for rhubarb in the home food garden; it is supremely easy to grow. From a seed catalogue order a couple of roots (not all seedsmen supply rhubarb) and place them in 8-inch-deep holes otherwise filled with humus or, in the old-fashioned way, with cow manure. Water them to the point of being well soaked and leave them alone for a few months to establish themselves by sending out roots to seek food. They require only watering often enough to prevent drying out. In the fall cover them with leaves a foot deep or more as mulch.

Come spring, it's fun to push aside the leaf mulch from each planting site and get a first glimpse of this unusual vegetable just putting forth its shoots. Sometimes they don't wait for you to clear away the mulch cover; they just rise and lift it up themselves.

After a day or two of warm spring sunshine, you will see the first foliage tight but beginning to unfurl. (See color page 76.)

Still encircled by protective mulch, each rhubarb plant spreads its broad leaves to the sun. Its growth characteristic is to utilize available plant nutrients, including any nitrogenous fertilizer you are disposed to bestow on it, and produce dozens of edible stalks. These are not cut or broken off but carefully pulled and twisted out of the crown itself. *Mirabile dictu*, the more stalks you pull, over the weeks, the more stalks replace them. At the rather immature stage shown here, rhubarb lovers delight to come into the garden, pull a tender stalk or two, and munch them raw. It doesn't even set their teeth on edge. They'll wait another week or so for the longer, thicker cooking stalks.

By the time your rhubarb is mature enough to appear like the bundles of stalks in supermarkets (at high prices, in these inflationary times), the leaves are approaching elephant size. It is an oddity of rhubarb that these leaves are strictly poisonous to humans. Perhaps that is why the leaves have been snipped off the bundles you see in the food stores. The plant in the picture will grow even bigger leaves, but its edible stalks can be pulled at the stage shown. Long considered a spring tonic, rhubarb continues to produce new stalks throughout the summer, which are both edible and delicious.

Asparagus, Cut Fresh Daily

When you decide to raise asparagus for the family table, do so with a view to enjoying a permanent asparagus bed. After the first year of getting established, you'll be cutting asparagus spears every spring for 15 or 20 years or even longer. You order from your seedsman's catalogue a dozen or more dormant "roots" or crowns, usually of the "Mary Washington" variety, which is tolerant to rust and a good producer.

Prepare for the arrival of the roots in the mails by digging out long trenches 8 to 18 inches deep and nearly a foot wide. In the bottom of the trench, spread a 3-inch-deep layer of old manure or humus in some other form and water this vegetative-nutrient base until it's soaking wet. When your asparagus roots arrive, you space them 18 inches apart in the trench, carefully spreading out the individual rootlets. These you cover with 2 inches or so of the soil taken from the trench. Gradually, at 1-week intervals, you shovel back all the trench soil. Each time you thus spread soil, you water it liberally. You can also cover the soil with mulch to keep weeds out of the bed, which must be weed free at all times thereafter.

Warm weather and moisture will one day, rather unpredictably, bring up overnight the "spears," as they are called, of your own fresh asparagus. But restrain yourself with all the firmness of character at your command, because you do not cut any stalks the first year. The second year you cut "lightly"; that is, only a few dozen spears within any month. The third year you can cut asparagus for, say, six weeks. You must cut every day or two, even if that means saving up stalks in the refrigerator till you have an adequate mess of them to serve all members of your family generously. If you don't cut the spears nearly every day (at ground level so as not to knife the crowns or dig up the tough white lower ends as commercial growers do to add seeming size and weight when you buy) each stalk proceeds to uncurl its buds and to "go to fern," as it is called. (See color page 73.)

After a reasonable cutting season (in most gardens ending in 6 weeks) you stop and let the asparagus plants take their natural course. In growing 4 feet tall or taller, they are making food for storage in the root system, which often reaches outward and downward a good 6 feet. This stored food will be used next spring to provide you with more fat, succulent spears. In your asparagus bed will be found male and female plants. The ladies end the growing season with a striking show of bright red seed berries. You could raise asparagus plants from seed if you wanted to spend the time bothering to do so. Many seed themselves anyway as "volunteers." Year-old roots or 2-year-old roots from your seed catalogue are much handier and yield results sooner.

Muskmelons Are a Luxury, When You Must Buy Them

If you can raise cucumbers, you can raise muskmelons, or cantaloupes, as they are sometimes called. And the ones you raise in your own food garden put those in the stores to shame. Those rubbery, half-ripened globes of expensive, shipped-in-crates fruit bear next to no resemblance to the orange-golden, tender-textured, nectar-juicy melons you put on the family breakfast table or serve as iced melon balls as a first course at a festive dinner.

You won't believe it till you've tasted the striking difference.

Given a sunny site, melons will grow prolifically with very little more attention than ample watering once a week. It is their nature as vines to spread out over a wide area of the garden.

That is why it is a good idea to assign them a section of their own where their expansion will not interfere with other crops.

Obviously, weeding any vine crop can be damaging because the weeds are hard to get at. A modern method of mulching solves this problem with finality. Stretch black plastic mulch (3 millimeters in thickness and 3 feet wide) over the strip or other area planned for melons. This sheet must be weighted down and held in position by stones or pipes or lengths of wood (such as two-by-fours) along the edges. Aside from weed control, the reason for the black mulch is that it keeps the soil at a higher temperature (i.e., above 68° to 70° F.). Melons ripen faster in the warmer soil. And black plastic mulch presents no great seeding problems. With a razor blade, cut a 6-inch cross in the plastic sheet every 2 feet or so, tuck the flaps under, and plant in each hole thus formed 5 or 6 melon seeds, watering them in. They'll sprout in about 10 days, when you thin to 3 seedlings (or 4 in very rich soil) in every hole. After that you need only stick a trickling hose under the plastic to give the melons water.

Now, with all this cheering-squad commendation of muskmelons as an easily obtained, luxurious delicacy, it may seem odd that the photographs seem to depict an elaborate, even complex, structure for their home culture.

The explanation is, having in one good growing year lost almost an entire bountiful crop of melons to an infestation of slugs, I resolved to prevent a recurrence. Hence the innovation of a lattice system of keeping the fruits off the ground and out of reach of slithering slugs. The first steps in this technique are the same as for any flat area as described above. Going to some pains to dig your soil 10 inches deep and introduce humus-making garbage pays off when you're raising melons far superior to the commercial growers'.

The melon patch was divided into 4 beds so as to provide walkways between the lattices, thus avoiding treading upon and possibly crushing the vines.

In using black plastic sheets for mulching purposes, one drawback is that you have to anchor them against the vagrant breezes. You can use soil along the edges or stones or rails. Shown here, the sheets have been "looped" at the ends to form a tube into which a pipe or heavy rod could be slid. Rotting hay surrounds the plastic sheets, in anticipation of the spreading growth of the melon vines during their season.

The slits having been razored in the plastc sheets, and each bed planted to muskmelon of the variety preferred, 4 lattices are carefully put in place. They rest upon foot-long pieces of two-by-four scrap lumber so that they are 4 inches or so above the plastic and the sprouting seeds. Or you can set them on inverted flowerpots.

It may take a week for the seeds to germinate and rise out of the soil (often raising their seed cases in the air if these haven't dropped off and released the tender cotyledons; they soon will). At this stage it is a little early to reduce the number of sprouts, but if all of them survive for another week you can pull out all but 3.

Predictably, the young groups of melon plants surmount the lathwork in another week or so, depending on the warmth of the nights. Above they look neat and orderly but they have riot in their eye. This becomes all the more imminent if you slide a hose under the plastic and allow a gentle flow of water to soak the soil every 10 days or oftener.

As the foilage makes growth, keep alert for the fun of spotting the first yellow blossoms. They start when the vines reach a length of 3 feet, or even less. You may see a brown honeybee at work on them.

Muskmelons do not develop all at the same rate. Like the one you see here, they are only thimble-sized when their flowers drop off per Nature's plan. Soon one noted that they are the size of Ping-pong balls and shortly after that resemble fuzzy tennis balls. As they approach full-size maturity, they begin to change color and to show the start of netting on their surface. This is ordinarily the time to keep an eye out for slugs, but if your melons are growing atop the lattice these pests cannot reach and damage them. Any young melons developing below the lattice can be lifted (but with extreme TLC) through the interstices and draped over a slat and off the plastic. Otherwise you can provide some protection from slugs by sliding a board or shingle under each fruit.

Your melon crop very slowly ripens to a tan color and the netting becomes more marked. A ripened muskmelon becomes seductively aromatic and a little soft and yielding at the end opposite its stem. But, prithee, be in no haste to pull it off the vine quite yet. Instead, test for "slip." This means very gently tugging at the stem where it joins the round fruit. If it doesn't come loose easily, give it another day or so and try again. Left to themselves, ripe melons "slip" naturally from their vines. When you harvest one or more melons, take your prizes into the house and let them "finish" their sweetness and flavor for a day or two before eating.

The Strawberry Crowns
Duke, Marquis, and Earl

You know how ceremonial the British are. Their lives are surrounded by symbols. Their dukes, marquises, and earls all wear coronets. And on each coronet is a band of conventional figures representing the leaf of the *strawberry!*

This prestigious insigne adds nothing to the refreshing flavor of the genus Fragaria, but you can breathe real deep over its dramatic implications.

Raising strawberries in your garden means buying selected plants from a reputable grower and arranging them in a semipermanent bed. They will continue to produce for at least three years if you give them a year to establish themselves. After the fourth year, their yield may begin to diminish to the point where you will want to replace them. Guaranteed and certified plants of named varieties cost you (in small quantities) about 10 cents to 15 cents apiece. Although some 5,000 varieties of strawberries have been identified worldwide, a modern supplier offers you only about 30 sorts, all carefully developed strains. So-called "ever-bearing" sorts are really 2-crop varieties, one early and one late, with a "breather" for the plants between. Still, if you are wondering why *any* strawberries at all are included in a book on vegetables, the logic for doing so is that we are talking about a food garden . . . and strawberries are indeed a food item, as you can see in the produce section of any supermarket. More important and perhaps more logical, most food gardeners yearn to eat their own fresh strawberries.

There are several slightly different techniques for growing strawberries. But they have in common a requirement for an acid soil, preferably light in texture (the sandier, the earlier fruit), thick with humus, large quantities of water all during the growing season, protective mulch cover against frost, and (of prime importance at the outset) placement of the plant's own central crown neither above nor below but exactly even with the ground level. Also, the first year that blossoms appear, they should be nipped off to make increased vegetative growth for a big crop the following season. Similarly, when the plants send out shoots called "runners" to drop roots and start new plants near the mother plant, these runners too should be nipped off for the same reason, namely to conserve strength for the following year. If, in the second year, you wish to allow such runner plants to establish themselves, they can either be left where they root themselves or they can be cut off and raised separately in your cold frame. They can subsequently serve as replacements for older, declining plants. Incidentally, severance from the mother plants should not be performed until the "daughter" is clearly flourishing and the connecting runner is turning red and dry. This vegetative umbilical will decay naturally in time, anyway.

The so-called "hill" system calls for planting your strawberries 10 to 12 inches apart in 2 or 3 rows, leaving 12 inches between rows. You can then leave an aisle or alley of 24 inches and put in another group of 2 or 3 rows, ad infinitum. Allow no runners to root, snipping them off as early as they appear (which they do with startling suddenness). This culture method results, obviously, in a plantation consisting entirely of separate, individual strawberry plants. These carefully nurtured specimens produce choicer fruit and often continue in longer bearing life. They can be replaced individually, should their productivity diminish and your best bearers left in the garden longest.

Another culture technique is the "spaced, matted row." If you choose this method, plan your rows about 40 to 42 inches apart and space out your plants in them 18 to 24 inches distant from each other. These increased spacings are for the purpose of allowing the first half-dozen (i.e., the most potent) runners to grow in a circle around each mother plant. You can easily position them in such a circle by covering their tips with soil and pinning down the connecting runners with weights (small stones will do nicely). Any additional runners are then cut off near the crown. This culture provides daughter plants from which you can pick fruit in their second year.

Perhaps the commonest commercial practice is the "matted row" system. To use this technique, plan aisles that are 18 to 24 inches wide with only 3 or even 2 inches between plants. Put in during spring, all your plants will develop into a thick stand. In the fall, thin them to leave 3 to 4 inches of space between them. Runners trying to escape from the outlines of the bed can be cut off. After all, you don't want them sneaking away and consorting with your carrots. Who knows what might happen?

In general, the closer together strawberries are planted, the lower the production of first-class fruit.

Let's suppose you have decided which cultural method you prefer to follow and have calculated the number of strawberry plants your garden area will allow you to put in. The decision and the calculation are abetted by a careful perusal of a catalogue from one of the reliable nursery growers of varieties recommended by the U. S. Department of Agriculture. They will sell you plants field-grown from virus-free stock furnished by the USDA's Bureau of Plant Industry at Beltsville, Maryland. Home gardeners used to be cautioned never to buy self-sterile or "imperfect" or pistillate strawberry plants. This precaution is largely superfluous today.

One day early in the spring (April is a safe month almost everywhere in the U.S.) your shipper sends along the plants you ordered, tied and labeled in bunches of 25. This is the optimum time of year for planting with an expectation of a bountiful crop. Your plants will arrive in a dormant state. Loosen the bindings on the bundles and moisten the roots. If you cannot immediately put the plants into the bed you have prepared for them, stow them in the refrigerator (never in the freezer compartment where temperatures go below 28° F.). Alternatively, you can keep them for several days in a trench, lying side by each nearly flat and covered with moist soil to the depth of their crowns. This is called "heeling in" because you press (not stamp) the covering soil down with your heel. If the soil seems dry, water it. Incidentally, if the roots look dried out when you open your package, by all means soak them in water for an hour or two. Just before setting them out in the garden plot, prune off all but 2 or 3 of the leaves on each plant. Some people also shear off up to one fourth of the root mass at the other end. I don't.

The orthodox way to plant is to dig a hole deep enough to accommodate the roots, heaping up a mound of soil in the center. The crown of the strawberry plant is set upon this mound in such a way that said crown is exactly even with the level of the soil. Spread the roots out around the sloping sides of the mound. Next, water in the plant, soaking the roots slowly. After that, fill in the hole, leaving the crown barely uncovered and free to start its growth. It's a good idea to cover each plant with a flowerpot, strawberry box, or paper cup for a few days to prevent drying out. It's an even better idea to keep the soil moist by watering liberally daily for a while. If you're extra lucky, it may rain for you. Strawberry plants should get lots of water right up to fruiting time.

Try to keep all weeds out of your strawberries. If you cultivate by hoeing every 2 weeks or so, you'd better not go more than 2 inches deep. A couple of geese will also do a good job of weeding and they won't disturb the roots.

Strawberry plants will stand a hard freeze after which 3 or 4 inches of hay will be needed to help prevent the tearing of their roots in heaving soil caused by freezing and thawing in turn. When the first warm days of spring return, most of the mulch can be pulled back off the rows. But do not trust the weather too far. Keep your mulch stuff handy in case temperatures threaten to drop some night. Use pine needles if you have some. They're nice and neat. And acid.

Any thrifty strawberry plant that has done its duty in giving you green foliage, white blossoms, runners, and a quart of berries is likely to have a tired root system. The vigor of such plants can be revived by cutting back the leaves to about 3 inches high. This pruning is quaintly called "renewing the plantation." Strawberry plants will generally do better if "renewed" right after the bearing period (when no more berries are coming along), especially if you are then nipping off all runners. At this time, too, they should receive some 10-6-4 or 8-8-8 fertilizer. You may prefer to use 5 pounds of ground cottonseed meal to 20–25 feet of row. It has an acid reaction.

When that blissful day arrives when the little green berries turn into big, red, luscious ones, pick them by snipping their stems without pulling the berries themselves. They might just squash in your fingers. And pick them daily, for they overripen suddenly and you thus lose some of the best ones. They should be chilled at once or they will continue to ripen. Freezing takes care of the surplus quarts you find on your hands without a friend to give them to. It's a simple process. Slide your berries into a bowl of clear, cool water and the dust will drop off them. Dry a little on a paper towel, as you would for eating. Hull and cut away the occasional overripe portions. Place in a covered plastic container, layering with a sprinkle of sugar as you fill it. Pop into the freezer compartment and you're all fixed for strawberry sauce for ice cream or shortcake or other desserts.

In big, bold black letters a grave warning should be uttered here (partly because it is commonly omitted from other strawberry literature) to stay out of the strawberry bed when it is wet, even if only with the morning dew. Mildew, the curse of these berries, is spread by handling when wet.

While many of us consider strawberries one of the most refreshing of all fruits, they do not agree with absolutely everybody's digestion. There is hydrocyanic acid in strawberries. To some human systems this is poison.

If you have selected, perhaps with the grower's advice, one or more varieties known to be suitable for your locality and your climate, you will find that your strawberry patch has survived the rigors of winter without harm. Among the earliest sights in your food garden is the refreshing green of the strawberry rows.

Even in the first week, the plants show good growth in soil that is on the acid side. In pH terms, that means below the index number 7. No lime, please.

You see here 4 rows, one for each of 4 different varieties. They will keep your breakfast table supplied daily (to say nothing of desserts) as each sort comes in bearing in turn, starting in June. You can expect about one quart from each plant, which makes it easy to buy enough crowns to keep your family supplied with this delicacy.

You will find blossoms and berries on the same plant. Strawberries' growth habit is to form clusters from a main stem rising from the plant's crown and the bud at the tip end ripens first and largest. Then you must pick the ripe ones every day before they become overripe.

Placed under the mother plant and one or more runners as well as a daughter plant, pieces of light-colored shirt board show up growth habit of garden strawberries. They send out "tentacle-like" stems to form new plants. Vigorous strawberry motherhood may produce a half-dozen or more offspring shoots, each rooting more than once.

Once you see where the runner is forming leaves for a new plant (usually at least 8 to 10 inches from the "mother" crown) and about to sink its roots to establish itself, you can divert this process into a soil-filled flowerpot. Nothing will easily stop a determined strawberry runner, and it will take up residence in an alien receptacle as readily as on the open soil. The reason for putting a pot in its path is to make it more convenient to lift it and reposition it when its attaching runner dries up and it is ready to leave home.

PART III

Cornucopia

Miscellanea Cornucopiae

Those who remember history well enough to recall Marcus Porcius Cato (234–140 B.C.) will refer to him, probably, by his surname, "The Censor." They may associate him only with his vehement slogan, "Delenda est Carthago." But this was just one of his many hard-nosed notions. It derived from no better data than his personal impressions, during a political visit, of Carthaginians' prosperous commerce. Their affluence, he decided, could be a threat to the security of Rome.

He was equally adamant when advocating the building up of his country's agriculture by adding compost and manure to the soil. Herein he was on more objective grounds, for he himself was born (at Tusculum) into an ancient plebeian family and bred to farming. His inspiration to replenish the Roman farmer's crop soil by restoring nutrients to it has bestowed a more lasting legacy upon subsequent society than his fantastic reiteration that "Carthage must be destroyed."

Today, 2,000 years later, we are still committed to feeding our garden soil so that it can feed us.

* * *

Weeding has for so many years been a farm and garden practice that it has given weeds a bad name as undesirables. How many backs have bent in the broiling sun, how many palms have grown horny on a hoe handle, laboring to "control" the weeds by slicing off their foliage.

But weeds can be proud of their superior root systems, which often go down farther for water than their socially superior food-plant competitors. And they store accumulated nutrients so efficiently that when we pull them up to get rid of them we can do worse than drop them in the aisles between rows, especially under mulch, thus returning them to the soil to complete their cycle.

Weeds deserve experimentation by food gardeners. For there is reason to suspect that weed roots can loosen the soil for our root crops. Purslane (or pusley, the old-fashioned name for it), like many another so-called "weed," has in earlier farming cultures been widely regarded as edible, tasty, and wholesome enough for the dinner table.

Some of the original Americans, the Indians, still raise selected weeds in plots where they are carefully thinned by the women of the tribe. Thinning gives weeds and cultivated plants alike more room to grow and thus encourages their roots to go down deeper into the soil for moisture and nutrients.

Incidentally, we owe it to one Jethro Tull that we today plant our vegetable gardens in drills or rows. It occurred to him that simply by hoeing between rows, he would greatly reduce the weeds. This was anno Domini 1731.

*   *   *

The processes of Nature being what they are, your vegetable garden is also a flower garden. The blossoms on your pea vines may not reach the size or vivid pastel tints of flowering sweet peas, but they do make a subtly delightful show, massed on their vines. Besides, they remind you that every single blossom means a whole pod of edible peas to come. In Nature, flowers precede fruits.

Suddenly it comes to you that vegetables' flowers have an appointed purpose and you are watching its fulfillment. One bloom will turn, perhaps, into a tiny green globe, a tomato in the very infancy of its ripening. Another may swell before your eyes into a finger-long "pickle" on its way to becoming an 8-inch cucumber.

In the meantime, the ecru of bean blossoms is still another satisfaction to the eye. The more so because you will see honeybees working on them. Then, soon after, you notice the tiny green scimitar emerging from the calyx of each bean flower. These are the early signs promising the flavorful beans you'll be picking in a matter of days.

Similarly, the suddenly opening blossoms on your cucumber vines are the size of a quarter and vivid yellow star shapes. Bees visit them every day for pollen and you can see the yellowish pollen bags on their dusty legs. In these bags they are carrying loads of tiny pollen grains, taking them home for raising brood in the hive.

It may relieve you to know that those little brown bees are always too busy at their nectar-gathering job to bother or to be bothered by the gardener. They won't sting you. (You would have to invade their hive and attempt to get past the guard bees posted at the entrance before these hardworking females, who never heard of women's-lib-bees, would attack.) You can even gently pick one up by her wings without penalty. She may wiggle and buzz but all she wants is to free herself to get back to her colony. There she delivers her load to another worker bee, proboscis to proboscis, who will digest it with enzymes before depositing it in one of the hexagonal wax cells being filled for capping. The lumbering bumblebee, who loves to spend the night asleep in a hollyhock blossom, bears you no animus. Hornets, called "yellow jackets," are a different matter. They sting painfully, with little or no provocation. Often these meanies nest in the ground and disturbing them can be disastrous. You might be well advised, especially if you have children in the family, to get a prescription from your physician (tablets, usually of two sorts, that are placed promptly under the tongue to dissolve), even before stinging occurs.

Irish children of an earlier generation used to capture honeybees one at a time and squeeze from them their droplets of sweet-tasting nectar.

Cornstalks bear no pretty flowers, but they do send up pollen spikes that spread a half-dozen arms to the breeze. A little later on and farther down the stalks, thin spears appear in the "armpits" or axillas at the base of some leaves. Almost as you watch, these spears unfold and put forth glossy strands of silk. It is the function of these silks to catch grains of pollen floating in the air, which will fertilize the kernels of the corn. Within a week, the spears have turned to ears. One silk filament, you find, leads to each kernel. They soon fatten in the sunshine, especially when the nights are warm and the days long. In due time, the silks will dry out brown. Any minute now, the ripe ears will be ready for pulling, plump with their "milk." Bring a dozen of them into the house about 20 minutes before mealtime. Let them be boiled for 3 to 6 minutes. Not a snap of the fingers longer. That's the way to taste corn on the cob.

There are more flowers in your garden full of vegetables.

If you neglect to cut your broccoli heads as they mature, they may just go on growing into masses of buds that open into yellow florets. These make an appeal to the eye but are by then a little past the eating stage.

After you've stopped cutting your asparagus spears for the season (usually limited with a great show of willpower to 6 to 8 weeks of early spring), the plants are allowed to grow up into tall foliage called "fern." Now they are full blown and mature. You stop cutting when you do because the plants need this foliage to build up a store of food in their root system under the soil's surface. This enables them to produce a crop for you next year. Unless you put some limit on cutting the edible spears, you may not get so much asparagus or such fat spears next season.

Some flowering vegetable plants smell so strong that they tend to repel raiding insects from the entire garden. Zinnias and marigolds are often given a place in the garden to serve this helpful purpose, too. In the humus-enriched soil you try to develop, year by year, these aromatics burgeon right up to the very frosts of fall. Sometimes they even seed themselves *in situ,* or you can save their seed after it has ripened. If you have space for it, there's no reason why you shouldn't have a "cutting garden" of flowers in your vegetable area.

More about odors.

Cabbage has its own characteristic odor. So do freshly dug parsnips. And a crushed tomato leaf will fill the air with an unforgettable perfume. It is hardly necessary to add that onions smell of onion, but you notice it only when pulling the young scallions or drying the full-grown bulbs.

Garden herbs like dill, parsley, basil, and mint are strongly scented, but you get the full effect only from the crushed foliage.

Cookbooks never tell you how to raise vegetables, so why should a garden book presume to tell you how to cook them? One thing about cooking, however, needs to be stated. And that is, your garden-fresh vegetables usually take less time to cook than do their opposite, store-bought numbers. Example: supermarket parsnips that require 8 to 10 minutes in boiling water to come to their peak of tenderness may mislead you. The parsnips you harvest, even though they are likely to be larger in size, will take not more than 6 or 7 minutes. In general, minimal cooking or saucing yields the truest flavor of garden vegetables.

*   *   *

Now, about planting your seeds by the phases of the moon. For aboveground crops (peas, corn, tomatoes, *et al.*) old wives plant from new moon to full moon. For root crops, plant from waning full moon to "the dark of the moon." Of course, this is all mere superstition, but in a civilization like ours there is always room for one more superstition. Besides, if you have ever watched a spring tide rising four feet above its normal flood and realized that ebb and slack and flow of salt-water tides is caused by the gravitational pull of that same moon, you may be more open-minded about old country people's notions of planting. Besides, aren't superstitions the origins of science, not to speak of religions?

*   *   *

Sharing surplus vegetables with neighbors gives you a curious sense of superiority. This is especially true when they ask how you get such sweet new peas or such large rutabagas. A sure way to achieve popularity among nearby housewives is to keep fresh dill going all during the season. There's something about fresh dill.

*   *   *

Experimenting, scientific or not, is an adventure no matter how it turns out. When Japanese beetles infest your asparagus at the fern stage, try knocking them off with a stick into a coffee can with an inch of water in it. Then compare the body count with the instant slaughter that follows a light sprinkling of the fern foliage with carbaryl (package name, Sevin).

Try positioning a large mirror north of a selected pepper plant and see whether the extra sunshine thus reflected will result in more peppers or bigger ones or earlier ripening. Ask an optometrist whether the mirror reflects the full spectrum of the sun, including the ultraviolet rays.

* * *

Dig a trench and every few days bury household garbage from one end to the other, covering each deposit as you go. Check from the "front" end, where the first canful went, to see how long it takes for the vegetative material to change completely into humus in the soil. It will depend on the weather: the warmer, the faster. Why do we call this "plate waste" by the term "garbage"? It wasn't garbage on the dinner table. For soil building, it can include everything edible but meat, fish, or fat. It's easy to collect, in a separate can, fruit rinds, vegetable peelings and leaves, coffee grounds, tea leaves, eggshells, cigarette stubs, and "blessed event" cigars.

* * *

Read garden books now and then. And state and federal government bulletins. Look for *reasons why*, or do they merely describe gardening procedures without much intelligible explanation? By all means, keep notes: you may someday want to write a book. Or make a talk before your local garden club. Three recommended books: *Vegetables for Today's Gardens*, by R. Milton Carleton, research director for Vaughan's Seed Company. Rich in varied advice, all plain spoken and authoritative. *Burrage on Vegetables*, by Albert C. Burrage, gentleman horticulturist; a classic in 1954, revised and revived in 1975. Notable for painstaking trial of countless varieties for flavor and quality. *Grow It and Cook It*, by Jacqueline Hériteau, French family style.

* * *

Everyone knows that pet owners talk to their dogs and cats. Horses, too, respond to their rider's voice and will whinny in answer to a recognized greeting from their stall in the barn. A knowledgeable rider wins a horse's confidence (they are very fearful animals) by talking to him and encouraging him while working. And horses are avid for their owner's praise; it's almost as good as a piece of carrot, apple, or bread.

What *not* everyone knows is that many gardeners regularly talk to their plants. It is a little like praying, in that you can't always be sure of immediate response, but you feel better. Your cheerful greeting when you come out to the garden in the morning surely does not go unnoticed by the growing vegetables or, in the end, unrewarded. They are so busy growing to fruition that they may not pause for a nod of a blossom or a wave of a leaf but, in one way or another, they will answer you.

Personally, I always address the sweet corn in two different tones. With the male pollen spikes I'm a bit hearty, because they are the masculine part of the plant; I admonish them to do their manly best. To the swelling ears themselves, however, I speak more gently. For they are the feminine part of the plant, they are the maternal aspect; in botanical fact, they are the womb. Woman-like, they love attention and compliments on their appearance, and I praise the progress they are making toward perfection in their function. Naturally, when the day comes for pulling the milk-rich ears, it is only courteous to thank the plants and praise them for what they have borne.

*   *   *

Your voice, however, is not the only one heard in your garden. As the rising tide of green approaches its crest under the warming summer sun, your vegetables will be visited by birds. They will be scouting for insects and so they will be most welcome. Birds pay attention to conversation too, although they enjoy even more a few whistled notes, repeated and repeated. They will exchange bird song for bugs. Catbirds are particularly familiar and nearly as fearless as the tiny chickadees. They will sit atop a bean pole while you are turning over the soil and wait for you to turn up a worm with it. Sometimes they don't even wait but come right close up to urge you to greater efforts. Robins and bluebirds, among others, are dutifully conjugal about carrying live food home when Madame Mère is setting on her eggs in the nest. And when the squawking fledglings are ravenous, both parents can be observed diligently carrying snacks from your garden to ram down the maws of their noisy offspring.

A pretty good way to ensure bird song all summer: put out free bird seed all winter. Birds, it should surprise no gardener to learn, frequently drop seeds upon the soil. One thinks of the Parable of the Sower, who "went forth to sow." Chance results in some unexpected drama. An overwintering sunflower seed, discarded by some careless blue jay, by Labor Day weekend may have prospered in the summer sun and reached a height of 10 feet or more. Every day, its dazzling golden flower turns slowly to face her sun god, from his rising to his setting. When her countless florets drop from her ripening seed head and the great sunflower bloom drops under its weight, that single seed, dropped by a tiny fluff of feathers, has "multiplied an hundred fold."

*   *   *

And as for the variety of tomatoes known, from their miniature size, as Small Fry, they seem to grow faster and produce more of their bite-size fruit than the hybrid tomato seeds I carefully plant for staking. Lacking the strength of character to remove these "volunteers" at the seedling stage, I watch helplessly as they take over space I had intended to assign to peppers. But they repay one with a plentiful supply of small tomatoes all season long. Like King Canute, I find I cannot forbid the flood.

*   *   *

You let oxygen into the soil by turning it over in the spring. Again in the fall, you dig with spading fork or, better, long-handled shovel so that winter's hard freezes can "reduce" the structure of the clumps of soil. Thinning seedlings, weeding out the ubiquitous chickweed, tying up the rising young tomato plants to stout stakes driven a foot or more into the ground, cutting off the runners from strawberry plants, and a dozen other incidental chores are all work. You may find them a pleasure but they are also labor. Like any other creative effort, a garden is not made productive by waving a wand. Fortunately, the work it involves is performed out of doors and, even when you are sweaty, is generally conducive to health. On the other hand, one can run an untidy, ill-tended garden and still reap some vegetables.

One encounters many published pieces by persons aspiring to celebrity, who complacently recite the superiorities of their own "system" without subjecting it to comparison with others. They play all nine innings without the competition of another team. Such innocence, in the twentieth century, of the "scientific method," of using a control!

*   *   *

Among the secret pleasures you will from time to time experience in your vegetable garden is one that leads directly to the sin of pride. Example: careful planning, aided by a stroke of luck in the weather, enables you to bring into the house the last ears of corn as late as October 31, long past the end of the sweet-corn season.

Or, example: your Butternut squash grew so robust and stored so well in your cool, dry cellar that you did not cut up and dine off the last of them until well into March of the following year. And by then you had started the new season's food garden by planting your onion sets and perhaps a row of lettuce.

These and other privately gratifying achievements, granted that they are attributable largely to luck, somehow crop up during skillfully manipulated cocktail conversation.

*   *   *

Also, you can forget about the seasonal chore lists that try to tell you in which month or even week you should plan to perform what tasks. Many garden books attempt to guide your hand according to some imaginary timetable. But it isn't the calendar that's best to rely on; it's the thermometer. When warm weather comes to your particular garden site, and your particular soil warms up and dries out, is the time to till and plant. When cold temperatures come in their turn, all growth in the garden slows, then stops. You pull down the drying bean vines or chop cornstalks accordingly. The date for any such seasonal attentions to the garden will vary from year to year. A long, hard winter, for example, sets a different timetable from that offered you by a mild open winter.

*   *   *

For a beginner, his garden is a kingdom . . . to come.

In truth, all gardeners inevitably become more religious, often unawares. Taking part in the natural processes of raising food that will support human life, they gradually discover a new meaning in that life. They see for themselves how the sun provides the energy for all living things on earth. No puerile superstitions, no only-on-Sunday rituals demean or distract from the profounder religion that life itself teaches in a garden. For more on this elevating theme, try Part I of *The Conquest of Civilization*, by J. H. Breasted, Ph.D., LL.D., D. Litt., Oxon.

At the same time, food gardeners are capitalists. Their gains from taking advantage of a national resource, the soil, are an enormous return on their investment. Yet any low-cost labor they exploit for profit is their own. Church-type religions have never frowned on the congregation making money, have they?

*   *   *

Working with the soil takes a sense of failure out of the mishaps of cookery. The cake didn't rise? Never you mind; just return it to the garden soil for recycling. Ditto for the beans or the spaghetti that burned the bottom of the pan, those raisins that dried in the package, the soggy undercrust from that apple pie, the vegetable leftovers left over too long. Back to the garden to make more humus!

Even the cut flowers that came into your house to grace the table. They may wither but they never die. For they, too, are returned to the soil from whence they sprang.

You will probably cease from using the word "garbage." You will save it as "ecological treasure."

*   *   *

Habit sometimes dies hard.

You meet many an earnest would-be gardener who persists in searching for sources of horse manure. Little doth he reck that this is merely a hold-over from the bygone days when farming invariably combined raising live-stock and food crops. He does not know exactly why he seeks animal excreta for his garden. He certainly is not aware that it contains little or no fertilizer in the sense of nutrient (usually less than 4 per cent of nitrogen at best). It helps him chiefly by improving the structure and texture of his plot soil as a rooting medium. His enthusiasm does not reveal to him that most of the nutrient value of his "well-rotted manure" is found in the liq-uid (i.e., urine) constituent, not in the more solid fecal matter itself. Urine contains an ammonia compound (as does rain) that breaks down chemi-cally to release nitrogen. But even this rapidly leaches away in rain water or melting snow.

That is a good reason in itself for adding any nitrate of soda or other ni-trogenous supplement in small quantities or as a light powdering, either broadcast over-all or dribbled four inches to one side of a row of growing vegetables. In any case, it's helpful to scratch in the nitrate particles lightly. One may also dissolve the stuff in a watering can and sprinkle it as a solution.

* * *

Food gardeners who are Jewish and keep kosher know that some animals may never, according to their faith's dietary laws, be eaten. Others may be kosher food only if slaughtered ritually under the supervision of a rabbi. For the word "kosher" means "proper," in the sense of being properly prepared and served to those of the faith.

Vegetables differ from meats in this respect. All are proper to eat; that is, all are "neutral" with respect to kosher, or, in the Hebrew tongue, all are "*parve*." Any given vegetable, moreover, may be served up with either a meat dish, a dairy dish, or a fish dish, whichever is being used for a particu-lar meal. (Shellfish are "out" completely because they possess no back-bone.) However, it is of interest (though doubtless thoroughly well known to Jewish gardeners) that, if vegetables are cooked with meats or sauced with a dressing containing meat, the Jewish homemaker must take care that the meat ingredient is in itself kosher. And, as she would know, any such sauce or dressing may not contain both a meat and a milk product.

* * *

Even after the growing season is over and snow covers the soil, your new knowledge of vegetable gardening may guide you to other wonders in Na-ture. Just raise your eyes to the heavens.

There, on a clear night, make acquaintance with the shining stars. The constellations and many individual stars have names for you to know them by. Some are Arabic, bestowed by ancient Mediterranean astronomers.

Begin to learn them, if you like, by starting with the North or Pole Star, formally called Polaris. To find Polaris, you first recognize the prominent Big Dipper. That's just what it looks like, so even school children easily find it. Its large "cup" or dipper proper is formed of four stars, and two of those, located at the side of the "cup" opposite the "handle," tell you where Polaris can be found. An imaginary line drawn from the lower of these stars through the upper one leads your eye directly to Polaris, the star situated above earth's North Pole.

Navigators and woodsmen have always tracked by Polaris because it is always there, never disappearing below the horizon as most stars do, in appearing to wheel clockwise around our globe.

Many can readily be located and remembered by reference to this same Polaris.

Our winter season, particularly, is notably glorified by the conspicuous constellation or grouping of related stars midway to the south and thus near the celestial equator. This is Orion. In ancient mythology, Orion was a mighty hunter in the sky and one of the Giants. He is marked for you unmistakably by the straight row of three bright stars in his sword belt. Outward from these are four stars marking the corners of a rectangular shape. The uppermost or northerly one is Betelgeuse; the lowest, southerly one is Rigel. The hunter himself is followed at heel by his hound, named Sirius, the Dog Star. This faithful companion, who never leaves his master, happens to be the very brightest star in our heavens.

And in summer, too, some balmy night, before you are quite sleepy enough to seek your pillow, you'll be standing contemplatively at the edge of your silently growing garden. Above you, in the friendly starlit sky, you will recognize Arcturus (the handle of the Big Dipper curves right into it) or the little group of seven stars named the Pleiades.

Soon you'll know, if you like to consult a star map, the direction and relative distance of "the bright star Vega," as it is always called, which with nearby Deneb and Altair form a vast, prominent triangle together.

One learns, too, to distinguish between the fixed or true stars and the ever-mobile planets. These are our sun's satellites, just as Earth is, and we all orbit along the ecliptic line. Chief among the planets are Venus, glorious goddess morning or evening, and Jupiter, and noticeably reddish Mars. (These, obviously, are their legendary Latin names.) Earth's own private satellite is Luna (but you may call her Moon) and, naturally, the most familiar planet because we see her nearest us and in all her monthly phases and because we have, with dubious propriety, landed men upon her.

As you commune with the stars, you may reflect that the long-forgotten scribes who left us the Book of Job and the legends of the prophet Amos, looked up at (and mentioned in Holy Writ) the same celestial bodies we view today. Perhaps they even stood in their own gardens or grove of olive trees. Quite possibly Amos lingered near his wood lot of sycamores.

There they are; the very same stars still, for you, too, to gaze and wonder at.

While you are thus contemplating your garden or listening to the noisy corn growing, perhaps the bright-as-day moonlight recalls to your mind Orlando, the love-smitten youth in Shakespeare's *As You Like It*. Affixing yet another poem to Rosalind upon a tree in the forest of Ardennes, he declaims his poetic plea to the moon above:

> Hang there, my verse, in witness of my love:
> And thou, thrice-crowned queen of night, survey
> With thy chaste eye, from thy pale sphere above,
> Thy huntress' name that my full life doth sway.

It's all there, passing above your home and garden, a breathless spectacle in the heavens. A bright, clear night in any season of the year can bring you a gardener's view of celestial magic.

As long as you like, you can stand there in the midst of your handiwork with growing things, conscious of a universe of eternal verities. You are riding our own orbiting planet, Earth, as she rolls eastward toward one more day's sunrise.

* * *

As soon as your own food garden has shown you how readily it can produce bumper yields for your family's diet, you will probably start sharing its bounty. But you cannot very well hand your neighbor or some town mouse at the office a half dozen tomatoes or a quart of beans in lose bulk. So you anticipate by folding and stacking brown paper bags from the food store. From the retailer's standpoint, this is a neat piece of irony—using his free bags to do him out of vegetable sales. Well, "competition is the life of trade." Besides, you can offer to sell him your zucchini.

* * *

We all boil up too much water for cooking vegetables. The canny cook who sticks to a minimum of water by observing the boil-off or vaporizing during the process, comes out with net gains—savings in fuel plus nutrients in rich solution for the next kettle of soup, or the next store-bought can of it that calls for adding water.

* * *

A generation ago, perhaps, there was introduced into gardening an innovative idea for planting narrow paper strips or tapes in which prespaced seeds were held. In conspicuously convenience-minded America (today the locution would be "convenience oriented" and used by many who do not relate it literally to the east or to the rising there of the sun) a seed tape promised to save bother. Regardless of its merits, the tape idea did not work well enough to survive. Trouble was, the paper would not always soften in moisture, sprout the seed and let it seek the soil. As you would expect, however, history repeats itself and the tape concept has been revived. This time the seeds are spaced in a gelatinous compound. This one works; it's worth trying, if your time, especially for thinning seedlings, and energy equate with its cost.

* * *

One salient reason for maintaining your own family food garden is the comparative cost of store-bought vegetables, even in the growing season. If you agree with Benjamin Franklin that a penny saved is a penny earned and if you notice that the proverb reads just as well in dollars, why not make some comparisons? On the very day that you pick four pounds of zucchini or a dozen corn or three nice blocky green peppers, send up a trial balloon: check their prices at the supermarket. A dollar-saved diary may show you in a few months that you have done better with your investment in seeds than if your broker had bought a hundred shares of Blue Chip, Limited, for your account.

* * *

You need not actually have served in combat infantry to excel in salvage. (The training is useful, however, and the term "salvage" is used liberally.) Item: a new neighbor's house is a-building and the contractor has some sand left over. Why let this be dissipated, when you can put it to good ecological use? Item: A nearby farmer couldn't quite get his hay in before prolonged rain spoiled the bales. Why not relieve him of these useless encumbrances, carting some of the loose hay or bales away free or even reimbursing him a few dimes per bale? (You won't need more than half a ton or so at a time, if that.)

Item: a local lumberyard or wood-working mill produces a surplus of scrap lumber. This they must get rid of periodically. What a way to pick up garden stakes!

There's no end to salvaging if you have the requisite acquisitive spirit.

* * *

For bean poles, saw off near the ground straight saplings in a wood lot, choosing those 8 feet long, approximately, and about 3 inches thick at their base. Don't be surprised if they sprout new green shoots from any twiggy branches you leave untrimmed. These probably won't endure the summer. But live poles themselves will go several seasons, especially if you brush the bottom 2 feet of their length with creosote.

* * *

Wire, if used for supported crops like beans and cucumbers, *et al.*, had best be rubber- or plastic-coated to avoid scorching tender tendrils and foliage in the heat of the sun.

* * *

If you need some baskets, bushel or half-bushel, ask your greengrocer. Same for mesh and burlap sacks.

* * *

Your local utilities, like telephone and electric light companies, often send out special trucks to chip the tree branches that must be cut away. Sometimes their crews would rather deliver these chips near your garden than cart them some distance away to a public dump. They make excellent walkways in your garden and keep down unwanted growth directly under your electric fence wires, respectively 2 and 6 inches off the ground.

* * *

If your child is offered an elementary course in botany, by all means encourage him or her to try it. The lessons, if given by a teacher with the twin gifts of explanation and inspiration, may give your child a life-lasting comprehension of natural life processes. The portions of instruction dealing with flower structure and pollenizing constitute first-rate sex education. (Any child can see the analogy with human conception and birth.) You yourself might enjoy, both as a gardener and as an enlightened human being, a summer extension course or a high-school adult education course in botany.

THE END

. . . yet it is never the end

The season is over, your garden's asleep. But the life of the soil has by no means ceased under that blanket of snow. The bacteria are slowed but not altogether stopped. And for garden and gardener there is always a new planting year ahead.

Appendix

You can trust your local hardware store or garden center to stock reliable seeds in packets. However, not all the good seedsmen distribute through retail outlets but instead rely entirely on their catalogues. I can speak from gratifying experience with only a few seed suppliers, but you can obtain the names of more firms than I list here from their advertisements or by applying to their trade organization:

American Seed Trade Association
Executive Building, Suite 964
Washington, D.C. 20005

Major suppliers by mail-order from their catalogues, listed in no particular order, include

Joseph Harris Co., Inc.
Moreton Farm
Rochester, New York 14624

Rayner Bros., Inc. (especially strawberries)
Salisbury, Maryland 21801

Agway (800 member stores and representatives around the country. For address, check local telephone directory)

W. Atlee Burpee Co.
Warminster, Pennsylvania 18974
Clinton, Iowa 52732
Riverside, California 92502

Stokes Seeds, Inc.
1204 Stokes Building
Buffalo, New York 14240

Burgess Seed & Plant Co.
P. O. Box 3000
Galesburg, Michigan 49053

Farmer Seed & Nursery Co.
Faribault, Minnesota 55021

Tate Fern's Nursery
Hampton, Iowa 50441

Henry Field Seed & Nursery
Shenandoah, Iowa 51601

Gurney Seed & Nursery
Yankton, South Dakota 57078

R. H. Shumway Seedsman
Rockford, Illinois 61101

Stark Bros. Nurseries
Louisiana, Missouri 63353

Geo. W. Park Seed Co., Inc.
379 Cokesbury Road
Greenwood, South Carolina 29647

F. W. Allen Company (strawberries)
1174-C
Strawberry Lane
Salisbury, Maryland 21801

Index